GLOBALHORIZONS

GLOBAL HORIZONS

AN INTRODUCTION TO INTERNATIONAL RELATIONS

[HENDRIK SPRUYT]

University of Toronto Press

LIBRARY AND ARCHIVES CANADA CATALOGUING IN PUBLICATION

Spruyt, Hendrik, 1956–
    Global horizons : an introduction to international relations / Hendrik Spruyt.

Includes bibliographical references and index.
ISBN 978-1-4426-0092-8

    1. International relations—Textbooks.   I. Title.

JZ1242.S67 2009   327   C2009-901086-0

We welcome comments and suggestions regarding any aspect of our publications — please feel free to contact us at news@utphighereducation.com or visit our internet site at www.utphighereducation.com.

North America
5201 Dufferin Street
Toronto, Ontario, Canada, M3H 5T8

2250 Military Road
Tonawanda, New York, USA, 14150

ORDERS PHONE: 1-800-565-9523
ORDERS FAX: 1-800-221-9985
ORDERS EMAIL: utpbooks@utpress.utoronto.ca

UK, Ireland, and continental Europe
NBN International
Estover Road, Plymouth, PL6 7PY, UK
TEL: 44 (0) 1752 202301
FAX ORDER LINE: 44 (0) 1752 202333
enquiries@nbninternational.com

This book is printed on paper containing 100% post-consumer fibre.

The University of Toronto Press acknowledges the financial support for its publishing activities of the Government of Canada through the Book Publishing Industry Development Program (BPIDP).

Edited by Betsy Struthers.
Designed by Zack Taylor.

Printed in Canada

To Sandy Sveine and Brett Blaze—noble, by noble deeds

CONTENTS

Part III: Global Challenges: Energy and the Environment

LIST OF FIGURES AND TABLES

Figures

Tables

PREFACE

Having taught both comparative politics and international relations for more than a decade and a half, I have concluded that our training too often falls short in one respect: we fail to make students think of themselves as *scholars*. Instead, intelligent and hard-working young minds are disciplined to digest endless dates, empirical facts, and organizational acronyms. Conversely, another approach tries to convey how the study of international relations is cross-cut with numerous debates, rival theories, different epistemological traditions, and various methodological techniques. We have many textbooks (and large and expensive ones at that) that try to do a bit of both.

No doubt such encompassing textbooks have a place. But when it comes to writing a research paper or essay, students at all levels, and at virtually all schools, seem stymied. They often lack the ability to ask a question in such a way that it could be answered in an analytic fashion. Even those who manage that lack the skills required to design research that has the potential to answer their own question. How many of us have been confronted by eager students who want to figure out "why the United States was attacked on 9/11?" or "what can be done to diminish HIV/AIDS in Sub-Saharan Africa?" I found this to be equally true of my students at private universities such as Columbia and Northwestern, as it was at public institutions that cater to large constituencies, such as Arizona State. (I will discount my time served as a graduate teaching assistant toiling in the salt mines, although that too would confirm my observation.)

Students, in other words, often think that learning means acquiring more information about facts or extant theories. They might understand that realism focuses on material factors and that constructivism places greater emphasis on ideational variables, and they might even be able to define dozens, if not hundreds of concepts and terms that populate our academic enterprise. But what this *means* for the purposes of thinking critically and creatively oneself remains largely unexplored. They acquire technical expertise but not critical thinking or a sense of methodological design. We teach them what realism or constructivism are as abstract theories, but we do not show them how these rival perspectives shed a different light on empirical issues.

This modest offering tries to fill this gap. I make no pretense that this book covers the vast array of competing theories, the long list of issue areas, or the large body of empirical knowledge that a successful scholar of international relations has to master in the end. It would, in any case, be impossible as issues, theories, and sometimes even "facts" change over time. Instead, I wish to show how one can usefully apply even a few theoretical approaches to empirical puzzles.

The book thus serves as an invitation to learn how theoretical approaches work in practice and to see how they can or cannot answer empirical questions. The hope is that the student acquires tools of the trade that she then recognizes in the extended case discussions and subsequently applies to cases of her own choosing. With these aims, this text avoids obsolescence in the face of rapid changes in global issues.

Each of the three parts of the book thus starts with some examples of theoretical approaches. It then applies them to two or three case studies, demonstrating how theories may explain "real world" empirical issues. Each part concludes with a reference section that may be used to further delve into the relevant theoretical literature and empirical background. Each Resources and Case Studies section further suggests several cases from the Pew Center at Georgetown University that link to the discussions in this book. I have found that students often welcome such hands-on involvement with case studies and have fruitfully used them in medium-sized lectures or smaller groups. The Resources are a list of relevant websites and give brief discussions of which sources are particularly relevant to the study of international relations.[1]

Aside from the theoretical and methodological aims of the book, I have sought to sensitize the reader to what I call the era of the global event horizon. In the not too distant past, we were separated from distant events spatially, temporally, and mentally. Foreign economic crises and distant wars were often regionally contained and experienced outside our own comfort zone. Indeed, more often than not, much of the general population lacked knowledge of those events. They were beyond our event horizon. Not only have modern communications, education, and transportation brought us in closer material proximity to one another, but we psychologically experience "the other" as immediately present in our environment. The consequences of this contraction of time and space—which the book hopes to illustrate—are felt in security, economic affairs, and concerns with resource scarcities and the global environment.

I owe considerable debts to many colleagues and students who have contributed, directly or indirectly, to making this book possible. I have had the good fortune to have encountered superb mentors across all subfields

---

1. The Bibliography contains the full information on all footnoted materials. Incidental references for magazine or newspaper articles are cited in full in the footnotes only. Each part of the book also contains a segment with suggested resources and case studies.

of the discipline. In one of the earlier drafts of this preface I endeavored to enumerate all of them. But having been trained as a graduate student at three institutions (Leiden, Ohio State, and the University of California, San Diego), I soon realized this would be a long list. Add to that the list of colleagues I have tried to emulate, and the list would have been longer still. Worse, I feared that failing memory might lead me to omit colleagues who rightfully should have been included. Consequently, I hope they will accept my collective thanks, which I hope to convey in person at our annual conferences and other occasions.

I am very appreciative of my graduate assistants Chris Swarat and Jesse Dillon Savage who tirelessly worked on correcting my idiom, grammar, and outright mistakes. Chris's work delving through materials and Jesse's careful editing were indispensable. Lucy E. Lyons, a bibliographer and collection manager at the Northwestern University Library, provided invaluable assistance in finding and annotating relevant sources and websites. I am greatly indebted to Greg Yantz and Anne Brackenbury of the University of Toronto Press for encouraging me to write this book, for working with me in bringing this book to fruition, and for their patience when I fell behind schedule. Betsy Struthers did extraordinary work in meticulously editing the manuscript. I would also like to thank Anna Del Col and the cover designing team for their creative work.

Finally, I dedicate this book to two friends, who, although trained in political science, have chosen a different line of work. Their continued interest in politics, however, and their belief that the study of politics—and, indeed, politics itself—should aim to improve the quality of life, has always been a source of inspiration.

INTRODUCTION

The Dawn of the Global Event Horizon

Event horizon: the boundary that represents the maximum distance at which events can be observed.

Real Time Communication and Spatial Contraction

At the great battle of Agincourt in 1425, English troops claimed a resounding success against the mounted knights of the French aristocracy. The battle was immortalized by Shakespeare in his play *Henry V* and still served to stir the hearts and minds of Englishmen 500 years later during World War II.

The harsh reality of modern warfare gives lie to such epic narratives. Pre-modern warfare involved relatively small numbers of armed forces and took place on relatively confined battlefields. Not more than a few thousand English and 10,000 French were engaged at Agincourt. But during the Somme offensive of 1916, the English suffered 21,000 dead and 40,000 severely wounded on the first day alone. World War I would cost close to 10 million lives in four years of fighting. War escalated even further, and hundreds of thousands of inhabitants of Hiroshima and Nagasaki were killed by two nuclear weapons. The total casualty list of World War II came, by some counts, to more than 50 million people.

Today, even after the end of the Cold War, the nations of the world collectively possess tens of thousands of nuclear warheads and other weapons of mass destruction. The superpowers can destroy any target in the world using nuclear missiles within 30 minutes of launch or even less if such missiles are launched from submarines. Edward Oppenheimer, on witnessing the first nuclear test explosion in New Mexico, had it right: "I am become Death, destroyer of Worlds."

At the time of Agincourt, Europe was decidedly an agricultural economy, still largely feudal in character. Some areas of the globe were known, but distant, and contact with such areas as the Middle East and Asia was infrequent, at least for the majority of the population. Other areas such as the Americas, the antipodal islands of Australia and New Zealand, and much of Africa were uncharted and unknown to Europeans. The more developed economies of Asia and the Middle East had more institutionalized long-distance trade, but even these economic contacts remained limited in their regional scope and volume.

Only the political and mercantile elites or small groups of scholars had any awareness of the world beyond their immediate confines. And even then, their knowledge was limited by the lack of communication and the long duration of travel over any distance. Today, we need only survey the everyday items around us. Products from every corner of the globe are readily available, sometimes at very low cost. International financial transactions take place in real time, with states becoming increasingly vulnerable to shocks elsewhere in the system. Foreign stocks are easily accessible to any purchaser in the developed capitalist countries. Governments sign international and regional agreements and join the World Trade Organization, the European Union, the North American Free Trade Agreement, and other regional organizations that to varying degrees limit state sovereignty. Here is one telling example of global economic interdependence: when in 2008 large financial institutions in the United States started to experience problems due to unsound loans in real estate, financial institutions everywhere came under stress. Stock markets in virtually every country retreated by about a third or more in the month of October (with poor Icelanders fretting about the 75 per cent drop in their equities).

The frequency and volume of interactions among states and between individuals, non-government organizations, and firms have increased exponentially. With material interactions has also come cultural dissemination. Students travel abroad, listen to "world music," adopt fashions and trends from Africa, Europe, and Asia.

This increasing density of interactions has also meant that our experience of time and space has contracted. Distant events affect us from across the globe and reach us in real time; as one politician phrased it, "every one is playing in everybody else's backyard." We might add that everybody is also in everyone else's backyard at the same time. National societies and politics have become intermeshed with the global community.

We once experienced distant events as remote, not only because of their geographical separation, but because the communication of such events took weeks if not months to reach their audience. As Fernand Braudel, the famous French historian, noted, it took two weeks for missives from Paris to reach the distant parts of the royal domain. Even in the nineteenth century, communications from the colonies would take many months to reach the imperial capitals of Europe.

Global Horizons takes this contraction of time and space as a premise of modern international relations. We will thus examine how international politics—that is, the relations between nations and states—has become global politics. For sure, territorial states remain critically important actors, but the current complexity of issues requires a more contextualized and subtle understanding of the problems that face humanity today.

Emile Durkheim and the Consequences of Dynamic Density

The French sociologist Emile Durkheim asked himself what differentiated pre-modern from modern societies.[1] He thought that pre-modern societies evinced a relatively low division of labor. Most individuals in such societies performed relatively uncomplicated tasks that could be duplicated by other members of the tribe or clan. Formal governance structures were few. Society was organized around mechanical solidarity.

Modern society by contrast evinces a high degree of complexity and specialization. Few individuals can readily step into a completely new line of work. Our governance structures are highly formalized and complex—think only of our legal codes and government regulations. In such a highly specialized and complex environment individuals must rely on each other for the provision of all kinds of goods and services. As do the components of the human body, we relate to each other as organs working in conjunction with and dependent on one another. Organic solidarity typifies our world today, at least at the national level.

How did many societies transform themselves from simple mechanically organized communities to larger, organically integrated, complicated social systems? How did we move from small tribal organization to the integrated nation-state, larger in territorial scope and population size, and vastly more complicated in its organization?

Durkheim believed that the transition depended on dynamic density. The transformation required that societies cross a minimum threshold of interaction. As long as communities were small with little interaction, specialization and development could not occur. But with population growth, and increasing exchanges of goods, knowledge, and people, societies could develop more intricate modes for providing subsistence goods and further economic development.

We are at the threshold of a similar process in international affairs. While we hold on to our national sentiment and identify ourselves as citizens of a particular state, the boundaries of national community are being tested and altered every day. Dynamic density operates not just at the national but at the international level as well. For all our attachment to Canada or the United States, and for all our ethnic and racial pride in our community, we cannot deny that the global problems facing us today will require us to imagine a future beyond the nation-state.

---

1. Durkheim 1933.

For much of human history, political communities (whatever their scale) were separated from other groups and polities by time and space. The globe encompassed many international systems with scant interaction between those systems. And even within each of those systems, interaction among the units making up that system might be slim. This is no longer the case. The event horizon is now truly global.

How to Think About International Politics

The main thread that will run throughout this book has to do with how we study international and global politics. Rather than survey a large array of issues and theories, the book aims to provide the reader with particular ways of thinking about politics. What are useful "tools of the trade"? How would one start to think about a particular problem or a particular occurrence in international relations? Which different perspectives might be usefully deployed to understand a given empirical puzzle? I do not intend to provide exhaustive descriptions of current events, long lists of facts, compilations of data, and exhaustive enumerations of which acronyms fit with which organizations. Instead, I will provide the means to sort through, and critically evaluate, current and historical events rather than a descriptive narrative. How, in other words, might one study international politics in an analytic fashion? Thus, each part first discusses modes of analysis that might be suitable to understand the particular issues in question and then applies them to empirical cases that demonstrate the use of such modes of analysis in practice. Finally, I will argue throughout that a historical and comparative approach must be part of any serious study. Whatever the merits of studying current events, or whatever the merits of devising complicated models to understand politics, no comprehension is possible without some study of the past. Where we are today depends on where we came from.

The book is organized around three main areas. First, we turn to a study of international conflict. What explains the outbreak of war? How might we foster conditions for peace? Part I starts by developing various analytic methods through which we can study conflict. It then applies these modes of analysis to three cases studies: World War I, the Cold War and its aftermath, and the outbreak of the Iraq War in 2003. It concludes with a discussion of how weapons of mass destruction raise unique problems and how these problems might be controlled.

In Part II, we turn to an analysis of international political economy through a typology of economic paradigms. After discussing several "tools of the trade" that are useful for understanding the global political economy, we turn to the study of diverse types of capitalism. Modern economies have developed unique approaches for managing their domestic economies and for competing internationally. These national styles have their roots in differing historical circumstances and ideological traditions. I subsequently discuss how the international economy has been organized in the twentieth century and why at times the international economic order has collapsed—as in the 1930s. We then analyze how the postwar order has developed in worldwide arrangements such as the World Trade Organization. Finally, we turn to the question of whether globalization has diminished the ability of states to determine their own economic fate. Is it still possible to speak of distinct national economic styles or are countries in essence similar in their economic arrangements? Are there, in other words, still diverse varieties of capitalism?

Part III focuses on a host of issues that have traditionally been given short shrift in international studies. Much of this no doubt can be explained by exigencies of the time. The Cold War impelled scholars to think about the unimaginable prospects of nuclear holocaust. The complexities of forging a more stable international economic order in the wake of World War II required study of economic leadership and cooperation among the developed countries. But already in the 1970s, observers started to draw our attention to truly global problems that crossed boundaries and presented new challenges to humankind. Environmental degradation, the oil crisis of the 1970s, and a rapidly expanding world population led some to conclude that we were approaching a turning point. Indeed, the very survival of humanity could be at stake. Such messages were forgotten by many international relations scholars in the economic boom of the late 1980s and the gradual reduction of tensions in the Cold War. Today's concerns about global warming, the depletion of natural resources, and the spread of contagious diseases have once again put such issues in the forefront. We have truly entered an era where we are confronted by a "global problematique"—transnational concerns that defy solutions by any one state.

Thus, *Global Horizons* aims at providing readers who are interested in international relations the means to think analytically. The case studies are meant as applications of specific theoretical tools to empirical events. Even if one is not interested in the specific cases mentioned in the book, the examples will demonstrate how one might apply the theoretical insights to a case that does interest the reader. The only limit lies in the reader's creativity. For example, while we do not discuss the outbreak of World War II, one might read the historical narrative and examine whether the causal variables that led to the start of World War I, such as the multipolar international system and a cult of the offensive, played a role. One might even ask whether the tools deployed for clarifying inter-state wars might, or might not, be useful for studying civil wars, and so on.

Similarly, while I focus in Part II on clarifying three variant forms of capitalism in the United States, Germany, and Japan, one could easily apply the theoretical model to other cases and explain why some states followed a liberal capitalist or neo-mercantilist model. And when we apply hegemonic stability theory to explain the emergence of the General Agreement on Tariffs and Trade, and contrast that with the lack of such leadership in the current environmental regime (such as the Kyoto Protocol), it raises questions about the need for hegemonic leadership in many other issue areas.

Simply put, the book is an invitation to do research of one's own beyond the empirical narratives provided here. My own view is that someone with a serious interest in international affairs cannot be content with a knowledge of only the cases under discussion here. Conversely, however, a serious student cannot do without knowledge of the important events and issue areas presented in *Global Horizons*.

PART I
INTERNATIONAL SECURITY

ONE

Tools of the Trade (1):
Understanding War and Peace
from Three Perspectives

The Rise of the Modern State and Organized Warfare

Organized conflict between groups seems to have been present throughout human evolution. We have forensic evidence of violent clashes between family groups and tribes well before the development of script and recorded history. The earliest written historical record, dating back to the first Egyptian and Mesopotamian dynasties, often tells the sad tale of violent conflict and destruction.

Arguably, one of the primary functions of political organization, even at the most rudimentary level, has been to protect the group from outside predation or, conversely, to inflict harm on rival groups. The methods through which human collectivities mobilized for war vary across time and space, but no empire, no local lordship, could escape the need to possess some means of violence, either to protect or to conquer.

How various forms of social and political organization have utilized military force, and how they have incorporated armed forces into their particular mode of organization, presents a fascinating line of inquiry. Michael Mann has traced the influence of military power on human organization from the earliest polities to the present.[1] For the purposes of this book, however, we will focus on war and peace in modern history and concentrate on the post-Napoleonic era, when nation-states developed war-making capabilities that today threaten humanity's very existence.

Large-scale warfare remains primarily the domain of sovereign territorial states. States are formal organizations whose authority extends to specific geographic borders but no further. Government within those borders is sovereign in that juridically no external power can claim authority within the state's borders. A state's government is thus supreme and recognizes no higher authority. German sociologist Max Weber suggested that the key defining feature of the state was its sole possession of armed force:

---

1. Mann 1986.

"A state is a human community that (successfully) claims the monopoly of the legitimate use of physical force within a given territory."[2]

While we need to be concerned with terrorism, mercenaries, and other non-state actors usurping military powers of their own, major armed conflict still remains primarily the domain of the state. Whatever the harm inflicted by private groups, it is only the public authority of states that can mobilize their societies for mass warfare on an unprecedented scale. Only states can send millions of men and women to battle. And only states can raise hundreds of billions of dollars and rubles to build arsenals containing tens of thousands of nuclear warheads and corresponding missile systems. Consequently, to understand war and peace today, we need to understand the rise of the state and the commensurate evolution of modern warfare.

The modern state finds its origins in the end of the feudal era, starting roughly in the eleventh century. After the fall of the Roman Empire (the Western Empire fell in the middle of the fifth century), local authorities usurped power to defend the population against invasions from the East. These Eastern tribes—Goths, Vandals, and others—were in turn being pushed forward by the steppe empire of the Huns who originated from far in the interior of the Eurasian landmass. Often it fell to the bishops of the Roman Church to take on the functions that previously had fallen to the governors of the empire.

For almost 1500 years after the fall of the Roman Empire, various polities would attempt to resurrect it and would claim to be its legitimate heirs. One such attempt was the Frankish Empire, which at its zenith united the European area from Northern Spain to the Elbe River in what is today the eastern part of Germany. Tellingly, its most powerful leader, Charlemagne, had himself crowned emperor on Christmas day of the year 800, thus alluding to his imperial status as well as his religious position as defender of the Church.

The Frankish, or Carolingian, Empire soon fell apart. Charlemagne's heirs could not agree on how to divide the empire among themselves. Worse still, invaders from the North (the Vikings), from the East (the Hungarian Magyars), and the South (Muslim raiders from North Africa) eroded the basis of centralized power. In its place arose a complex organization which revolved around the warrior chieftain and his retinue—the feudal system.

Feudalism has military, economic, and political aspects. The warrior chieftain formed the heart of the system. Local lords became the primary means of defense against external enemies. These lords wielded their power as mounted knights who built strongholds that gave the local population refuge in times of danger. In exchange, these commoners were obligated to provide the lord with particular goods. This exchange often took the form of in-kind transfers—peasants had to surrender a part of their harvest or perform labor services that the lord demanded. At the lowest rank of this

---

2. As cited in Gerth and Mills 1946, 78.

system stood the serfs who did not own property but held land from the lord, who thus doubled as warrior chieftain and large landowner. Often the status of these serfs resembled that of slaves in other periods.

Politically, this meant that centralized rule had eroded and passed on to the local lords. These lords had judicial powers to demand service from their subjects and penalize those who violated the lord's edicts. The higher lords also had the power to mint their own coin and levy taxes. In Germany alone, more than 10,000 castles were erected, each controlling the land in its immediate vicinity.

By the end of the eleventh century fundamental changes started to affect Europe. First of all, the invasions began to abate. At the same time, agricultural innovation and long-distance trade started to improve the position of the commoners in the feudal order. Finally, military innovations, such as the use of the longbow and massed pike-men, changed the nature of warfare such that the mounted knight no longer was the pre-eminent wielder of force.[3]

Whether economic changes or the innovations in warfare were the key factor in ending feudalism is a matter of debate, but whatever the causal dynamic the end result was clear: the primacy of the warrior aristocracy had started to wane. The balance swung back to rulers who could mobilize their populations at a larger scale, tax their populations, and create standing forces of mercenary troops. The saying of the day—pas d'argent, pas de Suisse (no money, no Swiss)—alluded to the fact that one needed money to buy the vaunted Swiss infantry in order to win wars. The adage also alluded to the general phenomenon that occasional feudal service based on the reciprocal military obligations of lords and lesser lords was being replaced by larger professional armies. Thus, by the end of the Hundred Years' War (1337–1453), the French king had created an army of more than 10,000 troops.

This growth in scale and scope of warfare necessitated a mobilization of government and society at a much higher level than before. In order to raise revenue, rulers needed an administration, tax collectors, and bureaucrats to write edicts and laws. The creation of a strong centralized state thus hinged on economic development. The more money one could raise, the larger the army one could equip, and the greater the conquest of new territories, which in turn raised one's taxing ability.

In short, the advent of centralized states, with kings as the primary authorities, came with a dramatic increase in not only the scale and scope of warfare but also the frequency of conflict. In terms of duration, feudal armies usually campaigned only for a few months, sometimes only a few weeks. Feudal military obligations were not uncommonly defined as service for 40 days. These armies usually mobilized no more than a few thousand troops. The largest army on record was probably the English campaign

---

3. For accounts of late medieval state formation, see Tilly 1990 and Spruyt 1994.

against the Scots, amounting to perhaps as many as 30,000 men. Most feudal campaigns were far more modest.

However, during the sixteenth century, military conflict changed dramatically. In 1470 Charles the Bold had an army of 15,000 in the Netherlands. A century later the Spanish King Philip II had a force of 86,000 in the Lowlands alone, with tens of thousands more scattered throughout the Spanish Empire. In the seventeenth century, countries such as Sweden were at war two years out of every three, while others (such as Spain and Russia) were engaged in war even more often. Warfare was ubiquitous and frequent.[4]

This remained the state of affairs until the late eighteenth century. Warfare was thus the business of rulers and their professional armies. No doubt the effect of these wars could be horrific for the population—as the religious wars of the sixteenth century and the Thirty Years' War (1618–48) proved. But warfare itself revolved around the ability of rulers to pay for military service. Territorial states defined areas of authority, but the governments of those states only imperfectly controlled and influenced their local populations. In the words of Ernest Gellner, they were capstone governments. The ruling strata did not dramatically affect the way of life, languages, and cultural expressions of the local population.[5]

The French Revolution changed all that. State and nation were gradually forged into one. Warfare now became the business of the state and its citizenry. With the cry of freedom, brotherhood, and equality came the identification of the individual subject with the goals of the state. Indeed, individuals became citizens and were no longer mere subjects. The French state could thus introduce the *levée en masse*, the mass mobilization of the entire populace for war. This coincided with the fact that France at this time was second only to Russia in terms of population on the European continent.

No one knew better how to exploit this advantage than Napoleon. Within two decades he conquered virtually all of Europe. Only the naval defeat at Trafalgar and the disastrous Russian campaign prevented him from conquering the entire continent. The Russian campaign foreshadowed the shape of modern war to come. More than half a million troops were mobilized for this ill-fated effort. However, due to military setbacks and the onset of winter, only a combined force of less than 10,000 soldiers remained by the end of 1812. Yet within months Napoleon could raise another huge army of more than 100,000. His fortunes waxed and waned in the years after, only to suffer final defeat at Waterloo in 1815.

The Napoleonic period, therefore, signaled a revolution in military affairs. Mass conscription armies became the norm. Only a state's population base and the ability to train these citizens into a fighting force created

---

4. Parker 1995, 147.
5. Gellner 1983.

any limit to what it could do. Moreover, as long as citizens identified with the goals of the state, and saw themselves as members of a shared community, they were prepared to make sacrifices as never before. Governments thus became actively involved in education and the standardization of languages. State making intertwined with nation building, the forging of a citizenry that identified itself with the state and the territory it occupied.[6]

By the twentieth century inter-state war had become inter-nation war. Nationalist ideals infused conflicts. Citizens would line up to die by the millions in service of their country. Wars became world wars, and humankind's very existence was placed in the balance. The atomic device dropped on Hiroshima in 1945 was probably the equivalent of 20 kilotons of TNT (20,000 tons of high explosives), killing well over 100,000 people. Less than two decades later the Soviets tested a thermonuclear device that yielded almost 50 megatons, almost 2,500 times the explosive yield of Hiroshima. The specter of nuclear war loomed for half a century, and the possible use of weapons of mass destruction (WMDs) remains a danger to this day. Even after the Cold War, the nuclear powers have tens of thousands of nuclear warheads at their disposal. Not only has the yield of such weapons dramatically increased humanity's destructive potential, but the means through which they can be delivered has made the entire world susceptible to virtually instantaneous destruction. To give one example, missiles launched from Russian submarines can hit any target in Canada or the United States in eight minutes. The possibility of thermonuclear war has contracted the globe in time and space.

It is thus critical that we understand the causes behind war and peace. With the stakes so high today, that age-old concern has become an imperative. So, in order to maintain peace, we must understand the causes of war.

Across the social sciences, the humanities, and the natural sciences, scholars have focused on why war occurs so ubiquitously and across time. Simply put, why do human beings engage in war? Other scholars in these disciplines have focused more narrowly on explaining specific events. Why did a particular war or wars break out? The literature that focuses on these two questions is so vast as to defy any attempt at surveying it in its entirety.

It is, however, possible to think systematically about why humans are conflict-prone and why specific wars have broken out. One method of doing so groups the literature in paradigms—theoretical perspectives that share views on what constitutes the nature of politics, on how one should study politics, and on which causal variables need to be investigated. Briefly stated, scholars of international relations group their analysis in three schools of thought. *Realists* tend to see international politics as a contest for power and security. The pursuit of security is the primary motivating

6. Posen 1993.

force, and the state's primary objective is to ensure the nation's survival. *Liberals*, by contrast, tend to place less weight on security concerns and see greater opportunities for cooperation among states, particularly given the possibility of mutual gains from economic interaction. Liberals share with realists the view that material factors rather than ideational variables are the key driving forces behind state behavior.[7] By contrast, *constructivists* tend to place greater emphasis on ideational causes, stressing that states and individuals have certain identities and hold certain beliefs. These ideas and beliefs in turn define how actors see their material interests.[8]

. All three of these theoretical perspectives might be further divided into subfields. Within the realist paradigm, classical realists place emphasis on historical context and ideational factors in addition to material distributions of power.[9] Structural realists, by contrast, place almost exclusive emphasis on the latter.[10] Within liberalism, economic liberals argue that economic interaction, and particularly liberal trade, is a key factor in preventing conflict. Democratic liberals, by contrast, tend to place more stock in the type of governments that the states in question have, as well as the rights conferred to their populations.[11] The assumption is that democratic states are less prone to war with each other than they are with authoritarian states. Finally, constructivism too can be divided into multiple camps that differ significantly in how they think politics should be studied. Some constructivists, such as Alexander Wendt, suggest that, although ideas and beliefs are critical for understanding behavior, it is still possible to develop rigorous scientific theories not unlike the natural sciences.[12] Others believe that the social world requires a fundamentally different analytic orientation. They favor greater emphasis on the study of how discursive practices and rhetorical framing influence ideas and beliefs.[13]

This book does not adjudicate among these different theoretical styles, nor does it place primacy on material or ideational causes. In many instances both might be at work. While choosing among these paradigms might be justified by theories of knowledge (that is, by particular epistemological considerations) or by views on the essential nature of politics (that is, by ontological considerations), I remain agnostic on those issues in this book. Instead, I will follow a pragmatic, problem-oriented approach, by

---

7. The most prominent scholar in the (neo)liberal tradition is probably Keohane, who challenged realist perspectives on international order; see Keohane 1984 and Keohane 1986.

8. Yet another logic for organizing the various perspectives might contrast liberalism with Marxism. I discuss the latter in Part II.

9. See the seminal work of Morgenthau 1966.

10. Waltz 1979 is the key proponent of neo-realism or structural realism.

11. An even finer-grained analysis of the various strands of liberalism is possible; see Zacher and Matthew 1995.

12. Wendt 1992.

13. Ashley 1986.

taking a given empirical puzzle—such as the question of why World War I broke out—and subject it to various different explanations that may well include and combine the three major paradigms enumerated above.

Kenneth Waltz and Three Perspectives on the Causes of War

Kenneth Waltz's earlier work provides us with a useful problem-oriented approach to the study of war and peace.[14] In *Man, the State, and War*, Waltz sought to explain the existence of conflicts in general, not specific wars. He suggests that there are three distinct ways of viewing, and thus studying, the nature of conflict.

One can best understand his approach as an ordering of variables at different levels of aggregation. In the first level, or first image of analysis, war is examined at the point of the individual. Why do human beings engage in war? Specifically, what is it about the make-up of human beings that makes them prone to violent conflict? Waltz notes how other thinkers have tried to find the cause of war by examining traits that occur in all humans. Extending beyond this, one might try to explain why a particular war occurred. Psychologists, for example, might focus on the character of specific leaders, such as Hitler or Stalin. In a related line of research, some analysts have drawn attention to how decision-making in groups is subject to particular dynamics that influence the processing of information or how the actions of others are perceived.

The second level, or image, sees war as the outcome of aggregated individual behavior. It focuses on the consequences of particular social and political organizations. War is, after all, not merely a conflict between individuals but is conducted by highly complex organizations. If we follow Weber's definition that states possess the monopoly over the means of violence, the question is: why do certain states wage war?

This mode of analysis has focused on several sub-areas of research. One line of inquiry explores whether particular types of government, that is, particular regimes, are more war-prone than others. Is it true that democracies are more benign than authoritarian states? Some have argued that the absence of war between democracies comes close to the status of a scientific law. Indeed, the assumption that democracies are peaceful has fed into the policy realm. If democracies are peaceful, then it stands to reason that powerful democracies should try to instill democracy elsewhere to ensure peace among nations. We have seen such assertions most recently in the stance of George W. Bush's administration, but it is worth examining whether that proposition indeed holds true. Another approach focuses on the internal relations between different components of the government or

---

14. Rather ironically, Waltz's later work (1979), for which he is better known, emphasizes almost exclusively structural factors. Indeed, the key variable to explaining international outcomes, in this view, is the distribution of power.

between public authority and social actors. How does the bureaucracy influence the decisions of elites? Do civilians exercise control over the armed forces in making foreign policy?

The third level, or third image, of analysis views international relations at yet a higher level of aggregation, emphasizing the particular architecture of the international system. It draws attention to the fact that individuals and states are part of a larger entity, the grouping of states that make up an international system. Individuals and states might thus be constrained, or conversely have opportunities, because of how that system is configured. Just as we are born into families with particular rules and with particular authority structures (our parents), so too are leaders and states part of a larger configuration.

The international system is distinct from domestic politics in that there is no higher authority to which one can appeal. States operate as sovereign entities without a formal higher authority. But, as we will see, this does not mean there is no structure to the system. The organizing structure might derive from particular rules, international law, and alliances, which in turn might derive from the particular distribution of power among states.

In short, moving from the first level to the third level we aggregate politics at an increasing scale and move up in the degree of abstraction. Individual leaders make decisions, but they are part of political institutions within the state. States in turn form part of an international system. This system constrains and perhaps determines how states behave.

The degree of structural determination differs as well across the various levels of analysis. Individuals must take the demands of the larger collectivity, the formal institutions in the state, into account. States in turn must heed the constraints and opportunities in the international system.

First Level Analysis

Examples of First Level Analyses in Psychology and Ethology

Like all Europeans, Sigmund Freud, the famous Austrian psychologist, was profoundly affected by the carnage of World War I. Almost 10 million people had died in brutal trench warfare. For the first time, the world had seen the use of modern chemical weapons (mustard and other gases), aerial bombardment of civilian populations (such as in the Zeppelin raids on London), and submarine attacks on civilian and military shipping alike. And all this occurred in what the Europeans professed to be the most advanced civilizations of their time. Until then the European imperial powers lorded over vast colonial territories, justifying their rule as a civilizing mission to inferior peoples. The carnage of the war gave lie to such high-minded claims. What had caused this ultimate regression of human progress?

Freud thought the answer lay in modernity itself. War resulted from the tension between innate individual desires and social organization. Modern civilization required one to develop particular characteristics in order to be socially acceptable. Individuals could not merely act upon their own preferences and desires but had to conform to what society thought was permissible and acceptable. This in turn necessitated the sublimation of instinct. Indeed, said Freud, human instincts did not merely have to be channeled but preferably buried altogether.[15] As a consequence, individuals in modern societies were in a state of constant tension between their inherent natural drives and societal demands. The result was external aggression, the desire to dominate the other. Tellingly, Freud referred to the political theorist Thomas Hobbes, who observed that *"Homo homini lupus,"* man was a wolf to other men.[16] More recently, Philip Slater employed a version of Freudian analysis. He explained American military involvement in Vietnam by the tension between American culture and innate drives. The war was caused by the materialist culture in the United States and a concomitant glorification of the individual.[17]

Ethology has presented a slightly different perspective but also seeks explanations for war at the first level. In his work *On Aggression*, Konrad Lorenz was particularly intrigued by the question of why the level of violence was higher within species rather than between species. Needless to say, he recognized that species could prey upon one another, but such contests, he argued, occurred primarily within species for territory, resources, and mating privileges. The answer lay in Darwinian selection. Biological competition rewarded aggressive behavior by opportunities for reproduction and subsequent selection and winnowing of the less fit. This dynamic thus led to convergence in behavior towards aggression, because the environment rewarded such behavior both in the short and long run. This was no different for *homo sapiens* than for other species. From his studies of animal behavior, Lorenz concluded that "it is more than probable that the destructive intensity of the aggression drive ... is the consequence of a process of intra-specific selection which worked on our forefathers for roughly forty thousand years."[18]

Some Problems with First Level Accounts

Freud's and Lorenz's works are but two examples of a much larger genre of scholarship. Their theories have subsequently been refined and amended by some and rejected by others. The purpose here is not to focus on these

---

15. Freud 1961, 44.
16. Freud 1961, 58.
17. Slater 1976.
18. Lorenz 1966, 39.

two particular arguments but to highlight some problems with providing a general explanation for all wars at the first level of analysis.

Although psychology and ethology suggest why organized conflict might be a generalizable phenomenon, the evidence remains inconclusive. For example, Freud's civilizational hypothesis that links warfare with modernity contrasts with anthropological evidence of warfare among tribes that until recently were barely exposed to modern political organizations. Thus, there seems reason to doubt whether warfare or organized group violence is fully attributable to modernity. Modern societies can wage war at unprecedented levels, but there is ample evidence to suggest the prevalence of warfare among many tribes in a pre-modern environment. From this perspective, warfare is not the creation of modern civilization or a particular environment. It transcends distinct historical periods, geographic regions, and distinct cultures.

To give one example, Chagnon's famous study of the Yanomamö, a tribal people of the Brazilian rainforest, dramatically illustrates how violence might be endemic among pre-modern peoples as well. He described how they frequently waged war on each other. Indeed, during his field work with them he counted 18 incidents in a year and half.[19] Violence was even endemic among members of the tribe itself, with wife and child beatings being common occurrences. One can find similar incidences of organized conflict across pre-modern tribes elsewhere. The Dajak of Borneo were infamous head hunters. The Zulu of Southern Africa not only subjugated other African tribes in the nineteenth century, they even routed a British force equipped with modern weaponry. The point is not whether pre-modern tribes are "uncivilized" and thus prone to war and violence but to illustrate that warfare is not restricted exclusively to modern or pre-modern collectivities.

Even within similar subfields the evidence is not uniform. Anthropological studies show many tribes who wage little if any organized warfare, even within the same geographic space. For example, in what is now the American southwest and Arizona, one tribe, the Apache, were well known among their fellow indigenous tribes as warlike, while another, the Hopi, were far less prone to raiding and violence.

Moreover, even if one accepts the premise that humans are predisposed to aggression, it is obvious that this does not always lead to war. That is, if innate drives are constant, what prevents war from breaking out at all times? If people have innate drives such as libido (sex drive) and thanatos (a death instinct), it seems to be society that causes those drives to manifest themselves or not. In other words, under which conditions do individuals act on those deeply held impulses?

---

19. Chagnon 1968. Chagnon was later criticized by others who wondered whether his presence among the tribe had accidentally contributed to the violence.

Similarly, one might wonder why the empirical evidence is mixed across relatively similar populations. Why do tribes or collectivities that face similar environmental circumstances, such as the Hopi and Apache, engage in different types of behavior? What other variables might account for the variation? These questions raise an old debate, the nature/nurture argument: are these drives innate, or are they actually socially constructed?

First level analyses also need clarification on how micro processes (at the level of the individual) lead to large-scale macro outcomes (at the level of the state and system). That is, warfare is conducted by organized groups and, in the modern era, by states that can mobilize their economies and their populations. How innate drives of individuals translate into foreign policy and international conflict needs to be explained. There is a vast difference between two individuals coming to blows in a bar-room scuffle and the massive organization for world war. As we observed when discussing third level analysis, the state works in a complex set of relations with other states (through treaties, alliances, and international organizations) that also determine state behavior.

Finally, some first level analyses border on the tautological. In sound explanations the causal variable—the independent variable—should be observable and measured independently from the phenomenon one wishes to explain—the dependent variable. For example, if we want to attribute the warlike behavior of the Yanomamö to their innate drives for warfare, we need to be able to somehow measure these innate traits (perhaps through psychological profiling, DNA research, etc.) independently from the observed pattern of violence. If we simply argue that we know that they are prone to war because we observe them waging war, then the explanation is tautological: the presence of an explanatory variable is derived from the very phenomenon one wishes to explain.

Political scientists thus admit that some of these explanations might be useful in understanding why there might be war in general—humans are not angels. But they do not help us in understanding the variation in the frequency and occurrence of war across time and space. Consequently, they also do not help us to prevent war. (Freud himself thought that prevention of conflict could only come from a centralized authority.) For these reasons, political science has tended to focus on a different form of first level analysis, which draws specific attention to individual decision-making and cognition. Rather than study war in general, this type of analysis focuses on the cognition, learning, and perception among individual leaders to examine why a *specific* war might have broken out.

Cognitive Factors in Decision-Making

Borrowing insights from psychology and social experiments, scholars have sought to explain how cognitive factors might influence the outbreak of conflict. But, unlike the approaches discussed above, this area of research seeks to explain how decisions emerge in specific conflicts rather than try to distill general proclivities in humankind.

Political psychologists have drawn attention to how individuals evaluate information and how they evaluate other actors in moments of crisis. Robert Jervis has been one of the most influential scholars in this line of inquiry, describing how various psychological factors influence perceptions and misperceptions on either side.[20] First, individuals' views become myopic, focused on the immediate, and so only certain limited aspects of the crisis are examined. Actors tend to see only a narrow range of options, and the options that they see are often colored by their evaluation of past history. For example, going into the first Gulf War (1991), decision-makers feared a long protracted war, as Vietnam had been. That quick victory by the alliance in turn influenced American leaders to think that the second Gulf War would be short and decisive. Internal inconsistencies in one's own position are overlooked as well. Group thinking might make matters worse. Individuals are reluctant to go against what they perceive to be the dominant position of the decision-making team. As the crisis progresses, individuals will converge further in their views, thus further diminishing the range of possible options.

Moreover, information is selectively processed or not processed at all. Actors fall back on stereotypical thinking and do not seek creative solutions to difficult problems. Indeed, complications are dismissed and contrary information ignored. Cognitive dissonance occurs, and information that might not fit the pre-existing opinions or mindset of the decision-maker is ignored or distorted so as to conform to the existing view. Furthermore, during a crisis situation, leaders sometimes tend to exaggerate the need to act swiftly. They see shortened time horizons, believing that there is only a small window of opportunity to solve the crisis or pursue an option that will favor their state. Finally, actors tend to shift the burden of solving the crisis to the other side. One believes one's own options are limited; conversely, the other side is believed to have greater room for maneuver. Thus, one expects the other to make concessions and back off from any demands previously made.

Such perceptions and misperceptions influence decision-makers to a considerable degree in many instances prior to the outbreak of war, as we will see in Chapters 3, 4, and 5. The results in each case were disastrous. Aware of these dynamics, some leaders, such as President Kennedy during

---

20. Jervis 1976. Such factors are particularly critical in nuclear crises given the objectively shortened time frame and the high stakes; see Jervis 1989.

the Cuban Missile Crisis, have tried to avoid these dysfunctional cognitive processes.

Second Level Analysis: Regime Type and the Internal Characteristics of States

Second level analysis studies conflict as the result of organized group behavior. Contemporary international conflicts are not caused by haphazard groups of individuals fighting each other but are the product of purposive acts of highly organized collectivities. In the twentieth century violence has been particularly virulent due to the ability of states to mobilize their societies for war in an unprecedented manner.[21]

As with first level analysis, there are many varieties and nuances in how scholars think about why states end up in conflict. One strand of literature focuses on the connections between economic and security policy. Another body of work asks whether regime type and the institutional structure of some states might make those states more war-prone. This literature examines such things as the influence of the military on decision-making, bureaucratic procedures, and the degree to which different components of government decision-making have been captured by special interests.

Economic Policy and War

Mercantilist policies and doctrine first emerged with the formation of territorial states during the late medieval period and developed further during the Renaissance. Although inchoate at first, mercantilism developed into an explicit economic and policy doctrine, which influenced the policies of many European states. Indeed, it continued to play a role throughout the nineteenth century, particularly in Germany, and arguably influenced politics in the inter-war period of the twentieth century. (The economic aspects of mercantilism are discussed in Part II.)

Mercantilism emerged with the gradual transformation of feudal decentralized rule into monarchic territorial states. In the feudal era, localized economies were characterized by the reciprocal exchange of obligations and trade of in-kind goods. The monetary economy was underdeveloped with no centralized coinage. Weights and measures showed bewildering diversity. The variation of laws, feudal customs, the lack of clearly established property rights, and the absence of a sound banking system all conspired to hold back economic development.

---

21. While our attention will be devoted to looking at inter-state war, this does not mean that civil wars could not be studied by our proposed method of distinguishing levels of analysis. Civil wars after all usually involve two distinct political entities, both of which claim to be the representatives of particular (rival) views of what the relevant boundaries of the state should be. Indeed, the secessionists seek to become a state of their own.

Given this situation, mercantile interests and aspiring territorial rulers could benefit from solving these problems. Consequently, by the late Middle Ages, the rulers of Italian city-states started to develop better weights and measures, regulate their coin, and pass all kinds of laws to benefit the commerce of cities such as Venice, Genoa, and Florence. These became the most important economic actors in the Mediterranean. By the time of the early Renaissance, territorial rulers in northwestern Europe embarked on similar policies.

Thus, consolidation of territorial rule, economic development, and centralized administration started to go hand in hand. One of the key tenets of mercantilism thus held that government had to be directly involved with state building and economic policy. A stronger state in turn could compete more effectively with other states.

At the same time, territorial consolidation meant that rulers clashed with the territorial claims of their rivals, increasing the frequency of warfare. Simultaneously, feudal warfare was being supplanted by professional, mercenary armies. Economic development had two sides. On the one hand, internal economic development was beneficial for the ruler's coffers. On the other, such economic development would allow a ruler to raise an army and conquer other territories. Mercantilism, or economic nationalism, thus aimed at creating an economically integrated state that was highly successful in territorial conquest and war. Territorial aggrandizement would further increase the revenue and resources for an even more powerful state in a mutually reinforcing, and self-perpetuating, dynamic of constant war.

Mercantilism thus holds two key tenets. Domestically, governments must intervene to create markets and facilitate economic development, which in turn will aid the war-making capacity of the state. Tellingly, some of the earliest capitalist enterprises were in military sectors. The Arsenal in Venice produced galleys both for the government and for private merchants in one of the first assembly line operations in history. Similarly, the King of France intervened to grant monopolies to key industries involved in gunpowder manufacturing.

Internationally, mercantilists view international politics as zero-sum: one state's gain corresponds with a commensurate loss for the rival state. States are thus concerned with relative gains. They are not just interested in bettering their own situation (by, say, acquiring natural resources) but in acquiring *more* than the other states. For example, if two states, A and B, both gain from trade between them, but A gains more than B, then B should refrain from trading with A.[22]

As a consequence, mercantilist governments pursue protectionism at home and support important industries. Foreign policies are driven by

---

22. Baldwin 1993 contains many of the key discussions concerning differences between realism (which shares many features in common with mercantilism) and liberalism.

competitive calculations, given that resources are finite—territory, natural resources, and gold bullion all become part of zero-sum contests that may initiate wars. A second level perspective thus sees mercantilist states as war-prone.

Liberals, particularly economic liberals, come to quite different conclusions. Liberalism's main tenets are often attributed to Adam Smith, who, in his *Wealth of Nations* (1776), argued explicitly against mercantilist doctrine. Smith asked one to consider a thought experiment. If a group of individuals were marooned on some deserted island, how would they organize their society? The answer was simple: they would readily gravitate towards those tasks in which they had a particular advantage or specific skill. People would specialize in what they did best and trade for the other goods or services that they needed to survive. Specialization would lead to efficiency, given that each individual would choose to do what they were good at. Subsequently, through trade, the overall good to society would be maximized as well. Rational self-interest would produce the greatest good. Individual desire for gain would correspond with society's overall gain. Smith called this the "invisible hand," which was at work in all human associations.

Smith transposed his metaphor of individual behavior and the benefits of market exchange to the realm of government organization and international politics. Rather than government intervention, market exchange driven by self-interest should be most efficient. When governments did intervene to protect or support a particular industry, this was more often driven by the protection of particular groups rather than the pursuit of societal gain.

As with individuals in a domestic society, states too would benefit from specializing in production in which they had a comparative advantage. Inspired by reading Smith's work, David Ricardo (1772–1823) formalized the argument even more forcefully. As I discuss in greater detail in Chapter 7, Ricardo argued that any state should specialize in production in which it has a comparative advantage and then trade the results of that production with other countries, even if it has an advantage in all the sectors concerned.

The implications for international politics are significant. For liberals, international interaction is not a zero-sum game, given that both actors stand to benefit from specialization and trade. Protectionism and exclusion of competition are not just desirable but in fact retard economic development and are contrary to self-interest. From this second level perspective, liberal states are thus less likely to be war-prone.

A third perspective on the relation of economics to war is provided by Marxism. Marxists, like mercantilists, see international politics as much more conflictual than liberals do. Marxists analyze the role of government in the domestic realm and combine this analysis with arguments regarding politics in the international realm. At the domestic level, society is divided into two classes—those who own the means of production (the bourgeoisie) and the laborers (the proletariat) who own only their labor but not capital, machinery, or land. We will discuss the conflict between these two classes further in Part II, but for now it suffices to understand that the capitalists and the proletariat have opposite goals. The capitalists seek to exploit the labor force efficiently, but in order to do so they require that the state intervene on their behalf. The state must uphold private property and enforce labor laws favorable to the bourgeoisie. Thus, the government in capitalist states is not a neutral institution. Only in socialist states where the proletariat has seized power can government be regarded as a beneficial organ. In such states government intervenes to allocate property rights communally and provide "from each according to his ability, to each according to his need."

This conflict between classes also occurs in the international realm. Socialist states, being run by the proletariat, do not have antithetical interests. Quite the contrary, laborers of the world—as Lenin was to proclaim—should unite. As they have coincident interests in furthering the laboring classes, they have no reason to engage in conflict. Capitalist states, however, have no such commonality of interests. Needless to say, they are opposed to socialist states in which the labor force has seized power, but capitalist states do not share interests. Given that markets and resources are limited, capitalism inevitably leads to conflict as capitalist states vie for resources and markets. For Marxists, international politics is conflictual because of capitalist states.

Adherents to Marxism did more than just expound such views. Lenin argued that World War I was instigated by capitalist states seeking access to resources and markets for their goods.[23] Not only should the working classes of Europe disavow involvement in the war, but a socialist state would not be part of the conflict. Banking on Lenin's desire to bring about a socialist revolution in Russia and pull it out of the war, the Germans actively supported his return from exile in Switzerland. After seizing power in the October Revolution of 1917, Lenin and the Bolsheviks did exactly that.

Regime Type and the Political Structure of the State as Causes of War

Another body of literature that takes a second level perspective focuses on the political organization and the nature of the regime of a country rather than on economic policy. The nature of civilian control over the military, bureaucratic procedures, and the influence of special interests have all been the subject of considerable scrutiny. One prevalent line of research argues that the influence of special interests and the armed forces, combined with a lack of public oversight, becomes particularly acute in authoritarian

23. Lenin 1939.

states. By contrast, democratic states are more peaceful. Indeed, some observers submit that the absence of war between democracies virtually constitutes a law-like phenomenon.[24]

For some observers, authoritarian states in and of themselves are more war-prone while democratic states are always more peaceful, regardless of the regime type of the other state. This constitutes the monadic view of the Democratic Peace argument. The dyadic view of this thesis suggests that democratic states are indeed more peaceful but only in their relations with other democratic states.

The Democratic Peace argument is arguably of long standing, and components of the contemporary theory can be found in much earlier thinkers. Joseph Schumpeter (1883–1950) thought that authoritarian states tend to be more warlike because of the influential and historically evolved position of a warrior aristocracy, which occupies an elite position in society based on their ability in combat.[25] This holds true not only for feudal aristocratic societies but also for authoritarian states where the military holds a privileged position in decision-making. Where the armed forces hold disproportionate power, civilian leaders are pushed to the background and military options rather than diplomatic solutions are pursued. Consequently, civil-military relations are a key factor in explaining the nature of foreign policy and the possible outbreak of war.[26] A somewhat similar argument is made by scholars who suggest that business interests might ally with the interests of the armed forces in creating a "military industrial complex." A combination of powerful economic interest groups and the military could hijack government and engage in risky ventures that might be beneficial for those particular interest groups but not for the state as a whole.[27]

In authoritarian states, such special interests—that is, pro-war business groups and the military aristocracy—can play a large role in the policy process because they exclude the public from decision-making. The public are less likely to choose war as a solution to conflict, as they might become its primary victims. However, if privileged groups dominate the political process, they can roll the costs of conflict onto the general population and try to isolate themselves from potential harm. Authoritarian leaders send others off to war, while escaping both the obvious physical dangers and the political consequences: they cannot be voted out of office when the war does not go well.

---

24. An excellent overview of the Democratic Peace literature can be found in Elman 1997.

25. Schumpeter 1961.

26. Feaver 1999 surveys the state of play in the research on this topic.

27. The theoretical argument got a public endorsement when American President Eisenhower, who, as a former general and leader of the allied forces in World War II, had intimate knowledge of the military himself, warned in his farewell speech of the dangers of the military industrial complex even in democracies.

Related to these hypotheses, Jack Snyder submits that authoritarian states subvert the regular decision-making process, because it is easier for privileged groups to logroll policies without public supervision.[28] For example, assume that one privileged group, the military elite of Country A, favors an aggressive policy towards Country B, which has a strong army. Another privileged group in Country A, the heavy steel industry, favors an aggressive policy towards Country C, which has a strong navy. A buildup of Country A's navy would benefit the steel industry. The military might support the heavy industrial sector if, in turn, the big business group supports the military. The result then will be an aggressive policy towards both countries B and C.

Unlike the monadic view, which considers certain democratic states as inherently more peaceful than other types of states, the dyadic view argues that democracies are less prone to go to war only when they are dealing with other democracies. Democracies might be less conflict prone due to their ability to signal clearly to other states what they intend to do. They are transparent, because they have free speech and media. Authoritarian states are distrusted because their leaders can more readily defect from their promises and because of the lack of transparency in decision-making. Why should we trust the words of a dictator if he can break his word or withdraw from a treaty without consequences? In a democracy, however, a leader can be held accountable by the population. She must take those demands and voices into account.

Second level perspectives also pay attention to bureaucratic factors that may influence security policy. Inter-agency quarrels and turf battles can lead to different outcomes than one might expect if one used a unitary state perspective and assumed that the state's elites behaved as a unified, strategically rational actor. As Graham Allison has shown in his analysis of the Cuban Missile Crisis, parochial bureaucratic interests can subvert calculations by political elites who pursue the overall state interest, even when the stakes are extremely high.[29]

Second Level Explanations are Necessary but Insufficient

In the following chapters we will spend considerable time using second level perspectives to illuminate why war broke out in 1914 and also played a role in the invasion of Iraq in 2003. Yet we cannot rely on this level of analysis exclusively.

First, given that the world is populated by countries with different economic systems and with many different forms of government, we need to find ways of preventing conflict even between unlike actors. Indeed, it is

---

28. This forms a critical part of Snyder's 1984 explanation of the outbreak of war in 1914.

29. Allison 1971.

clear that democracies and authoritarian states are not always at war with each other. There are many examples of peaceful relations between such states. Even during the Cold War, when two superpowers with starkly opposed economic systems and different regime types faced each other, overt hostilities did not break out. There must be other factors that also play a role in explaining the absence of war.

Thinking in term of policy prescriptions, if one accepted the argument that only certain types of states are peaceful, then one might even call for aggressive policies on the part of purportedly peaceful states. Indeed, if it is true that democratic states are more peaceful than authoritarian states, does this mean that democratic states should enter into particular conflicts or initiate wars to try to change the other form of government? Democracies might then enter into a war to "end all wars," as Woodrow Wilson claimed. Or a democratic state might attempt to violently change the nature of another country's government, as the United States and Britain attempted to do in Iraq, despite the objections of many allies, such as Canada, France and Germany.

Finally, there are historical anomalies to some of these second levels. Looking at dyadic arguments, we know that similar types of government have fought each other. The Soviet Union and China engaged in low-level but violent border clashes in the 1960s. Vietnam and China ended up in a full-fledged war. We might add the Soviet interventions against Hungary in 1956 and Czechoslovakia in 1968 to that list. All these states were socialist countries, so the Marxist argument at least seems to contain some anomalies.

Even the dyadic view of the Democratic Peace thesis has its critics, although counterexamples seem less obvious. Some argue that the dyadic view is not statistically relevant. Others suggest that on closer inspection some allegedly democratic states were less democratic than supposed while some allegedly authoritarian states were not all that different from democracies.

In short, while second level perspectives provide keen insights, they cannot give us the whole story. We need other levels of analysis to get a clearer picture of the larger context. Which constraints and opportunities do states face at the international systemic level that might explain the prevalence of war in general and specific wars in particular?

Third Level Analysis: A Systemic View

Systems theory looks at the larger structure in which actors operate. A system is a set of regularly interacting elements within a particular organizing structure. In other words, the behavior of the individual elements that make up the system is explained by their placement within the larger pattern of interactions.

Intuitively, one can understand this by thinking of a family. The moment one is born one becomes part of a larger whole. There are particular sets of rules that govern how one should interact with siblings. There are authority relations between parents and children. The family in turn is part of a network of social rules and even formal legislation that sets parameters for how parents and children should interact. In other words, individuals are part of larger social entities that present themselves as a given and that provide opportunities for certain behaviors while constraining other types of actions.

The same holds true for international politics. The international system consists of regularly interacting units. Today those constitutive units are sovereign, territorial states, but historically there have been systems that consisted of empires, feudal lordships, and city-states (as in Ancient Greece). The system thus privileges some organizations over others. Aside from a few exceptions, only internationally recognized states can take part in key international organizations such as the United Nations (UN), the World Bank, and the International Monetary Fund.

The international system, moreover, has a particular structure, a particular arrangement of the constitutive parts. Most importantly, the international system lacks any central authority that can legitimately exercise coercive power over its constituent units, the states. Thus, we can say that the international system is anarchic.

Anarchy and the Distribution of Power

Structural realists such as Kenneth Waltz argue that the international system shows dramatic differences from domestic politics.[30] He draws upon two analogies to make his point. First he compares the international system to pre-modern forms of organization. Based on the work of Emile Durkheim, the late nineteenth-century French sociologist, Waltz notes that pre-modern societies such as tribal organizations lack formal hierarchy and complexity. Individuals perform functionally similar tasks that require little training and little specialization. In other words, in these societies government is not formalized and the level of economic development is low.

Modern societies, by contrast, possess hierarchy and complexity. They are replete with many formal rules and regulations, not only in terms of legal and political organizations but also in the private sector, as with rules governing corporations. As a consequence, individuals can specialize in very narrow tasks, allowing for an advanced division of labor and thus economic development.

Drawing on this view, Waltz argues that the critical element distinguishing the two forms of society revolves around the ordering principle.

---

30. Waltz 1979.

Does the society possess hierarchy (government) or not? The international system resembles pre-modern societies since there is no world government and states must rely on self-help. The elements of the system, the individual states, are poorly integrated and the division of labor is low. States resemble each other in providing similar functions for their population, such as defense of the nation's territory, crime control, and national legislation.

Waltz then draws a second analogy between economic markets and international politics. In competitive markets with lots of producers, all firms are price-takers. No firm by itself can determine a price, but given that companies have to compete with one another to lure customers, the price that a firm can charge for a given product will be determined by supply and demand. But this is not always true. In some markets, a few firms may dominate production and thus control how much is produced and at which price. Cartel arrangements between firms allow companies to charge more for their products by limiting the supply available to customers. It might even be the case that one firm dominates production and occupies a monopoly position. The consumer, if she wants to continue buying this product, is at the mercy of the monopolist. In other words, in oligopolies and monopolies firms are price-setters not price-takers. Smaller firms and consumers can only react to what the larger firms do.

Waltz suggests that this provides insights into how the international system works. If there are a large number of actors, and if they are relatively equal in strength, then states behave as firms would in a competitive market. There will be few constraints, and states will engage in open competition with other states. All states will be similarly placed. However, when a few major powers dominate, then the international system will resemble an oligopoly. Similarly, if one actor dominates, the states that compose the system will show behaviors that look like firms in a monopoly situation. Dominant states will face few restraints whereas smaller states will have to go along with the dictates of the larger states.

The key point for Waltz is that just as the division of market share allows us to make predictions about how firms will behave, so too will the particular balance of power—the relative strength of states—allow us to predict state behavior. We do not need to know much, if anything, about a particular state, other than whether it is strong or weak. Simply knowing what the international system looks like in terms of the balance of power—are there many equal states? is one state far more powerful than others?—will tell us how any rational state would behave given that particular configuration. We do not necessarily need to know anything about the individual make-up of individual leaders (the first level of analysis) or the internal characteristics of states (second level analysis).

Waltz identifies two critical elements in the international system: anarchy and the distribution of capabilities. The condition of anarchy gives us the permissive cause of war by creating an enabling condition. If we had a world government (hierarchy), wars would not occur. The distribution of power in turn provides us with *a priori* expectations about whether war or peace might be more likely. Assuming that actors are rational, we can thus predict that systems with a balance of power are more stable than systems in which power is distributed unevenly.

Waltz's neo-realist, or structural realist, perspective also leads one to examine whether the stability of systems depends on the number of great powers. Are systems with two dominant powers, as during the Cold War, more stable than systems with four, five, or more great powers? These questions, as we will see, have important ramifications for policy. Waltz believed that a world of two superpowers was desirable. Former American Secretary of State Henry Kissinger, by contrast, favored a world with a larger number of great powers that could act collectively against expansionist powers.

Besides the distribution of power in a system, the nature of alliances might also have important effects.[31] As we will see in our analysis of World War I and World War II, the types of alliances that states concluded at the time limited the options for other states. Indeed, some alliances created incentives for other countries to go to war. It was an issue not just of how many great powers were present in the system at that time, but of how those states created particular arrangements that for others changed the nature of their calculations. The Franco-Russian alliance thus drove Germany to seek closer ties with Austria. In this sense, the alliance structures presented themselves as given sets of conditions that confronted decision-makers as static constraints rather than something they could control or change.

---

31. In Waltz's earlier work (1959), he argued that alliances have an independent effect on state behavior. In his later work (1979), he suggests instead that the distribution of power should be measured as the distribution of power among states alone, not among alliances. The effect of alliances can be subsumed under the distribution of power among states.

TWO

Tools of the Trade (2):
Game Theory

Game Theory as a Third Level Perspective

Game theory examines how rational actors behave strategically in a particular structural configuration. In this sense, game theory takes a third level perspective. The particular context compels actors to cooperate with each other or to take advantage of the other player. Indeed, it is possible that actors might wish to cooperate with one another but that the structural situation creates impediments to doing so. Actors might very well prefer mutual cooperation over conflict, but due to anarchy (the lack of an overarching authority who can enforce compliance and cooperation) they are driven by self-help. Consequently, they must rationally pursue their best strategy not knowing what the other actor will decide. Thus, game theory can provide a useful set of tools to help us understand the outbreak of World War I, as well as nuclear crisis management and strategic interaction in general.

Game theory can be highly mathematical and plays a prominent role not only in the study of international politics but also in economics and business literature. Even the simple modeling of a game between two actors who face a one-time decision to cooperate with each other or not cooperate (defect) has dozens of possible solutions. In this context we will examine only a very small subset of possible games. Situations in which actors prefer mutual cooperation will be denoted as CC, with each actor preferring cooperation over antagonism, which will be denoted as DD, for joint defection. Thus, mutual cooperation CC is preferred over mutual defection DD, but for a variety of reasons cooperation might nevertheless not end up being the outcome. Cooperation games are games in which actors perceive mutual benefits from cooperation and prefer this over mutual defection. Three such games are Staghunt, Prisoner's Dilemma, and Chicken. Many other types of strategic games do not have this structure, and actors do not prefer CC over DD.

We also simplify by only examining two-person, one-time, or single play games. Each actor faces a decision to cooperate or defect, and each faces this decision only once. There is no second round play. In many real life situations, games will involve more than two actors and often will have multiple stages. Nevertheless, we will be able to derive important insights from even this rudimentary understanding of games.

I will use the following notational conventions. There are many ways of setting up the logic of a two-person game. For our purposes, I model the game as a two-by-two matrix. Each actor will have the choice to cooperate (C) or not cooperate, that is, defect (D). This gives us four possible outcomes. In the matrices, the first number denotes the horizontal actor's first preference, the second number the vertical actor's preference. Thus, (1, 4) signifies that the actor on the horizontal axis chose this particular outcome as his first choice, while the second actor saw this outcome as her worst choice.

Surveying all the four outcomes, we can use the greater than symbol (>) and the less than symbol (<) to show how actors ranked one preference over others. So, if my preference ordering has mutual cooperation ahead of mutual defection, I would write this as CC > DD. Similarly, the following preference ordering for one player—DC > DD > CD—denotes that this actor prefers to defect while the other player cooperates. Moreover, that outcome is preferred over mutual defection, which, in turn, is preferable to cooperating while the other player defects.[1]

Types of Games

Staghunt

This game derives its name from a reading of the work of Jean-Jacques Rousseau, the eighteenth-century French political theorist. Rousseau argued that all would benefit if actors cooperated with one another in hunting a stag. Conversely, if each actor hunted for himself, each could, at best, catch only a hare. If each did their duty in the cooperative venture, all would share the fruits of the larger kill. However, if individuals believed that not all would do their duty, it might be possible for the stag to escape, in which case those faithfully adhering to the agreement to collectively hunt for the stag might be left with nothing. Thus, a lack of confidence in the other player(s) might lead the game to unravel, even though mutual cooperation (CC) was objectively the best outcome.

---

1. For an introduction to game theoretic logic and its applications, see Oye 1986. Two non-cooperation games are Harmony and Deadlock. In Harmony at least one actor will prefer to cooperate no matter what the other player does: CC > CD > DC > DD or CC > CD > DD > DC. The latter two do not really matter, nor does the ordering of the first two. The point is that I will pursue cooperation no matter what the other player does. A second game might be Deadlock. In this case at least one actor prefers DD over CC: DC > DD > CC > CD. One actor will thus pursue a hard-line policy no matter that he thinks the other player will do.

Figure 2.1 | **The Staghunt Game**

Player II

		Cooperate	Defect
		1	**2**
	Cooperate		
		1	4
Player I		**4**	**3**
	Defect		
		2	3

In the Staghunt game the preferences for either actor are CC > DC > DD > CD. (Note that in Staghunt, Prisoner's Dilemma, and Chicken the preference orderings are symmetrical.) Each player prefers mutual cooperation over anything else (CC), but if one does not follow up on the agreement, then the person chasing the stag ends up with nothing (the stag can escape), while the other manages to catch a hare. This would be Player I's worst outcome (CD). If Player I thinks that Player II might defect on his duty, it would be rational for Player I to defect as well. With both actors engaging in this line of reasoning, it is possible that the least preferred outcome (DD) will result.

The point is not whether the Rousseau parable is empirically correct. Instead, the thought experiment is intended to draw our attention to particular types of structural situations in which cooperation might not occur if one does not trust the other actor to comply. The chance of achieving mutual cooperation in these types of games is relatively high, given that both actors have mutual cooperation as their first preference. It is a question of transparency and knowing what the other actor is up to. Mutual cooperation might be achieved if monitoring can be improved.

Pure liberal trade theory is an example of a Staghunt scenario. According to this economic perspective, if a state defects from liberal trade by raising tariffs to keep foreign goods out, then that country hurts itself. Tariffs raise the price of goods for the consumers of that state and protect non-competitive industries. Rationally speaking, then, any state should pursue liberal trade. However, if one fears that another country might

Figure 2.2 | **The Prisoner's Dilemma Game**

Player II

		Cooperate	Defect
Player I	**Cooperate**	2 2	1 4
	Defect	4 1	3 3

choose protectionism, perhaps because of domestic political reasons, then one might defect from liberal trade as well. Even though both countries rationally prefer liberal trade (CC), distrust of each other creates incentives for both to defect (DD).

Prisoner's Dilemma

Intuitively, everyone will recognize this game from the many police shows on television. Imagine the scenario in which the police have caught two criminals red-handed for a serious felony offense, say, car theft. The prosecutor has enough evidence to convict both suspects, whom we shall call Curly and Moe. However, the law enforcement officials suspect that the suspects might be implicated in a more serious crime, that is, the fatal shooting of a nearby storekeeper. Lacking reliable eyewitnesses, they have no evidence to convict either one of the more serious crime. At this point, the prosecutor can take each of the suspects aside and offer a deal (without either knowing what the other suspect is doing). The suspect who provides testimony against the other will be treated leniently on the minor violation (car theft), while the other is treated harshly for the more serious violation (armed robbery and murder).

The prosecutor counts on the rational calculation of each of the suspects. If both keep their mouth shut, that is, if the criminals cooperate with each other (CC), the prosecutor will manage to convict both of them for the lesser offense, but they will avoid being linked to the more heinous crime. If both of them rat out their partner in crime (DD), both of them will be found guilty on all counts. Mutual cooperation is thus preferable to mutual defection.

However, since neither knows whether the other is keeping his mouth shut, it is rational for each to testify against the other. The suspect, say Curly, who provides testimony against Moe will get the best possible outcome, with only minor punishment (DC), while Moe takes the rap for the murder if he maintains his silence. This would be Moe's worst outcome as he would be held fully responsible for the crime (CD). Even mutual defection (DD) would be preferable as both would then share in the responsibility and thus the penalties would be less severe for Moe. In other words, given that it is rational to testify against the other person, the result will be that both suspects will provide evidence linking them to the more serious crime. Each player will choose to defect, not knowing what the other player will do, with both of them ending up with mutual defection.

The preferences for both players are thus ordered as DC > CC > DD > CD. Each player's first preference is to take advantage of the other player (provide testimony against him), while the other player cooperates (keeps his mouth shut and does not provide testimony to the police). Conversely, keeping one's mouth shut (thus cooperating with the other player) might yield the worst possible outcome, if the other player defects.

Cooperation in this game is far more difficult to achieve. If Player I defects, he can achieve his first and third preferences. If he cooperates, he can achieve only his second and fourth preferred outcomes. Regardless of what the other player might do, it is thus rational to defect.

This type of game typifies situations where states fear for their security. States might be better off cooperating with one another than going to war. But not knowing whether the other state will attack, it is dangerous to pursue diplomacy or disarmament. Indeed, if one believes the other state will attack (defect), it might be prudent to try to attack first (thus opt for defection as well). As we will see, at the eve of World War I leaders engaged in exactly such calculations.

Chicken

Playing chicken revolves around a strategy where each player threatens the other with a terrible result for both, unless the other complies with one's demands. The game has many everyday analogies but became popularized as a real life game in which two drivers head towards each other on a collision course. The first one to veer off is deemed scared and is branded as the "chicken." The player who veers off can be seen as the one who complies with the other (cooperation). The one who drives straight on is the player

Figure 2.3 | **The Chicken Game**

Player II

		Cooperate	Defect
Player I	Cooperate	2 2	1 3
	Defect	3 1	4 4

who does not cooperate (defection). If both veer off, one might deem this mutual understanding to save both reputations (mutual cooperation, CC). If both hold the course, a frontal collision with disastrous consequences will be the result (DD).

The game's preference ordering is DC > CC > CD > DD. Player I's first preference is to have the other player veer off while Player I drives on (DC). Player II is the chicken and Player I gains in prestige. Should that not happen, the players hope that both will veer off so that Player I's reputation is still somewhat intact. Player I's third preference would be to veer off, once he concludes that Player II will hold the course (CD). If both try to force the other player to veer off and both keep driving straight on, both end up dead (DD, mutual defection).

Nuclear crisis bargaining can be understood as a game of chicken. Both sides, the United States and the Soviet Union, threatened each other with nuclear retaliation in order to force the other state to change its policy. Both sides tried to win the game, threatening to hold the course and go to nuclear war if necessary (defect). Each tried to put the burden on the other nation to pull back in order to avoid nuclear holocaust (cooperate with the threatening state). The danger in these situations is that if both states had persisted in their hard-line policy, this might have led to nuclear war (mutual defection). During the Cuban Missile Crisis in 1962, political leaders in Washington themselves referred to the crisis dynamics in terms of a game of Chicken.

Factors Influencing Cooperation

It is important to keep in mind that these games assume that actors cannot communicate with one another, or, if they can communicate, they do not trust each other. Hence, they do not know what the other actor will do. The game is also modeled as a single play situation.

Two conditions can dramatically alter the nature of the game. First, the payoff structure might influence the likelihood that actors will choose to cooperate or defect. Imagine, for example, that the differences in outcomes between CD and DC in the Prisoner's Dilemma are slight. In short, the cost of being taken advantage of, and the gain that might result if one player tries to take advantage of the other player, are quite similar. In such an environment, Player I might be willing to take some risk and try to cooperate with Player II. If the differences are significant (as they were going into World War I), then cooperation might be more difficult.

An even more important feature of the game is the possibility of repeat play. Research shows that actors who engage in Prisoner's Dilemma games can diminish the likelihood of mutual defection. A relatively simple strategy of Tit-for-Tat dramatically improves the likelihood of cooperation. In Tit-for-Tat, an actor punishes the other actor if she defects, but only once. Conversely, if the other actor cooperates, one continues to cooperate as well. In this sense, games can evolve to become more cooperative.[2]

---

2. Axelrod 1984.

THREE

World War I

Eight to ten million soldiers will swallow each other up and in so doing eat all Europe more bare than any swarm of locusts. The devastation of the Thirty Year War compressed into the space of three or four years and extending over the whole continent ... Crowns will roll by dozens in the gutter.[1]

The Historical Prelude

The French Revolution (1789) forms a watershed in European history. Until then many countries still had semi-feudal economies and were largely ruled by aristocracies. In much of continental Europe—Prussia, France, and Spain—these dynasts ruled as absolute monarchs. Only a few states had developed more republican forms of government, particularly where urban and commercial interests prospered, as in some parts of Northern Italy and the Low Lands (the Netherlands and Belgium). Consequently, in most countries people did not identify with their governments. They were subjects, not citizens, and had no voice in the political system.

The French Revolution shook that foundation to its very core. Partially influenced by ideals expounded by the new United States of America, the French intellectuals and populace challenged the ruling classes. Starting with the storming of the Bastille, the Parisian prison, the Revolution engulfed France for the next decade. Thousands of aristocrats, including the monarchy, were executed, the Church was stripped of many of its assets, and the feudal system came to an end. The ambition of the Revolution manifested itself strikingly in the introduction of a new calendar starting in the year zero, the introduction of the decimal system, and the standardization of measures. The social, political, and economic worlds were redesigned under the political battle cry of fraternity, equality, and

---

1. Friedrich Engels proved uncannily prescient in 1887 in foreseeing the consequences of World War I; Engels, cited in Joll 1992, 206. For another general overview of the war, see Taylor 1980.

{ 53 }

liberty. Individuals would be citizens, not subjects. Popular sovereignty replaced absolute rule.

The military implications of the Revolution were startling. Now that people identified with *their* country and *their* government, they could be asked to serve the state. Thus, instead of having to hire mercenaries, government could conscript its citizens to fight. As a result, mass conscription—the *levée en masse*—dramatically raised the number of troops that France could place in the field. Since France, at that time, was also the most populous country in Europe after Russia, the combination of a large population base plus the new type of conscript army gave it a decisive edge on the battlefield.

Eventually, the Republican government gave way to a form of military dictatorship under Napoleon Bonaparte in 1799. Napoleon's military prowess and his imperial ambition soon brought ruin to Europe. Over the course of 1805–07 he defeated the combined armies of Austria, Prussia, and Russia. His invasion of Russia in 1812 mobilized an army of perhaps 600,000, a huge army even by today's standards. Russian stalling tactics and the infamous Russian winter, however, proved insurmountable. The combined army of France and its satellite states was decimated. Nevertheless, a year later Napoleon had managed to raise another large army, which could be defeated only by a combined force at Leipzig. After his defeat, he was exiled to Elba, but escaped and once again challenged a combined force at Waterloo in 1815. With some luck on their side, the English-Prussian force defeated him for once and for all.

The French Revolution and the subsequent Napoleonic conquest of much of continental Europe had significant consequences. First, revolutionary ideals carried over to many of the European states. A rationalized economic system and greater access to government appealed to large segments of the population. Second, in order to meet the French challenge, even absolute rulers, such as the Prussian king, had to emulate many of the advances in administration and government that the French had introduced.[2] In short, the nation-state gradually started to take shape. In the nation-state, the population first identified itself as a particular group, the nation, which was distinct from other groups, and second, identified itself with the territorial state that it occupied.

The European wars had also resulted in horrendous losses. Two million people perished in the various conflicts. Millions more were displaced, and the economic damage was incalculable. This presented the quandary facing the European statesmen of the time. How could the five Great Powers of Europe—Britain, France, Prussia, Russia, and Austria—work together to prevent such cataclysmic events from recurring? How could they maintain the peace when, in this multipolar system, each could affect

---

2. See Craig 1955, ch. 2.

the stability of the international system? The answer lay in a cooperative regime that would prevent major wars from breaking out for almost 40 years.

The Concert of Europe 1815–48

In 1814–15 the Great Powers of Europe convened in Vienna to discuss how they might prevent another bid for imperial domination by France or any other great power. Their representatives came up with a deliberate design to maintain the peace. Lesser states were consulted, but ultimately the agreement revolved around the Great Powers' design. This system was named the Congress of Vienna after the place of the negotiations, but the other name given to it is perhaps more descriptive: the Concert of Europe. Working together the states could maintain harmonious relations.[3]

The Concert was based on several key provisions. First, all agreed that none of the key actors could be eliminated. Thus, each of the Great Powers could be assured of its own survival as an independent state. Should one state nevertheless launch a bid for imperial domination, then the others would jointly create a countervailing alliance. In the Napoleonic period, by contrast, France had been able to engage and thus defeat its rivals one by one. Second, should wars nevertheless break out, the Great Powers would try to keep them limited in scope, aimed at redressing particular objectives or grievances rather than destabilizing the other state or advancing radical ideals. Third, alliances should be flexible. Each state was to band together with any other state against a possible aggressor. Fourth, buffer zones were established. Intermediate powers, like the Netherlands, were propped up, and Bavaria would act as a buffer zone to separate Prussia and Austria. Finally, the political leaders considered the overall situation as non-zero sum. One actor's gain need not come at the expense of the other. For example, new colonial gains in other parts of the world did not come out of territories already held by another Great Power.

The Concert was a success. It managed to adjust the balance of power among these states and to avoid a major confrontation for roughly 40 years. This is not to say that this system of realist politics was benign or beneficial for the other, smaller states. Indeed, some of these were partitioned or integrated against their will. Populations were moved across borders or forced to live in states not of their choosing. However, compared to the Napoleonic wars, this seemed like a moderate price to pay.

The lessons to be drawn from the Concert had a long legacy. Some saw in this conscious design for peace among multiple Great Powers a strategy that could be used to avert major wars in general. Henry Kissinger, National Security Advisor and then Secretary of State during the Nixon

---

3. Gulick 1955 describes the intricacies of the settlement; see particularly chapters 7–9.

and Ford administrations in the United States (1968–76), had studied the Concert system as a student at Harvard. When he came to office, his intention to balance the Soviet threat by a multi-power condominium consisting of the United States, China, Japan, and Europe was similar to the Concert's logic. Moreover, by engaging in a policy of *détente*—the deliberate attempt to downplay differences and foster closer relations—he attempted to provide incentives to the Soviet Union as well. This was not altogether different from what the Concert actors had done with France. In other words, the logic of the Concert system informed American foreign policy more than a century and a half after its conclusion.

The Bismarckian Period (1862–90)

By the late 1840s the situation in Europe had started to deteriorate. By then the new generation of leaders had scarce memory of the Napoleonic conflicts. The dread of another great war had receded, and the common fear that united the diplomats at Vienna had dissipated. Other issues aggravated the problem. The Ottoman (Turkish) Empire that had controlled large parts of the Middle East, Northern Africa, and Eastern Europe was in decline. Both the Austrian and Russian Empires had ambitions in Eastern Europe, and each sought to fill the power vacuum left by the Turks. Russian attempts to capitalize on the Ottoman weakness led to the Crimean War (1853–56), in which Russia was defeated by a combined French-British expeditionary force.

Nationalist tensions and reform movements also destabilized some of the European continental powers. Revolutionary movements swept through many countries in 1848, while nationalist tensions led to rebellions against Turkish rulers in Eastern Europe, which led to several new independent states. These same nationalist sentiments also threatened the Austrian Empire that contained Slovaks, Czechs, Austrians, Hungarians, Slovenians, and others.

Nationalism also inspired the unification of two countries that until then had consisted of aggregations of smaller units. What is now known as Italy consisted of a set of smaller independent units—Piedmont, Savoy, Tuscany, Venetia, the Papal States, and the Kingdom of the Two Sicilies—until unification (1859–70). Count Camillo Benso di Cavour, the Prime Minister of Sardinia-Piedmont, and Giuseppe Garibaldi, a patriot and military leader, played key roles in uniting these disparate territories into one state, which, although not immediately a great power, certainly had to be reckoned with.

The German unification was even more startling. When Bismarck came to power in 1862 as the Prussian Minister-President, Germany consisted of several dozen independent territories and cities. Bismarck embarked on a process of state-building and united the territories into a

German Empire with Prussia at its head. The Prussian King became the new Emperor Wilhelm I, and Bismarck was given the title of *Reichskanzler*, or Imperial Chancellor. In order to unite Germany he waged three wars, defeating Denmark in 1864, Austria in 1866, and France in 1870. In one fell swoop Prussia, which already had been a strong state, now transformed itself into the strongest power on the continent. Interestingly, Bismarck limited his objectives: rather than destroy Austria, he was satisfied with its defeat in 1866 and saw it as a potential ally for the future.

One other change occurred in the overall situation facing the Great Powers: the European empires could no longer expand into heretofore uncolonized areas. Even Africa had been carved up among the European states. By 1881 every corner of that continent had been divided in the "Scramble for Africa." Thus, expansion had become a zero-sum contest, and the empires started to fight each other for the last territorial spoils.

How could the Great Powers maintain the peace in this difficult environment? A Concert system was no longer viable. Instead, Bismarck devised a complex alliance system through which he managed to prevent a major war for three decades after 1870. He sought to oppose any strong state that could threaten Germany, particularly France. Satiated after German unification, he also planned to oppose any power that would threaten the European order, whoever that might be. We might describe this system as a revised balance of power system, with Germany aiming to be, in Bismarck's words, "one of three in a world of five"—meaning that Germany would aim to be in alliance with two other Great Powers in a system of five Great Powers. This balance of power system, like the Concert, was premised on the notion that all major actors should be assured of their survival.

In order to keep aggressive states in check, Germany concluded various alliances to neutralize the incentives for any state to go to war.[4] First was the "Three Emperors League" with Russia and Austria (1872). This was directed against any attempt by France to seek revenge for its defeat of 1870–71 and left France isolated without a continental ally. Second was the "Dual Alliance" with Austria (1879). This was, in one sense, a mutual defense treaty, though it had other objectives as well. It aimed to keep the peace between Russia and Austria by checking both their ambitions in the Balkans. Under the terms of the agreement, Germany would come to Russia's aid should Austria seek to expand in the Balkans at Russia's expense. Conversely, if Russia were the aggressor, Germany would side with Austria against Russia. Third was the "Triple Alliance" with Austria and Italy (1882). Bismarck feared that border disputes between these two countries might lead to war. To prevent such a conflict, he promised that Germany would not oppose Italian ambitions in Africa. Conversely, Italy

4. Craig and George 1983, ch. 3.

was to desist from provoking Austria. And should Austria and Russia end up in a war over the Balkans, then Italy was not to side with Russia against Austria.

Finally, Bismarck concluded an understanding—an *Entente*—with Britain, who did not sign formal alliances but called its agreements *Ententes*. The Chancellor made clear that Germany had no ambitions to challenge Britain in its imperial holdings, nor would Germany seek to match Britain's naval pre-eminence. Should Britain and France end up in colonial disputes, Germany would offer qualified support for the British.

The crux of the system was to isolate France, Germany's main opponent, and maintain the status quo that Germany had established on the continent in 1870. It differed in one important way from the Concert system of 1815: it did not include all the Great Powers but was instead premised on a highly complicated balancing of five Great Powers (six if one includes Italy). Bismarck had performed a high-wire act of diplomacy. Once again, competing aims in a multipolar world could be managed. But when the system unraveled, the result was the cataclysmic war that Europe had avoided for a century.

The Demise of the System (1890–1914)

By 1890 Bismarck was out of power. Wilhelm I had passed away and his grandson, Wilhelm II, became the new emperor. He had far greater ambitions for Germany than his grandfather. Bismarck's realist politics had no place within his administration, and he had to resign.

The situation in the Balkans worsened as the Turkish Empire continued to slide. Whereas Russia was initially constrained by Germany through the Dual Alliance, it now wanted Germany to stand aside in the Balkans. The lack of German support led to Russian withdrawal from the Three Emperors League in 1887. For the time being, Russia concluded a German-Russian Reassurance Treaty, but in secret it turned to the one great power that had been isolated by Bismarck: France. Moreover, France still had territorial claims against Germany stemming from the war it fought in 1870 in which it lost the province of Alsace-Lorraine. The French and Russians concluded a secret alliance in 1892, although spies soon revealed its content.

The agreement was more a battle plan than a mutual defense treaty. It specifically noted that both France and Russia would engage in full-scale mobilization at the first signs of potential war. It thus anticipated that war would be massive rather than limited. It also explicitly targeted potential enemy states by naming the Triple Alliance (Germany, Austria, and Italy). Most importantly, it called for the simultaneous, two-front engagement of Germany if either Russia or France was attacked. There need not be prior consultation. Speed was of the essence. If Germany and Austria were to be defeated, it was critical that France and Russia attack from both sides and as quickly as possible. Memoranda exchanged within the Russian camp reveal how the participants thought the war might be decided in the first few weeks, even days: "Whoever first concentrates his forces and strikes against a still unprepared enemy has assured himself of the highest probability of having the first victory, which facilitates the successful conduct of the entire campaign."[5]

A hair-trigger situation was created. If France and Russia were less poised for war, they might be swiftly defeated if the other actor (the Triple Alliance) attacked them. The converse also held. If France and Russia attacked first, with Germany and Austria unprepared, then the latter two would be overrun. Each side thus had to devise a lightning war strategy.

During these years, Germany experienced rapid economic, military, and industrial growth. Although Britain had industrialized earlier, Germany surpassed it by 1900. This in itself might challenge Britain, but things were made worse by Wilhelm's naval ambitions. When Britain developed a new type of battleship category, the Dreadnought, Germany decided that it would develop a similarly high class fleet of such types. The Dreadnought race was on.

Britain had long maintained a two-power standard. This was interpreted in various ways, but basically the intention was for the Royal Navy to be strong enough to meet a challenge of the two next most powerful fleets combined. Germany's naval ambitions threatened that standard and Britain's supremacy of the oceans. From London's perspective, Britain needed to rule the waves to maintain its ties with the empire and the Dominions (Canada, Australia, and New Zealand). Given that Germany was a continental power, its naval buildup and colonial pursuits in South West Africa, Tanganyika, Togoland, Cameroon, and the Pacific islands could only mean that Germany had its eye on the British Empire. Consequently, Britain joined the alliance that was already in place to deal with a German threat: the French-Russian agreement. Britain formed an *Entente* (again an understanding, not a formal treaty) with France in 1904 and with Russia in 1907.

The consequences of these alliances were significant. In declaring its support for Austria, Germany now lacked any means of control over the Austrians in the Balkans. Similarly, with British and French support, Russia now could count on their support should Russian policy in the Balkans lead to a confrontation with Austria and Germany. Thus, by 1914, the multipolar system had transformed into two alliances and had become virtually bipolar. True, the states of each alliance were still independent entities, and in that sense one might say the world was a multipolar one, but for all intents and purposes they were shackled to their alliance partners. The Triple *Entente* of Britain, France, and Russia now stood toe to toe with the Triple Alliance of Germany, Austria, and Italy.

5. As cited in Kennan 1984, 264.

The Outbreak of World War I

By 1914, tensions were building around the globe. In Africa, France and Germany confronted each other in colonial crises. On the seas, Germany and Britain were vying for naval supremacy. But the Balkans—rife with nationalist sentiments, Turkish decline, and Austrian and Russian rivalry—proved to be the powder keg that started the first truly global war. In earlier epochs wars were largely confined to regions or groups of states. By the twentieth century, however, the war-making capacity of states had evolved to the point that the most powerful states could operate in any country or region of the world. The density of interaction meant that the conflict would be fought on an unprecedented scale and intensity.

In the early summer of 1914, a terrorist attack killed the heir to the Austrian throne, Archduke Ferdinand. Austria suspected Serb complicity and posed an ultimatum to Serbia. Russia, Serbia's traditional ally, came to its aid and threatened Austria. From then on things spiraled further and further out of control. With Russia and Austria confronting each other, France and Germany were quick to mobilize as well. With mobilization almost indistinguishable from a build-up for attack, all countries on the continent geared up for the great conflict. Britain initially tried to stave off disaster but to no avail. War broke out on 28 July 1914.

In Western historiography, many have noted how the war resulted in horrendous losses through endless (and fruitless) trench warfare. Some will recognize the sacrifices made by the Dominions, such as the Canadian naval contributions and the Australian and New Zealand lion's share of the burden of the ill-advised campaign in the Dardanelles. Less well known are the 1.3 million Indians who served in the British forces during the war or the more than 600,000 Africans who fought for France. German and British forces fought in East Africa, while parts of their fleets chased each other around the globe. The war was truly global in its geographic scope.

It also marked a watershed in global history. For the first time, the United States broke out of its isolationist shell, which had led it to focus primarily on the Americas, and sent large numbers of American troops across the Atlantic. Already by far the strongest economy in the world, it was poised to become the most powerful military machine in the decades ahead. Indeed, so successful was the United States that the twentieth century was to become, in the words of some observers, the American century. Four great empires—the Austrian, the German, the Russian, and the Turkish—would fall. In the East, Japan had stayed out of the conflict, coming to an agreement with Britain, which realized it could not simultaneously engage Germany while having to defend its oriental possessions against Japanese encroachment (a portent of things to come).

If the American Civil War is sometimes described as the first modern war—with devastating consequences, as it killed more than half a million

men—World War I capitalized on every military technology that mankind
had devised: aerial bombardment, the machine gun, submarine warfare,
mass troop movement, and chemical weapons. The trenches became a
slaughterhouse. The most advanced and most "civilized" nations of the
world killed each other by the millions. In the battle of Verdun alone, a
quarter of a million perished. On the first day of the Somme offensive,
the British counted 60,000 casualties, dead and wounded.[6] War on the
Eastern Front and in the Alps was equally devastating. By the war's end in
1918, almost 10 million had died, and the world had changed forever.

How can we explain the outbreak of this war? Obviously, given its
importance, this is a critical question in its own right. But World War I
also provides an interesting example of how we might deploy our methods
of analysis. In looking at this war through various lenses, we can see how
to study the outbreak of other conflicts.

First Level Analysis: Perceptions and Misperceptions among the Key Decision-Makers

The various political and military European elites suffered from several
factors that hampered their decision-making ability. First, they misper-
ceived the intentions of other leaders, and, at the same time, they engaged
in burden shifting to those leaders. When we look back at the historical
record, we see ample evidence that the attention span of many leaders was
impaired. Both sides missed or discounted diplomatic overtures from the
other side. Germany did not see Britain's proposals as a genuine attempt
to broker a settlement. It believed that Britain could choose to stand aside
in the conflict if it wished. Without British support, the French might have
been more reluctant to confront Germany and Austria. Britain in turn
argued that it had commitments to France and Russia and that the burden
for averting war lay on Germany. Both sides thus ascribed to the other
actor greater room for maneuver, while leaders perceived that they themselves were hopelessly constrained and had little choice but to fight.

Political and military elites chose analogies that fitted their preferred
course of action. In the beginning, all sides believed the war would be
short, and German leaders, in particular, invoked the memory of the
quick victories of 1866 and 1870–71. As noted above, Russian politicians
and military elites thought the war would be decided in the very opening phase. German staff officers similarly believed it would be all over by
Christmas, and some generals even claimed it would be over in two weeks.
The German Crown Prince looked forward to a happy, merry war.[7] Few

---

6. For an unsurpassed account depicting the horrors of trench warfare, see Keegan
1978.

7. Joll 1992, 214. The phrase *"frisch fröhliche Krieg"* is ascribed to him, and alludes to
a hunting song, further suggesting how sport and war seemed virtually indistinguishable to
the participants.

cared to think about the evidence from the American Civil War, which was one of the first wars fought with the use of railroads and which introduced early submarines and prototype machine guns. That war had dragged on for four long years, killing more than half a million people.

Second, leaders suffered from cognitive rigidity and inflexibility. War was seen as inevitable. Bethmann Hollweg, the German Chancellor, thought that "the great majority of the peoples are in themselves peaceful, but things are out of control and the stone has started to roll."[8] Others likened their situation to mountaineers shackled together, who had to follow where others fell. Opponents were cast as diabolical and untrustworthy. The British soon referred to the Germans as Huns; Germans disparaged the uncivilized Slavs, the Russians, and the Serbs. Everyone found some way of seeing the opponent as subhuman or, at the very least, inferior. Evidence that conflicted with pre-set beliefs was brushed aside. Thus, although Britain had signaled it would support France and Russia, particularly if Belgian neutrality were violated, the German government thought Britain would stand aside. Disconfirming evidence was simply ignored.

Third, leaders believed that they confronted a shortened time horizon. Indeed, the belief that the war would be won by the alliance that struck first was perhaps the most critical element in the decision-making process. The various governments not only wanted to believe in a quick war because that would be less costly, they also thought that military technology favored the one who attacked first. This belief was then superimposed on the psychological trait that befalls all leaders in moments of crisis—they believed that they had only a very limited amount of time to react. Unless they acted with speed and urgency, the situation would be out of their control. In thinking that they had to act immediately, and thus that their room for diplomacy was limited, the rulers of the various countries in fact created the very condition they feared.

Beliefs among the intelligentsia and general population also fanned the flames of war.[9] Indeed, the idea that war could be quick and short was widespread. Some also thought that war was an inevitable and beneficial product of human evolution. These sentiments contributed to a cult of the offensive.[10]

Analysts and military planners examined the implications of the new military technology and concluded that these favored the state that first took the offense. Railroads, for example, could quickly bring massive numbers of troops to a particular sector and so allow the attacker to build up a dominant force that could overwhelm the defender. In earlier times, any

---

8. Joll 1992, 23.

9. Collective belief systems methodologically straddle the first and second levels of analysis. We are not just looking at individual cognition or specific leaders, but we are interested in a larger aggregate, the collective consciousness of the populace at the time.

10. See particularly Snyder 1984.

movement to the front was ponderous and slow, giving the defender time to react. Even the machine gun was thought to be an offensive weapon. An infantry man advancing with a machine gun could lay down a withering pattern of fire that the defender could not resist. (That defenders in their fortifications could mow down advancing infantry in the open field was apparently considered less plausible.) Not only could troop mobilization and movement proceed faster in the new environment, it was also thought that armies could position themselves in secret. There was the constant fear that the other side might launch an unexpected sneak attack.

German leaders also thought, incorrectly, that the Russian economy was undergoing successful modernization. Russia had started to modernize its economy and political system after its defeat by Japan in 1905. Since they believed that the Russian reforms were so successful that Russia would soon overtake the German economy, the German leaders thought they had to attack Russia soon, before it became invulnerable to defeat. "Today war is still possible without defeat, but not in two years," lamented Bethmann Hollweg.[11] The longer Germany waited, the more likely it would be that Russia might actually attack.

Beliefs in bandwagoning rather than balancing also lent support to the idea of an offensive war. Bandwagoning meant that lesser states would side with the stronger state rather than try to form an alliance and construct a balance against that stronger state. German decision-makers, therefore, thought that Belgium would not oppose the German advance through its territories in order to attack France.

Social Darwinist philosophies and nationalist views made matters worse. In a distorted reading of Darwin's theory of evolution, people believed that competition and selection were beneficial for the progress of human society. For the more fit to weed out the less fit (the weaker states) was thus a natural process. Nationalist mythology that expounded the virtues of one's own nation state, while disparaging the accomplishments of other nations, provided additional justification for going to war.

These widespread views, combined with the perceptions and misperceptions of leaders, led to aggressive foreign policies. States opted for military strategies that favored the offense rather than defense. Consequently, politicians considered that a preemptive, decisive war was feasible. The one to attack first would win. Those who sought a diplomatic solution to the crisis following the assassination of the archduke were severely constrained due to the short time frame imposed on them.

Finally, the belief in the offensive advantage led leaders to try to create secret alliances and build up their militaries. Instead of trying to prevent war by strengthening their defenses or by creating strong and clear alliances that would deter a possible attack, the political elites prepared for war.

---

11. As cited in Van Evera 1985, 81.

A Second Level Perspective: The Primacy of Domestic Politics

While the first level perspective focuses on explaining political outcomes by looking at psychological traits and the nature of decision-making within groups, the second level perspective focuses on regime type and the state's domestic organizations and institutions. As we have seen earlier, various second level approaches are possible. One can examine relations of civilian governments and their military, or the nature of bureaucracies and their influence on policy, as well as the particular type of regime that a country has.

These questions figured front and center in the debates surrounding the culpability of Germany in causing World War I. Some argued that international politics, the balance of power and the nature of alliances, were the key causes. Others, such as the German historian Fischer, rooted the cause in Germany's internal politics, at the second level of analysis. Speaking of a primacy of internal politics (*Primat der Innenpolitik*), he drew attention to the particular features of Wilhelmine Germany and its implications for foreign policy. Rather than argue that external circumstances influenced Germany (an outside-in explanation), Fischer submitted that the internal politics of Germany influenced its external disposition (an inside-out explanation).[12]

The following discussion of the internal politics of Germany and briefly that of Britain is meant to suggest how one studies the relationship between domestic politics and foreign policy. This is not a comprehensive account of the internal politics of all the protagonists; we lack the space and time to do so. However, the analysis serves two purposes: 1) to clarify the internal influences on the foreign policy of two key protagonists, and 2) to demonstrate the importance of the second level in explaining the war.

German Historical Development

In the sixteenth century, what is now Germany consisted of many autonomous political entities, such as duchies, margraves, cities, and bishoprics. Although in principle part of the Holy Roman Empire, many of these were in fact independent states. Among these entities, Prussia occupied areas in what is today eastern Germany and parts of Poland.

---

12. See the discussion in Berghahn 1973, 1. In a similar vein, in the early years of World War II, a prominent historian examined why the United States found itself in a war with Germany. More specifically, Rosenberg (1943/1944) asked why Germany had become an aggressive state in the late nineteenth century during the Bismarckian era, again during World War I, and now in World War II. The answer lay in the long-term origins of authoritarianism in Germany. Unlike states such as Britain that had gradually developed as democracies, the Prussian and then the German political system at key junctures had chosen the route of authoritarian state development rather than democracy. For Rosenberg, the origins of World War II simply concluded the long political development of Prussia and then Germany which had its origins in the fifteenth century.

Prussia was ruled by the Great Elector, who, as one of the high aristocrats of the Holy Roman Empire, cast a vote in affirming the emperor. The very fact that the emperor had to rely on such support from the high nobles suggests how weak the empire was. The elector shared power with other nobles within the Prussian realm. These were the landowners, the Junkers, who managed their estates in a feudal manner. Below the elector and the aristocratic Junkers were the commoners—the townsfolk and the peasantry.

In the middle of the seventeenth century, Prussia was still relatively weak. Its army numbered only around several thousand, and it was frequently set upon by stronger states such as Sweden, Austria, and Russia. It lacked a centralized government and strong bureaucracy, with much of the power residing with the landed aristocracy. According to Rosenberg, "Government of, by, and for the landed aristocracy was the preponderant pattern of rulership in the east German principalities."[13]

The elector, nobles, and commoners had different interests. Each also had various views regarding how Prussia should be run and how it should combat the external threats posed by the greater powers of the day. The elector wanted to establish a stronger state by centralizing political authority, thus giving himself more power. In order to create a more efficient administration, he wished to raise taxes, build an effective government bureaucracy, and create an army that could check external threats. However, the Junkers were reluctant to cede more power. They wanted to manage their estates with minimal intervention, dealing with the peasantry on their lands as they pleased. They also were not keen on the elector's plans to raise taxes. The peasantry and commoners, by contrast, wanted substantial political reform that would give them greater political influence. The peasants still worked the lands in feudal circumstances. Commoners, such as town dwellers, were not locked in serfdom, but they too did not have much influence. Moreover, the urban centers of Prussia were small when compared to the towns of northwest Europe and Italy. And, as in the traditional feudal structure, commoners occupied the bottom of the social hierarchy.

The bargain eventually struck between the elector and the Junkers solidified the development of Prussia as an absolutist state—a strong monarchy without much parliamentary oversight. Under the terms of this political alliance, known as the Second Serfdom, the elector gained greater powers and ultimately became the King of Prussia. The Junkers consented to the king's request to raise taxes from the commoners and peasantry for a much larger army. In the following decades, the Prussian army became one of the most formidable in Europe, and Prussia became known as the

---

13. Rosenberg 1966, 31.

"Sparta of the North."[14] In exchange for the Junkers' support, the king made them tax exempt.

The exemption of taxation is a key feature of all absolutist governments. In early medieval times, parliaments had originated as counsels of the nobles of the realm in support of the king—most famously captured in the medieval agreement contained in the Magna Carta. The nobles insisted on such rights of counsel on various issues, particularly the king's levying of aid and taxes. Consequently, in countries where rulers wished to tax the nobility, parliaments were strong as the nobles had a vested interest in curtailing the authority of the king. In Spain, France, and Prussia, where nobles became tax exempt, only weak parliamentary systems emerged. The big losers in this deal were the commoners and peasantry who were forced to bear the burden of new obligations.

The Prussian alliance also gave the Junkers other advantages. With the resources to create a strong army, the king could fight external wars more effectively. At the same time, the army could be used to repress possible internal revolt by commoners and peasants. (As is the case in some systems today, when authoritarian civilian government conspires with the military, the armed forces can serve for external defense as well as internal repression.) To complete the last element of this alliance, the Junkers—besides being given tax exemption and greater autonomy to control their peasants (hence the term Second Serfdom)—became the key suppliers of the officer corps. Thus, Junkers and king could use the military forces for their own purposes.

By the mid-nineteenth century, the political and social environment in the German lands had changed sufficiently to re-open the prospects for a democratic system. In Prussia, however, the king still ruled in an authoritarian fashion. The landed aristocracy still occupied an important political, military, and economic position. They were a privileged tax exempt class, occupied the high ranks of the officer corps, and were important producers of grain, specifically rye. However, the emergence of an industrial sector and the growth of an urban middle class, particularly in some of the more industrialized German lands, threatened their privileged position. Excluded from the decision-making structure, industrialists and bourgeoisie now demanded greater say in the affairs of their respective states.

Once again, however, the alliance of king and nobles curtailed these demands for democracy. The Prussian king had several objections to change. First, he aimed to squelch democratic reforms so that, ruling as an authoritarian monarch, he could maximize his power without interference. Second, he favored unification of the several dozen distinct polities that still existed in the 1850s into a larger German state. Brandenburg-Prussia

---

14. Rosenberg 1966, 40; Craig 1955, 4. Craig's book remains the locus classicus on the Prussian army.

was one of the strongest of these states, but there were other areas of economic and military importance such as Hessen, Bavaria, the independent cities of Hamburg, Bremen, and others. If he could unify these under his rule, Prussian influence would grow exponentially. The Junkers opposed democratization as well. Like the king, they favored unification and for very similar reasons. Economically, they were particularly interested in obtaining controls on the import of grain, particularly from the United States. By then American exports were starting to go up as the United States expanded westward. To protect their own markets, the Junkers favored tariffs on agricultural goods.

The middle class and some of the industrial sectors were the big proponents of political reform and democratization. The industrial sectors, particularly big business, were less keen on democratization, because they feared the rise of the left and a more militant class of laborers. Both classes also favored unification but largely for economic reasons. The many borders and tariffs raised transportation costs and stood in the way of achieving greater efficiencies of scale. Not dissimilar to the demand for European integration today, big business thus supported the diminishing of local barriers to trade. They also favored protectionist measures against all but agricultural goods to keep out industrial goods from the leader of the industrial era: Britain. In order for German industry to be able to sell its products, it wanted to keep English goods out (or at least raise their prices through tariffs), making German industrial products more attractive.

Prussian Chancellor Bismarck completed the master plan. As we saw above, he unified the country by waging three wars against Denmark, Austria, and France, but he also managed to keep the international peace thereafter by carefully designing alliances that isolated France. The other components of his plan had internal consequences. His forceful unification satisfied the preferences of the king, Junkers, and the industrial and middle classes. He also raised tariffs benefiting the Junker elites and heavy industry. Given the economic interests of the Junkers in the protection of their domestically produced grain (rye) and the interests of heavy industry in the protection of domestic steel production and manufacturing (iron), this alliance of aristocracy and industry is referred to as the Iron and Rye Coalition. As a result, the Prussian king became emperor of the new German Empire. Both Junkers and heavy industry got tariff protection. However, democratic reform was the casualty. The aristocracy and the industrial elites controlled the policies of the Second German Empire, with only a weak parliament, called the Reichstag, to offer it advice. In a nutshell, Junkers and big business supported continued authoritarianism and exclusion of foreign economic goods.

Although the Reichstag gained some powers, it was restricted from intervening in military affairs, particularly the budget. This particularly became important as Germany prepared for war and built up its army and navy, which directly threatened British naval supremacy: "Just as the survival of Prusso-German Constitutionalism necessitated exclusive control over the Army as an instrument of internal repression, the power-political problems raised by the need to build up a Navy directed William [sic] II towards an 'absolute monarchy'."[15]

In sum, at the eve of World War I, the authoritarian government of Germany combined with the armed forces to form the ruling strata of German politics. With both predisposed to war, and with political opposition of no consequence, they could do as they pleased. German authoritarianism and the influence of the military on civilian decision-making must thus be considered as causes for the outbreak of the war.

The English Experience

Almost at the same time as Prussia entrenched an absolutist system, the attempt of the English king to rule without parliament was dramatically reversed. In the early seventeenth century, England found itself embroiled in conflicts in Ireland and Scotland. The king desired to levy taxes to equip an army to fight these wars. His fellow nobles in Parliament, however, rejected his demands for greater financial resources. Subsequently, Charles I proclaimed he would rule without parliament, making decisions with his own council, the Star Chamber. This decision, combined with other grievances, resulted in a civil war that lasted from 1640 to 1649. In the end, the king lost the struggle as well as his head. After several more decades, this victory was reaffirmed in the Glorious Revolution of 1688–89, a bloodless coup which established the supremacy of Parliament over the monarchy. Thus, whereas the Prussian elector had succeeded in establishing royal absolutism, the English king's attempt ended in abject failure. Thenceforth, the monarchy ruled side by side with an active Parliament, though one dominated by nobles, that consented to being taxed in exchange for oversight over the king (or queen).

Similarly, events in Britain in the nineteenth century provide an interesting contrast with simultaneous developments in Prussia. The industrialization of England changed the social landscape. New towns emerged almost overnight. Manchester, until the late eighteenth century a small town of less than 10,000, multiplied tenfold in three decades. Yet it lacked representation. Other boroughs, however, some of which no longer existed, were represented. The emerging industrial class thus lacked power even though their economic might had increased with industrialization and trade. In various Reform Bills, the king's prerogatives were gradually reduced. Parliament underwent major reform in which borough representation changed dramatically. With mercantile interests in favor of free trade—given that Britain

---

15. Berghahn 1973, 34.

was the leader in the industrial era—political reform resulted in increased democratization combined with a free trade policy.[16]

Aside from leading to two different regimes in the two countries, the three-way contests between monarchy, aristocracy, and the industrial middle class also led to different sets of relations between civilian government and the armed forces. In Germany the two were virtually indistinguishable. The Junkers had an important political position and retained their dominance of the military. At the eve of World War I, well over half the officer corps above the rank of major was of aristocratic birth. At higher ranks the ratio was even starker. It must come as no surprise that the military exerted a great deal of influence on political choices. In Britain, by contrast, no such obvious linkage existed. The dominant political and economic classes sometimes had interests in common with the military, but they were distinct groups with divergent preferences and with distinct policy choices. Additionally, with Britain's security more dependent on the navy than the army, the armed forces could not be readily used for internal repression. The navy could serve to forestall any invasion of the home islands but obviously could not be used to squelch urban protests.

Given significant public hesitancy, and with civilian oversight over the military assured, the British Parliament was less inclined to go to war than were some of the continental powers. However, when Germany would not guarantee to respect Belgian neutrality, Britain was drawn further into cooperation with France to stop German aims on the continent.

A Third Image Explanation of the Outbreak of World War I

Are Bipolar or Multipolar Systems more Stable?

As we have seen, the European Great Power system proved ever more difficult to manage once the Congress of Vienna started to unravel. The Congress had worked because of a momentary consensus on the need to avoid a war between the Great Powers. In the decades after 1815, statesmen understood what the consequences would be of such a conflict and designed mechanisms to prevent it. But managing the competing claims of various powers all at once was far from easy. Indeed, some have seen the number of contending powers as the heart of the problem. The discussion of whether a system of two powers is more stable than a system with a larger number of great powers is more than a purely theoretical exercise. It informs policy prescriptions today.

Some scholars, such as former American Secretary of State Henry Kissinger, argue that multipolar systems are more stable. Kissinger studied the Congress of Vienna and drew from it the lesson that an international

---

16. Gash 1968, ch. 2, 7.

system consisting of several contenders could be adequately managed and that such a system would be more stable than if the number of great powers was small.[17] Putting his ideas into practice, Kissinger believed that superpower rivalry between the United States and the Soviet Union was less stable than a world with multiple centers of power. Consequently, he argued for American support for a united Europe, close ties with Japan, and better ties with China.

Others drew different conclusions. Looking back at Europe in the nineteenth century, they concluded that an astute (and ruthless) statesman such as Otto von Bismarck might be able to manage this complexity momentarily, but that multipolar systems tend to be more fragile in general than a two-power or bipolar system. Proponents of this view lamented the decline of the two-power system that characterized the world from 1945 to 1991.

In what ways might a system with multiple powers be more stable? First, with more states, it is more likely that there will be cross-cutting and overlapping loyalties. For example, an adverse economic relationship with one state might be compensated by benign security relations with that same state, because one needs it as an ally against a third party threat. So states will have diverse relations with various states depending on the issue at hand.

Second, conflicts are less likely to be all-out conflagrations. Given that multiple possible allies are available, other states will aid in balancing against a rising hegemon. For example, after Napoleon defeated Austria and Prussia, Britain and Russia combined to halt and end the French bid for European dominance. By contrast, in a bipolar world each state has to rely primarily, perhaps entirely, on its own ability to balance between the two major powers. Moreover, defeat in war will be very costly as there will be no other actors who can redress the balance. Related to this point, we can see that adjustment and balancing in a multipolar system are possible, even for states that are relatively weak. And, consequently, because states might be less fearful, they will be less likely to engage in massive arms build-ups, and arms races will be less prevalent.

By contrast, if one actor in a bipolar system believes the other might be pulling ahead, this might precipitate a war. Rather than wait for the ascending power to have a preponderant advantage, the declining state might go to war while it still has a reasonable chance of victory. Indeed, there is a large body of literature that suggests wars tend to break out when a declining great power is challenged by a rising great power. These hegemonic conflicts correlate with changing patterns of growth and decline.[18]

---

17. Kissinger 2000 (first published in 1957).
18. Gilpin 1981.

Despite the arguments in favor of the multipolar system, advocates of bipolarity maintain the latter is preferable. In a two-power system, such as that during the Cold War, peripheries are relatively unimportant. Given that the two powers have to rely on their own resources to balance against the other state—that is, they must balance internally rather than externally through allies—they will be less concerned with control over peripheral countries. As long as the control over a third state does not affect the balance of power between the two dominant powers, the periphery will not matter as much. Thus, during the Vietnam War, proponents of bipolar stability such as Kenneth Waltz argued against the war, since it did not have any bearing on the balance of power between the Soviet Union and the United States.

Moreover, because the two dominant powers manage the balance internally, there is less danger of buckpassing. With buckpassing, states hope that another state will confront the aggressor rather than balance themselves. Each state hopes to reap the benefits of the actions of others who have confronted the aggressor, without bearing the burden of such confrontation. If each state engages in such calculations, no state might act decisively, and the end result will be that nothing is done to stop the aggressive state, with all eventually falling one by one to the imperial power. Napoleon's success in defeating various powers sequentially comes to mind. So, as long as the two powers can match each other's build-up, war will be less likely. The two dominant states cannot pass the buck, and each will act to rectify any imbalance.

A bipolar system is also likely to be more transparent. Each of the dominant powers will understand which state might threaten its security. Consequently, each power will monitor its rival closely. The system is clear, and as long as the actors have information about each other, it will be stable. In multipolar systems by contrast, newly formed alliances may transform the international landscape.

The Question of Polarity and the Outbreak of World War I

Unfortunately the situation leading up to World War I seemed to inherit all the drawbacks of both multipolar and bipolar systems with few of the advantages of either. On the one hand the European system consisted of five (or six if one includes Italy) major powers: Britain, France, Germany, Austria-Hungary, and Russia. Thus one might hope that cross-cutting cleavages and loyalties and flexible alliances would mitigate the chances of war.

However, as we have seen from our description of the post-Bismarckian era, the European system had congealed into two tight alliances: the Triple Alliance and the Triple *Entente*. Political leaders differed on how to read the situation. German leaders thought that Britain might not enter the war. If the system had been truly bipolar, and was understood by the actors as being such, then Germany would not have misinterpreted the signals from Britain that it would come to the aid of France and Russia. Moreover, the alliances were not quite so tight that one could describe them as a single entity. Italy indeed defected almost immediately from the Triple Alliance and entered the war on the side of the Triple *Entente*. Even Austria and Germany disagreed during the war about the best course of action, with Austria making overtures for peace while Germany resisted such attempts.

From one perspective, the system looked bipolar in that all the major powers were involved and redress could not be obtained because the alliances were rigid. Yet, on the other hand, each alliance did not appear as a coherent unit, as would be the case in a truly bipolar system, leading to misunderstandings and a lack of transparency.

The Balance of Power in World War I

The material balance of power provides another structural explanation. In its simplest form, balance of power theory suggests that if a state has a military advantage, it will act belligerently. An asymmetric distribution of power is thus unstable, while power symmetries correlate with stability and peace.

Can we explain the outbreak of the war by the strength of the respective actors? As Paul Kennedy shows, there were no dramatic differences in the relative strengths of the two alliances.[19] Together, Germany and Austria possessed a stronger industrial base than France and Russia. In the key sectors of coal and steel production, the Central powers outweighed them. However, if Britain were included with France and Russia, then the *Entente* had the upper hand over Germany and Austria. In manpower numbers, all sides could mobilize considerable forces without any great difference in numbers. In short, the balance of power did not clearly favor one alliance over the other.

A more fine-grained analysis of military strength, however, indicates that the development of particular types of military technology contributed to upsetting the balance. Particularly, Germany's choice to develop a navy with the Dreadnought class battleship challenged Britain's supremacy. With British security relying on control of the seas, Germany's choice to try to match its technological lead in battleship development threatened what had been the status quo. Germany was a land-based power with interests on the continent. Britain, as a maritime empire, had vested interests in its overseas Dominions and its many colonies. The fact that Germany now sought to develop advanced naval capabilities, while also maintaining a strong continental army, greatly concerned the British government.

---

19. Kennedy 1985.

The perception of the balance might have been even more important than the material indicators of that balance. Let us blend third level research on the objective distribution of material resources with first level analysis—what did political elites make of these facts? We know from the historical record that German leaders looked at the objective data of the balance but read it in such a way that it supported the decision to go to war. While they realized that the Triple *Entente*'s industrial and economic strength matched that of the Triple Alliance, they excluded Britain from their calculations by assuming it would stand aside and included Italy in their favor, assuming incorrectly that Italy would fight with Germany and Austria.

German leaders made another mistake. As we already saw, their information indicated that Russia was growing at a rapid pace. And, indeed, Russia had engaged in an attempt to modernize its underdeveloped, almost feudal society. In 1905 Russia was defeated by Japan—the first instance in the modern era of an Asian country defeating a European state. This had propelled reform in the backward Tsarist empire. However, Germany was wrong regarding the pace of the reform taking place there, believing that it would soon overtake the German annual rate of growth, which in fact exceeded that of Russia. But the misperception led German leaders to conclude that they had to attack now, rather than risk defeat several years into the future. In other words, looking at the evidence at hand, German leaders believed that the trend in the balance of power provided them with a window of opportunity that they had to seize in 1914.

World War I as an Aggravated Prisoner's Dilemma

As we have seen in our previous discussions, the structure of the international system creates a Prisoner's Dilemma. Interacting states do not know what the other state intends to do. Without an overarching authority, each state must rely on its own military capabilities and has no higher redress to counter aggression, given the incapacity of international organizations to exercise force.[20] In these situations, each actor rationally has an incentive to distrust the other actor. In an environment where the very survival of the state might be in question, this means that the state should prepare for war and take any means necessary to ensure its continued existence.

While states would be better off cooperating and thus avoiding going to war with each other, the danger that the other state might attack will lead each state to prepare for war or try to preempt the other. Thus, the preference ordering for each actor would look like this: (1) go to war while the other state is unprepared and defeat that state; (2) both states

---

20. The League of Nations failed to check Japanese expansion in Asia and Italian aggression in Africa. And while the UN can authorize the use of force, the organization itself lacks military means. Although some plans were put forward shortly after World War II and again after the Cold War to develop a standing UN force, these plans came to naught.

cooperate and avert war; (3) both states go to war; (4) the state does not prepare for war, the other country attacks and is victorious. (I denoted this earlier as a DC > CC > DD > CD preference ordering.)

The conditions leading up to World War I exacerbated this preference ordering, making the structural situation even more precarious. First, as we have seen, the perceptions in various capitals led decision-makers to believe that their rivals were getting ready to attack. These views did not derive solely from psychological factors and misperceptions but also from the alliance structure. Starting with the 1892 alliance of France and Russia, the participants realized that in a war on the continent, each state had an incentive to attack first. France and Russia had an incentive to attack Germany together from both fronts, thus maximizing their chances for victory. The Franco-Russian alliance could not be more explicit in its aims: "In case the forces of the Triple Alliance or one of the partners of that Alliance should mobilize, France and Russia ... will immediately and simultaneously mobilize the totality of their forces and will move them as close as possible to their frontiers."[21] The agreement went on to specify the number of troops to be mobilized, "in such a manner as to oblige Germany to fight simultaneously in both East and West." Far from merely constituting a defensive agreement, it was in fact a plan for attack—stipulating numbers of troops and a specific target.

Germany in turn realized that, in order for it to win, it would have to first attack one opponent and then swing around to deal with the other. The German Von Schlieffen Plan hinged on the ability of German troops to wage an offensive war on the western front and, after the defeat of France, move the troops quickly by train to attack Russia. The war, it was said, would be decided by the timetable of the railway. This offensive plan was the only one on the table for German decision-makers. A.J.P. Taylor remarked: "Schlieffen ... though dead, was the real maker of the First World War ... In 1914 his dead hand pulled the trigger."[22]

This structural situation was worsened by the view that technology gave the attacker the advantage. As we know with hindsight, soon after the war commenced, all participants got mired in static and appalling trench warfare. But the belief that offense had the upper hand at the beginning of the war made the Prisoner's Dilemma worse. Given these misperceptions and given the incentives for each of the alliance partners to attack, decision-makers viewed the structure of the game as imposing dire consequences if one pursued peace and did not mobilize for war. If one tried to cooperate with the other state, and that state attacked, then the latter would be victorious in a matter of days. Not mobilizing, while the other state prepared for a lightning war, would be tantamount to self-annihilation. Conversely, if one managed to attack first, while the other

21. Kennan 1984, 181.
22. Taylor 1980, 20.

state was caught ill-prepared, one could get rid of a mortal enemy. Not only was there a benefit for not cooperating (DC) but that benefit was very high. Conversely, the costs of cooperating while the other prepared for war (CD) could be disastrous. And thus, even as states realized the nature of the game, they did not see a way out of this predicament. If one indicated a willingness to halt mobilization and the rush to war, this would simply create an opportunity for the opponent to strike first with success.

Conclusion: The Causes of War in 1914

Needless to say, any event as complex as World War I has many causes. The purpose of this extended case study is not to clarify every aspect of this particular war or to give a complete description of its causes. Instead it is intended to show how one can go about studying any conflict from a variety of perspectives and reduce the bewildering array of data to a reasonable discussion.

First level variables played a role in various respects. Elites ascribed to other leaders nefarious motives, engaged in wishful thinking, and were blind to evidence that contradicted pre-existing mindsets. At the same time, while elites acknowledged that a major war was imminent, they believed that their own room for maneuver was limited. If war was to be averted, it was the responsibility of other leaders to prevent it. Thus, politicians of the time shifted the burden to each other. Not only individual leaders, but society at large seemed infused with a bellicose spirit, a veritable cult of the offensive. Tragically, many thought that if war was going to occur, it would be short, and it would yield a victory for the state that took the offensive. Nationalist fervor compounded the mistaken assumption.

Second level variables mattered as well. From this analytic perspective, the belief that the offensive party would have the upper hand was not due to miscalculations but to institutional dynamics. Military elites benefited from offensive strategies, as these justified larger military expenditures and gave the armed forces greater autonomy. In authoritarian states such as Germany and Russia, but also to some extent in democratic France, the armed forces rather than civilians exercised considerable influence, and they could thus implement their preferred strategy in the conduct of overall foreign policy.

Authoritarian governments not only gave the military undue influence on political decisions, but they precluded meaningful oversight and input from the civilian population. As Jack Snyder notes, in the authoritarian states where the military played a key role in decision-making—such as Russia, Austria, and Germany—the armed forces logrolled their preferences.[23] The various service branches supported each other and chose

---

23. Snyder 1984.

offensive strategies. Given their prominent position in the overall political structure, their chosen strategies became their countries' foreign policies. Consequently, small groups of privileged classes made decisions that would send millions to their death.

Finally, a third level view sheds light on other aspects of the outbreak of war. One can debate whether the polarity of the system contributed to the start of the war. However, this debate is somewhat inconclusive as it depends on how one sees the alliance structure. Were European politics complicated because there were five or six major powers vying for position, or was the European system in effect a bipolar one with tightly aligned countries? The very opaqueness of commitments, particularly the commitment of Britain to France, made matters worse. Leaders could assess the balance of power in favorable terms depending on how they saw the strength of the rival alliance.

In terms of military assets or material resources for heavy industry and war production, there did not seem to be a dramatic imbalance. However, the belief that the technology gave the offensive party the upper hand suggests it was not the imbalance per se, but the type of military technology of the time, and the perception of the material distribution of power, that made the balance a precarious one.

Taken together then, first, second, and third level analyses provide different angles of view. Every conflict or potential conflict can be approached by looking through these different lenses. Why did some of these variables conspire to lead the world to war in 1914 and again in 1939? Why did they not lead to a confrontation between the United States and the Soviet Union during the Cold War? How do such causal dynamics continue to affect leaders in today's decisions to choose to go to war or not? We will discuss some of these questions in the following two case studies.

FOUR

The Cold War and After

*If we are honest with ourselves we have to admit that unless
we rid ourselves of our nuclear arsenals a holocaust not only
might occur but will occur—if not today, then tomorrow.*[1]

*The first implication of the nuclear revolution is that military
victory is not possible. From this it follows that if statesmen are
sensible, wars among the great powers should not occur.*[2]

Our study of the causes of World War I in the previous chapter indicates
how different levels of analysis contribute to a fuller understanding of why
the conflict started. More generally, first, second, and third level perspectives can illuminate how other wars might erupt. Understanding how such
events might happen can give decision-makers some insights into how
conflict might be avoided.

World War II brought home the costly lessons of war in the starkest
terms possible. By one estimate, 55 million people perished. In the Soviet
Union alone, more than 20 million people died. Many millions more were
wounded. Entire nations lay in ruins and economies drained. Moreover,
the technology of war had made huge leaps. At its outset in 1939, even
advanced nations such as Britain had biplanes in their air forces. Less than
six years later, Germany could send missiles—the v2—from the continent
to bomb London, and two atomic bombs destroyed the cities of Hiroshima
and Nagasaki in Japan.

At war's end, two superpowers remained that dwarfed all others
in economic and military power. Before long, the Soviet Union and the
United States combined had more than 50,000 nuclear warheads in their
arsenals. Missile technology evolved to such a degree that each state could
destroy the other country in less than half an hour. Submarines capable
of launching missiles and patrolling the coast of the enemy could do so in
even less time. As the Cold War threatened to become a hot conflict, the

---

1. Jonathan Schell, as quoted in Harvard Nuclear Study Group 1983, 233.
2. Jervis 1989, 23.

fate of humanity was put into a precarious balance with both sides poised to strike at a moment's notice.

Even today major powers maintain vast arsenals of nuclear weapons, as well as other weapons of mass destruction. Additionally, the prospect of such weapons falling into the hands of non-state actors has added other dangers. How have we avoided a major power conflict until now and how might we maintain the peace in the future?

The Advent of Global Thermonuclear War: From Massive Retaliation to Mutual Assured Destruction

At the end of World War II, the United States was the sole nuclear power. Although Germany had launched its own nuclear program, it had failed to develop the bomb. This was partly due to Allied efforts to thwart Nazi Germany from acquiring such weapons and partly because Germany could not muster the immense effort to develop the fissionable materials required.

Even though the Soviet Union soon developed nuclear weapons of its own, the United States continued to lead the weapons race, first in developing larger numbers of nuclear warheads, and then in the development of a thermonuclear warhead. Unlike the fissionable materials used in the atomic bomb, the hydrogen bomb used nuclear fusion, yielding warheads that were hundreds of times more powerful than the bombs dropped on Hiroshima and Nagasaki.

In the first decade after the war, the United States enjoyed a comfortable lead in nuclear weapons. It had more warheads than the Soviet Union, and its European allies provided a geographic advantage. From its bases in Europe, it could strike at the Soviet Union, which lacked any similar forward position to attack the United States. However, the Soviet Union enjoyed an advantage in conventional, non-nuclear arms. Unlike the United States, it did not decrease its troop strength after the end of World War II, and it continued to maintain more than 5 million troops under arms. It also built up a sizeable force in aircraft and particularly in heavy armor, enough so that the United States was concerned that it would use its proximity to Western Europe and its conventional advantage to threaten or even attack and occupy those European states. So large was the Soviet advantage that the French military staff calculated in the late 1940s that it could hold out for only eight days against a massive Soviet attack.

When perceived in terms of a global struggle of capitalist democracies versus authoritarian communism the problem became even more acute. How could the United States defend itself and its allies in all the corners of the world that were seemingly menaced by communist states?

Early American nuclear strategy approached this quandary by developing the doctrine of massive retaliation. The Truman and Eisenhower administrations adopted a posture that threatened the Soviet Union and its Warsaw Pact allies with a nuclear response to any level of challenge in any location that the United States deemed within its sphere of influence.[3] This nuclear doctrine in turn formed part of the American "containment strategy," foreshadowed in the famous Long Telegram sent under the pseudonym "X," but written by George Kennan when he was attached to the American embassy in Moscow and published as an article in the journal *Foreign Affairs* in its 1946/47 issue:

> In these circumstances it is clear that the main element of any United States policy toward the Soviet Union must be that of long-term, patient but firm and vigilant containment of Russian expansive tendencies.[4]

The containment strategy called for a policy of maintaining alliances in all areas where communists threatened to expand and was directed at deterring the Soviet Union and, after 1949, the People's Republic of China. These alliances were backed by an American nuclear guarantee to use nuclear weapons if necessary to prevent or roll back communist aggression.

American pre-eminence, however, was relatively short-lived. Several years after the United States had developed and used atomic weapons, the Soviet Union developed such weapons as well. When the United States developed the hydrogen bomb, its lead was shorter still. A nuclear arms race ensued throughout the 1950s with both sides building ever larger nuclear arsenals and ever more destructive bombs. The United States developed and tested a thermonuclear device in the 13 megaton range (13 million tons equivalent of high explosives, or TNT). The Soviets built even larger bombs, ultimately testing a device that yielded 50 megatons. By contrast, the Nagasaki and Hiroshima bombs had produced a yield equivalent to about 12 to 20,000 TNT or 12 to 20 kilotons. In short, the hydrogen bombs were thousands of times more powerful than the bombs that killed more than 100,000 people in Hiroshima and almost that number in Nagasaki in 1945.

Under such conditions, no side could realistically expect to fight and win a nuclear war. Gradually the United States shifted to a nuclear strategy based on "mutual assured destruction" (MAD). This had several components. First, it envisioned that nuclear war would be "all out" rather than limited in scope. A nuclear exchange would not be limited to a few strikes but would involve the use of the entire arsenals at the disposal of both superpowers. Military as well as civilian targets would be hit.

Moreover, because the United States wanted to deter a Soviet attack on its allies as well, it extended the threat of MAD to incorporate those countries. Thus, if the Soviet Union invaded or attacked key American allies,

---

3. Snow 1991, 237.
4. Kennan (X) 1946/1947, 575.

particularly its partners in the North American Treaty Organization (NATO), then the United States would retaliate with the nuclear weapons at its disposal. Article 5 of the NATO treaty stipulated that an attack on one would be considered an attack on all. Thus, in common parlance, it guaranteed "New York for Paris." If the Soviets attacked Europe (Paris), the United States would strike back even though the Soviet nuclear counterattack would in turn destroy American cities such as New York. When President Kennedy traveled to Berlin in 1962 and pronounced *"Ich bin ein Berliner"* (I am a Berliner), he meant more than just to signal his identification with the plight of the citizens of that city, surrounded as it was by communist East Germany. He was signaling to the Soviets that an incursion on Berlin would be dealt with as if they had invaded an American city.

Secretary of Defense Robert McNamara described the essence of MAD in 1967:

> In that eventuality we must be able to absorb the total weight of nuclear attack on our country ... and still be capable of damaging the aggressor to the point that his society would be simply no longer viable in twentieth-century terms. That is what deterrence of nuclear aggression means. It means the certainty of suicide to the aggressor, not merely to his military forces, but to his society as a whole.[5]

As a strategy, however, MAD contained a paradox. On the one hand it made nuclear war less likely. Given that neither side could realistically expect to survive a massive nuclear exchange in any meaningful way, it diminished the incentive to start such a war. The previous massive retaliation strategy made sense only if one could use nuclear weapons to counter a threat without suffering annihilation oneself. It was based on the ability of the United States to fight a successful nuclear war. But this no longer held.

On the other hand, because a nuclear war would be suicidal and thus the superpowers would be less likely to provoke it, MAD might create incentives to act aggressively at a lower level of conflict. Because a nuclear exchange would be disastrous, any actor threatening to initiate such a war in response to conventional attacks faced a credibility problem. Why would the Soviets believe that the United States would jeopardize its own security by launching a nuclear attack on the Soviet Union in retaliation for a Soviet conventional invasion of Western Europe? McNamara realized that MAD revolved around the credibility of the threat:

---

5. Robert McNamara, speech in San Francisco, 18 September 1967. Available at http://www.atomicarchive.com/Docs/Deterrence/Deterrence.shtml.

> The point is that a potential aggressor must believe that our
> assured-destruction capability is in fact actual and that our will
> to use it in retaliation to an attack is in fact unwavering.[6]

In other words, mutual perceptions were critical in this game of Chicken.
Each side had to convey to the other that it would indeed launch a nuclear
strike if its fundamental interests were threatened. Given the inherent
paradox of MAD, both sides sought ways of making their nuclear threat
more credible.

Consequently, in the late 1960s, during the Nixon and Ford administrations, the United States shifted its strategy gradually from MAD to a
counterforce doctrine, which targeted Soviet nuclear capabilities and its
fighting capability.[7] American doctrine still contained a MAD component,
which entailed the destruction of the 200 largest Soviet cities and 34
per cent of the population (as was estimated in 1978). The counterforce
option thus lowered the nuclear threshold. Nuclear war was less likely
to be an all-out catastrophe but more limited in scope. It was hoped that
the deterrent would be more credible because nuclear war might not be
suicidal after all but simply a very costly war. In this way, the doctrine
would deter lower level conflicts.

For counterforce to be plausible, the United States had to develop two
technologies. First, it greatly expanded the number of nuclear warheads. If it
could drop several warheads on Soviet missile silos, it would stand a greater
chance of knocking out the possibility of a Soviet nuclear counterattack.
Second, it developed greater precision in its delivery systems. The principle
was the same: if American missiles could destroy Soviet missiles before
the latter were launched, then the United States might prevent a Soviet
counterattack. In this sense, counterforce made nuclear war more plausible
because one side might hope to win without self-annihilation, but at the
same time it lowered the probability of conventional conflicts, because the
deterrent was more credible.

During the Carter administration (1977–81), the United States
completed its move away from MAD and adopted a strategy that emphasized selective targeting, particularly of military installations. The Reagan
(1981–89) and Bush (1989–93) administrations continued this doctrine
with some variations, labeling it a counter-value strategy. In this view,
nuclear war could be limited in nature and scope. The development of
more accurate missiles, and missiles that could carry multiple warheads,
gave the planners the technical means to consider the possibility of a precision strike against the enemy.

The Soviet Union also developed the capability to launch a knock-out
blow, that is, first strike capability. Although it lacked the precise delivery

---

6. McNamara speech of 18 September 1967; see note 5.
7. See Snow 1991, ch. 3.

systems of the United States, it made up for that flaw by building very large missiles. While these were less accurate, their higher explosive yield compensated for that weakness by destroying a wider territory. They could be used to disable American bombers and missiles still on the ground.[8]

But paradoxes remained. The two superpowers aimed to enhance the credibility of a nuclear threat by making a nuclear war potentially less costly. Conversely, however, their strategies raised the fear of a first strike. As in World War I, both sides had to fear that the other party would adopt an offensive strategy and attempt to achieve victory in a knock-out blow.

Managing the Nuclear Predicament: Contributions from Three Levels of Analysis

With the decline of the communist regime in the Soviet Union and its fragmentation into 15 successor states, the Cold War has come to an end. Consequently, the danger of a large-scale nuclear war has diminished. Nevertheless, both superpowers continue to maintain large stockpiles of active and reserve nuclear weapons. At the peak of competition, the Soviet Union and the United States maintained more than 20,000 nuclear warheads each. Indeed, by some estimates the combined total might have escalated to close to 60,000 of such warheads. Since the end of the Cold War, the superpowers have diminished the number of atomic weapons in their arsenals but they still maintain several thousand.

How did these ideologically rival superpowers avoid a nuclear conflict even though the arms race and competition between them could very well have led to such an event? Following the theoretical thrust of this book, we will consider how war might have erupted due to causes at the first, second, or third level of analysis.

Perceptions, Misperceptions, and Credibility Problems

Individual miscalculations and misperceptions of hostile intent might have had disastrous consequences during the Cold War. Indeed, as we will see in our discussion of the Cuban Missile Crisis, the nuclear strategies of both sides exacerbated and complicated the problem of transparency, credibility, and shared information. In addition to the psychological problems that plague decision-makers in moments of crisis, and in addition to the particular problems created by nuclear deterrence, both sides also had antithetical ideological systems and believed the other state to be aggressive and dangerous. Since nuclear deterrence hinges on making the other actor believe that one is willing to wage nuclear war, even though such war would be suicidal, the possibility of miscalculation and misunderstanding was significant.

---

8. A useful overview of nuclear doctrines, the arsenals involved, and related issues is the Harvard Nuclear Study Group's publication (1983).

Few nuclear crises have been more studied than the Cuban Missile Crisis of 1962. Perhaps at no other time did the two superpowers come so close to the brink of nuclear war.[9] The problem arose when the Soviet Union deployed intermediate-range missiles in Cuba to support the communist regime that had seized power there just a few years before. Fearing an American invasion—the United States had earlier sponsored an effort led by the Central Intelligence Agency (CIA) to bring down the Cuban government by a small invasion force—Fidel Castro sought the support of the Soviet Union. To defend Cuba and to give itself a strategic base close to the enemy, the Soviet regime decided to place there nuclear-tipped missiles that could strike at virtually any location in the United States. Washington saw this as a direct challenge to its supremacy in the Western hemisphere and threatened to destroy the Cuban missile sites and to implement a blockade around the island. Both sides thought that nuclear war was imminent.[10]

President Kennedy was aware of the pitfalls surrounding decision-makers during moments of crises. Indeed, he saw close parallels between the developments leading up to World War I and the crisis of 1962. Without imputing any irrationality on the side of his own administration or to the administration of his Soviet counterpart, General Secretary Nikita Khrushchev, Kennedy understood that both were potentially subject to miscalculations and misperceptions.

As we know from our earlier discussion, during crises individuals tend to neglect contrary evidence and to evaluate information according to pre-existing belief systems. Kennedy feared that information that did not fit the established mindset of his advisors would be passed over and ignored. To remedy this situation, he solicited different points of view from the armed services as well as from his own civilian administration. He was also aware that actors tend to conform to other positions, particularly to those of the leadership, during periods of escalating tension. Such "groupthink" could eliminate alternate solutions to the crisis. In order to avoid this problem, Kennedy would leave the Executive Committee (the key decision-making group during the crisis) to explore various possibilities and to speak freely without the president in the room. His brother, Robert Kennedy, Attorney General at that time, sometimes sat in for him and operated as a conduit for some of the president's messages to Moscow.[11]

To make his own team understand the psychological issues involved in crisis decision-making, Kennedy suggested that his advisors read Barbara

---

9. A fine rendition of the crisis is provided by the WGBH/PBS video series (an Annenberg/CPB project). See *War and Peace in the Nuclear Age*, Episode 5: "The Cuban Missile Crisis: At the Brink." Allison 1971 remains the starting point for any serious study of the crisis.

10. Munton and Welch 2007 provide an overview of the research on the Cuban Missile Crisis, with the benefit of new information that has emerged after the fall of communism in the Soviet Union. Their book also contains a good bibliographic essay for further research.

11. Robert Kennedy 1969 provides a gripping inside account of the tension in the White House, even if it provides only a partial view of the crisis.

Tuchman's *The Guns of August* (1962), which chronicles how the leaders of the European states had seen the events of 1914 spiral out of control, leading to World War I. The president wanted to make sure that neither his government nor the Soviets, unlike the decision-makers of 1914, would see no other option but war.

Khrushchev was also aware of these dynamics. He realized that leaders tend to see the other actor as having more room for maneuver than themselves. Thus he, or Kennedy, might think that his hands were tied and shift the burden of extrication from the conflict to the other actor. "We must not tie the knot of war so tight that neither cannot undo it," he noted in a telegram to Kennedy.[12] Both had to make an effort to allow the other leader a means of retreat.

The Cuban Missile Crisis was not unique. However, as one of the most dramatic events of the Cold War, it serves as an example of how mutual perceptions might have triggered a superpower conflict. Yet, in this instance, both leaders acted together to avoid such misperceptions from spiraling out of control.

Joseph Nye has noted how the United States and the Soviet Union engaged in nuclear learning.[13] Both sides gradually came to share the same views and beliefs about the nature and consequences of nuclear war. If the Soviets had continued to believe, as Stalin expounded, that nuclear weapons were merely a step up from heavy artillery, the likelihood of war would have been much higher. Similarly, the exchange of information on weapons technology and nuclear strategy led to shared understandings of arms control, the danger of arms racing, and the problems associated with various nuclear strategies as well as nuclear proliferation. Going even further, the Gorbachev administration (1985–91) engaged in more complex and profound learning: not only was nuclear confrontation dangerous and to be avoided, but the very nature of the Cold War could be changed. The West and the East need not be political enemies. Gorbachev engaged in fundamental reforms in his government, opening the door to the end of the Cold War.[14]

Second Level Perspectives

At the second level, both states had dramatically different political and economic systems. The Soviet Union was dominated by a (seemingly) monolithic Communist Party. Individual rights were frequently violated, and citizens lacked meaningful control over their government leaders. In terms of the civil-military relation, it appeared that if there was reason to

---

12. As mentioned in *War and Peace in the Nuclear Age*, Episode 5: "The Cuban Missile Crisis: At the Brink." WGBH/PBS video series, Annenberg/CPB project.

13. Nye 1987.

14. A fine set of discussions on this topic is contained in Breslauer and Tetlock 1991.

be concerned with a military industrial complex in the United States, this was even more worrisome in the Soviet Union. The Soviet system had set out to alter every aspect of public and private life, carefully monitor its citizens, and punish potential opponents in the harshest terms, particularly during the Stalinist decades. Pitting such an authoritarian—arguably a totalitarian—regime against a democratic state suggests a recipe for disaster, especially if viewed in light of the Democratic Peace argument.

Graham Allison's study of the Cuban Missile Crisis presents a convincing account of the importance of second level factors during the crisis.[15] On the American side, President Kennedy at times had to wonder about his control over the military. Inter-agency quarrels between the CIA and the Air Force, between the various branches of the armed services, and between other organizations at times jeopardized the interests of the state. During one infamous episode, the CIA and the Air Force squabbled about who had authority to conduct U-2 flights over Cuba. As a consequence, flights by these spy planes were not conducted at all, and the United States lacked critical intelligence. Khrushchev's position was no different. He too had to worry about his control over the military. Similarly, he had concerns about his own political position, since the de-Stalinization campaign had not been fully completed.[16] Nevertheless, both leaders managed to retain control over their armed services in spite of all the military blustering— American general Thomas Powers once scoffed that he would bomb the Soviets back into the Stone Age, and Soviet generals similarly pronounced how the Soviet Union would emerge victorious in a nuclear exchange.[17]

Consequently, bureaucratic incentives to expand military budgets or to opt for strategies that might have been beneficial to the armed services but were not necessarily in the interest of their respective nations were checked by leaders who evaluated the militaries' preferences in the overall context of their state's foreign policy. Unlike the situation preceding the outbreak of World War I, overall foreign policy concerns determined military strategy, rather than the reverse.

Consequently, when Mikhail Gorbachev rose to power and suggested dramatic changes not just in the political system but also in the size of the armed forces, the military was in no position to oppose him. Indeed, he could actually count on considerable support from the armed forces against his political rivals, the hard-line communists who favored the old system.[18] The subsequent changes in the Soviet regime, and the emergence of a nascent democracy in Russia, ended the Cold War and the fear of a nuclear holocaust—at least for now.

---

15. Allison 1971. For a recent perspective, see Munton and Welch 2007.
16. Linden 1990, ch. 8.
17. For a discussion of the Soviet case, see Colton 1990.
18. See Desch 1993.

Third Level Issues: Bipolarity and the Dangers of Games of Chicken

Unlike the Great Power situation in World War I, there was no ambiguity about the nature of the international system in 1962. Only two key powers were critical to maintaining the balance of power in the world. Both the United States and the Soviet Union were keenly aware that they had to take the lead in balancing against the opponent of the other bloc. Internal balancing, rather than buckpassing, characterized the decades after 1945:

> The post-1945 bipolar structure was a simple one that did not require sophisticated leadership to maintain it. The great multipolar systems of the nineteenth century collapsed in large part because of their intricacy; they required a Metternich or a Bismarck to hold them together.[19]

Consequently, a key contributing factor to avoiding nuclear war was the clarity of the international structure. Both actors knew what the stakes were and from which corner danger might emanate.

Nevertheless, despite the clarity of bipolarity, the nature of the nuclear predicament raised dangers of its own. While the risk of misperceptions always looms large in any conflict, the particular logic of nuclear deterrence exacerbated this problem. Even if both sides engaged in rational calculation and tried to prevent miscalculations, the fact that they were locked in a game of Chicken raised the ante as both sides threatened to fight an unwinnable war. The Soviet Union and the United States each preferred that its opponent would concede and retreat, but if neither side backed down, both would be annihilated—obviously the worst possible outcome.

This forms the crux of the problem: in order to win the game an actor must tie his own hands. If, for example, the American leaders believed that the Soviets would engage in nuclear war if the United States did not back down, then the burden of avoiding the war fell on the American executive. This was not its first preference, but conceding would be better than nuclear holocaust. The actor who thus successfully put the burden on the other player could force the other to retreat or run the risk of all-out nuclear war.

The danger comes when both players tie their own hands in order to obtain their first preference, that is, to force the other state to retreat. Tying one's hands can be achieved through various means. The United States put troops in Europe as a tripwire. Although it was not a large enough force to repel a Soviet conventional invasion, the annihilation of these forces would likely precipitate an American nuclear response. Thus, the placement of American conventional forces made their threat of nuclear

---

19. Gaddis 1993, 10.

retaliation to a Soviet incursion a credible threat. Similarly, politicians in democracies can go public, thus staking their political fortunes on a successful conclusion of the crisis in their own favor. When Kennedy addressed the nation, stating that he would not back down and would confront the Soviet Union militarily if necessary, the signal to the Soviets was that he was now tied to forcing the issue. Khrushchev could counter that hard-liners in the party prevented him from yielding and that he could not alter the Soviet placement of missiles.

However, if neither side believes that the other state will go to war—although in reality they have actually tied their hands so as to make a nuclear response unavoidable—they might then inadvertently stumble into a nuclear exchange, the equivalent of two drivers hurtling towards each other expecting the other to veer off, not knowing that both actors are in fact unable to veer off.

In a game of Chicken both actors also have an incentive not to reveal their true preferences. The more one can keep the other guessing, the higher the burden on the other actor to decide whether to retreat or not. Indeed, it might even be beneficial to convey how irrational one's own decision-making is or how limited one's room for maneuver might be. But, conversely, the other actor also knows that this might be a ruse and thus discount such information. The game is thus fraught with potential miscalculation.

As the Cuban Missile Crisis indicates, both sides came to understand the particular dynamics of nuclear games of Chicken and tried to avoid such a danger. Nevertheless, given the continued presence of thousands of nuclear warheads in the world (more on this below), the danger of such games of Chicken remains with us.

The Nuclear Balance and Lessons from World War I

The nuclear era resembled the prelude to World War I in another manner—it threatened to give the offense the upper hand. If a state could expect to win a conflict if it launched a nuclear attack, this would heighten the probability of war. Consequently, if any side developed a first strike capability—the ability to carry out a strike against an enemy such that the opponent is not able to effectively retaliate—then the international system would become less stable. Even if both sides had roughly similar numbers of warheads, a first strike capability would entice an aggressive state to entertain thoughts of a successful nuclear offensive. Even a defensively minded state might feel compelled to launch an attack if it feared being attacked itself. In short, this scenario would be very similar to the fear of a lightning offensive in World War I.

By contrast, if both sides had second strike capability—the ability to sustain a nuclear attack and retaliate with a nuclear strike of one's own—

the superpower relation would be more stable. A second strike would take away the incentive for any state to attack first.

During the Cold War, both superpowers engaged in technological innovations and arms races to try to gain the upper hand. The United States originally had the lead, but the Soviet Union's nuclear arsenal and its delivery systems increased rapidly to close the gap. When both sides had a MAD capability, the incentive for any potential attacker was minimal. As the name implies, both sides would be destroyed. Thus, even though there were dangers involved in games of nuclear crisis bargaining, the stalemate induced caution.

However, as noted earlier, political leaders feared that MAD lacked credibility. The Americans thought that the Soviets would not take their threat to escalate to the nuclear level seriously, given the obvious consequences for the United States. How could the United States deter Soviet encroachment on its spheres of influence if it could not hope to survive a nuclear war itself? The American response, as we discussed above, was to develop a nuclear war-fighting doctrine as evinced in counterforce and counter-value postures. But in order to develop this doctrine, the Americans, followed quickly by the Soviets, developed technologies that in fact made the world less stable.

This instability particularly showed up in the development of strategic delivery systems. Nuclear weapons systems can be grouped by their modes of delivery into tactical-battlefield weapons, intermediate-range or continental weapons, and strategic-intercontinental systems. This is not a matter of the destructive potential of these weapons (their nuclear yield) but of their geographic range. The superpowers developed tens of thousands of nuclear warheads in each of these categories.

American and Soviet decision-makers and planners competed in all these areas with a multitude of delivery systems, but they also gradually started to negotiate how to manage this competition, particularly since the détente policy of the Nixon administration of the early 1970s. Of particular importance were the strategic weapons systems that could strike at the heartland of either superpower. Both used three types of weapons systems to deliver strategic warheads: long-range bombers, submarine-launched ballistic missiles (SLBMs), and inter-continental ballistic missiles (ICBMs). In the United States these three were sometimes referred to as the Triad. If an opponent destroyed one of the systems, then one of the others could still deliver a devastating counterstrike.

Each of these systems had distinguishing characteristics, but two features in particular were critical. First, the systems differed in their ability to destroy enemy targets. Here, precision and nuclear yield were key. If a country could deliver its warhead(s) in a very precise manner or if it had very large warheads, one could destroy the enemy's arsenal with a knock-out blow—a first strike.

Systems also differed in their vulnerability to detection and destruction. If one's systems could not be detected, they could not be destroyed, and thus they could be used to retaliate with a devastating nuclear attack. That is, invulnerable systems gave one second strike capability.

During the 1960s and 1970s the weapons systems by and large showed these features:

	Precision (ability to carry out first strike)	**Vulnerability** to First Strike
Bombers	High (but can be recalled)	High (necessitates scramble procedures, some planes kept continuously aloft)
SLBMs	Low	Very low
ICBMs	High	High (use them or lose them)

Bombers, provided they could penetrate the opponent's air space or use bomber-launched missiles without doing so, could deliver their warheads in a relatively precise manner. But, conversely, when they were on the ground they were vulnerable to destruction by enemy attack. (To counter this threat the United States maintained bombers with nuclear warheads in the air round the clock.) SLBMs, by contrast, were considered less precise and had less range because they had to be launched at sea and underwater (since then such missiles have become far more precise and have acquired longer range). However, submarines were very difficult to detect and destroy as they roamed the oceans submerged. ICBMs were considered more precise (in the American case) or could deliver powerful warheads (in the Soviet case) and had longer range, but they were also more vulnerable given that the location of each other's missile silos could be pinpointed by spy satellites and other means.

In World War I both alliances believed that each possessed a devastating first strike capability. Indeed, the attacker would be able to destroy the opponent within months, perhaps within weeks. The defending state would not have the chance to recuperate and strike back, and thus lacked a second strike capability. Each state had to fear an imminent attack that would lead to utter defeat. High threat and uncertainty subsequently led to war.

The same holds true for nuclear weapons today. If one state develops precise weapons systems, it will create incentives for itself to contemplate the benefits of an attack. Conversely, the other state will feel less secure, fearing a "bolt out of the blue." By the same token, if a state develops less vulnerable weapons systems, it will diminish the incentives for an attack, since the defending state can strike back and thus feel more secure. In order to prevent nuclear war, both sides have to feel secure, and both sides need to feel sure of their ability to launch a second strike.

Consequently, the arms control negotiations that took place during the Cold War between the United States and the Soviet Union were much more than simply discussions about the number of warheads or weapons systems. If both sides could be sure of a substantial second strike capability, the overall political climate might improve. The Americans and Soviets, therefore, set out to limit the number of warheads that missiles could carry and the size of missiles. A very large missile could carry many warheads with a very high yield. This would give the attacker the ability to destroy the defender's missiles in their silos, thus diminishing the chances of a retaliatory second strike. ICBMs had these characteristics but were themselves vulnerable to attack. SLBMs were not particularly large, carried fewer warheads, and were less precise, but given their invulnerability, they gave a defender more certainty that it could launch a counterattack against the attacker's population centers. So, although they were not suitable as first strike weapons, SLBMs provided stability.

For these reasons, both the United States and the Soviet Union had doubts about the wisdom of developing anti-ballistic missile (ABM) systems, which could launch smaller missiles to intercept incoming nuclear-tipped missiles. If developed and deployed, they would in effect diminish the ability of either state to launch a retaliatory strike. Thus, while the system at face value seemed defensive, the ability to negate the opponent's missile attack made the other state feel less secure. For example, if the Soviet Union had deployed a successful defensive system that would make it invulnerable to an American nuclear attack, the United States would feel less secure, because the Soviets might now launch a nuclear attack with impunity. The two countries signed a treaty limiting ABMs in 1972. However, in 1983 President Reagan launched the Strategic Defense Initiative (more commonly called the "Star Wars" program), which aimed to achieve ABM capability, much to the dismay of the Soviet Union. The end of the Cold War halted the project, but it was revitalized under George W. Bush's administration (2001–09), ostensibly to knock out missiles from "rogue states" such as Iran or North Korea.

It is impossible to discuss all the agreements reached between the United States and the Soviet Union, but several are worth noting because they demonstrate the logic of the argument above. Aside from the ABM treaty, agreements were also signed to change the composition and nature of nuclear arsenals. In 1985 the United States had 10,830 strategic warheads. Of these 20 per cent were on ICBMs, 52 per cent on SLBMs, and 28 per cent on heavy bombers. The Soviet Union by contrast had 9,490 strategic warheads, of which 68 per cent were on ICBMs, 26 per cent on SLBMs, and only 6 per cent on heavy bombers.[20] Simply put, a large

---

20. Mayers 1986, 62.

number of Soviet warheads were on systems that were both vulnerable and accurate. This made the Soviets less secure from an American attack but gave them considerable first strike capability. This in turn made the Americans feel less secure. Moreover, the United States could argue that its arsenal, primarily placed on submarines, did not give them a first strike capability.

The Bush/Yeltsin agreement aimed to remedy these issues.[21] First, it reduced the total number of warheads and particularly the number of warheads per missile, leaving both sides with roughly a similar number of warheads. However, they agreed to deploy such warheads on systems that gave both countries a greater guarantee for second strike capability. As a result, the Soviet composition changed dramatically. The United States' nuclear composition ended up with deployments of warheads on ICBMS (500), SLBMS (1,728), and bombers (1,272). The Soviet Union put its warheads on ICBMS (500), SLBMS (1,744), and some bombers (752). In short, more than half of each force was put on less vulnerable delivery systems, making both sides more secure.

Weapons of Mass Destruction after the Cold War

With the end of the Cold War in the late 1980s and the dissolution of the Soviet Union in 1992, the hope for a more peaceful international order emerged. However, many problems still remained. Although a superpower conflict had been avoided, conventional and civil wars raged in many parts of the world, particularly on the African continent and parts of Asia. We cannot delve into these in great detail as they involve numerous issues of racial and ethnic identity, religious tensions, and long-standing historical grievances. Each historical context brings its own particularities to any given conflict.

Instead, we continue the previous line of inquiry. Humanity has in the course of history devised ever more destructive means to inflict injury on one another. As we have seen, the medieval wars that lay at the basis of the transition to the emerging state system gave way to national armies that could use mercenaries and gunpowder. These in turn transformed into huge national armies that mobilized millions, leading to the unprecedented slaughter of the two world wars in the twentieth century. Weapons of mass destruction (WMD), which are devastating in scope and can cross entire continents in minutes, have put our very survival at risk. Whereas WMD were previously monopolized by the superpowers, other countries have now acquired them, and it is not inconceivable that non-state actors, such as terrorist networks, might gain access to them as well. What is the

---

21. "Summit in Washington; Excerpts From Bush-Yeltsin Conference: Working Toward a Safer World," *New York Times*, 12 June 1992.

nature of the current predicament, and how might this global problem be managed?

We typically differentiate several types of WMD. Nuclear weapons are the most obvious, and these have been the primary source of concern. As we have seen, the superpowers as well as France, Britain, and China have developed such weapons in the tens of thousands. Sometimes this category also includes radiological weapons. These are not nuclear explosive devices, but bombs that are meant to spread radioactive waste and materials in the atmosphere. The effects are intended more to spread fear among the population than to achieve an immediate military victory. Given these effects, and given the relative simplicity of their manufacture, these might be weapons of choice for terrorist groups in the future.

Biological and chemical weapons have also been part of the superpower arsenal even though they have taken a secondary role. Chemical weapons, particularly various types of poisonous gas, were used in significant quantities in World War I. Biological weapons were used even earlier. Historical records show that warring states used to deliberately spread disease and pestilence among each other's populations. Enemies have poisoned each other's wells and tossed the corpses of plague victims over city walls.[22] In the current arsenals of the world, viruses and bacteriological agents have been developed and can be spread with devastating effect among millions of people.

During the Cold War, many countries had programs to develop these weapons. The Soviet Union in particular had an active bio-chemical warfare development program. Some of these went awry when bio-agents escaped confined laboratories and contaminated humans and livestock, killing them quickly. The Soviet government denied that one of the more infamous incidents, the Sverdlovsk accident of 1979, had occurred. Russian President Yeltsin, however, after the fall of the Soviet Union, admitted it had happened.

The United States placed modest emphasis on these types of weapons. The American strategy, which remains in effect today, is to treat all types of attacks by states using any types of WMD—nuclear, chemical, and biological—as similar. That is, an attack by another state using bio-chemical WMD will be treated as a nuclear attack and will lead to massive retaliation by the United States with the possible use of nuclear weapons.

The Different Context of the Post-Cold War Era

The end of the Cold War, however, has complicated the situation in various respects. First, the collapse of the Soviet system completely changed the nature of the superpower rivalry. The Soviet Union divested itself from

22. Guillemin 2005, 3.

its sphere of influence in Eastern Europe and its Warsaw Pact allies, and it-self dissolved into 15 new states. Even though both Russia and the United States continued to maintain sizeable nuclear arsenals, the superpower rivalry for all intents and purposes had come to an end.

The subsequent economic collapse of Russia left the United States as the far stronger of the two. Indeed, the Russian economy in the late 1990s was outmatched by much smaller advanced capitalist countries such as South Korea and the Netherlands. The United States remained the pre-eminent military power. Even though the Soviet threat had decreased, the United States did not lessen its military expenditures as initially expected. Even though the Clinton administration diminished the American presence in Europe, it maintained a sizeable American deployment in the Pacific, and although the defense budget declined, it still required hundreds of billions of dollars a year. Some observers even spoke of a unipolar world, with only one, rather than multiple, great powers.[23]

A second change in the global system had to do with nuclear prolif-eration. By the beginning of the Cold War, the United States had developed both atomic and hydrogen bombs, but it was in each of those categories quickly followed by the Soviet Union. Britain, France, and China—all, ironically, permanent members of the UN Security Council—developed their own systems in the 1950s and the 1960s. But many other states of various sizes had nuclear ambitions as well and continued to pursue these even after the Cold War ended.[24] Israel might have had nuclear warheads as early as the late 1960s. India and Pakistan similarly had long-standing nuclear programs and engaged in several tests of such weapons in 1998. Both Brazil and Argentina were interested in developing nuclear systems but did not see these programs through to their end. South Africa devel-oped several nuclear warheads, but when the apartheid regime unraveled in the late 1980s it relinquished its nuclear program.

Of particular concern are the WMD programs in the Middle East and North Korea. The latter has had a highly secretive, dictatorial regime ever since Kim Il Sung assumed power in 1948 and installed a communist regime. It has also displayed an aggressive posture towards South Korea and the Western allies, and it has in addition a very large standing con-ventional force.[25] Libya, Iraq, and Iran have for decades tried to develop nuclear weapons programs. Iraq's government under Saddam Hussein also developed chemical weapons and used these against Kurdish insurgents in Iraq and against Iran during the Iranian-Iraqi war of the 1980s.

---

23. Layne 1993 submits that other powers will rise to balance against the United States.

24. Sagan 1996/1997.

25. For a theoretical overview of how and why states in different regions have chosen alternative paths, see Solingen 2007. Park 2004 describes the North Korean withdrawal from the Non-Proliferation Treaty in 2003 (for the second time since 1993), while vacillating in the multilateral negotiations.

A third threat emanates from the collapse of established states and from the desire of non-state actors (including terrorist networks) to acquire WMD. Of particular concern has been the swift dissolution of the Soviet Union and the lack of command and control over Soviet forces as it disintegrated. How could one manage the proliferation of nuclear weapons, given that Belarus, the Ukraine, Kazakhstan, and others were seemingly poised to gain them on their (now sovereign) territories? How could one avoid one of the warheads falling into the hands of rogue military or other networks?

Three Tiers of Issues

The current predicament can be divided into three sets of issues. First remains the traditional problem of how to manage *relations between states* that currently possess WMD. Second is a subset of this area of concern. Here we are concerned with interactions between states, some of which might wish to fundamentally challenge the existing international order. These are sometimes described as rogue states, not merely because they oppose the United States or the West, but because they violate international agreements that they have signed, or because they have transgressed rules of international behavior. These states might already have WMD or are seeking to acquire them. Third, we are faced with how to manage WMD given that non-state actors are actively seeking to acquire and use them.

Inter-State Management of Nuclear Weapons

Despite the end of the Cold War, nuclear weapons continue to play a critical role in international politics. Indeed, whether states desire these for reasons of security or prestige, it cannot be denied that while the arsenals of the traditional nuclear powers have diminished, many states are expanding theirs.

Given that many of the new nuclear states have acquired their weapons for regional purposes, the distinction between strategic systems and tactical delivery system is perhaps less relevant than during the Cold War. India's nuclear capability, for example, is directed towards its rival Pakistan and also serves a purpose in signaling its military capabilities to China.

Russia and the United States aim to reduce their arsenals further. The Moscow Treaty (Strategic Offensive Reductions Treaty) aims to reduce Russian and American arsenals by 2012. Russia would maintain 1,040–1,240 strategic and 2,750 tactical nuclear warheads, while the United States would keep about 3,700 strategic and about 850 tactical warheads.

Table 4.1 | **The Nuclear Powers and Their Arsenals (2003)**

Country	Strategic	Non-Strategic
China	250	120
France	350	0
India	60	?
Israel	100–200 ?	?
Pakistan	24–48	?
Russia	5,600 (approx.)	4,000 (approx.)
United Kingdom	180	5
United States	8,646 (including inactive)	2,010

Source: Center for Defense Information,
http://www.cdi.org/issues/nukef&f/database/index.cfm.

Because of their destructive capabilities, decision-makers and strategists differ on whether nuclear weapons in and of themselves induce peace. Here again, thinking of the nuclear predicament through three different lenses might guide the discussion.

The Argument that Nuclear Weapons Induce Stability

Those who argue that nuclear weapons will deter war between states that have them by and large make the following assumptions. First, they view the world as consisting primarily of states that exercise a monopoly of violence within their territory (that is, these states have effective sovereign authority). Furthermore, when it comes to critical decisions of foreign policy, such as conducting nuclear deterrent strategies, most governments operate as unitary, rational, decision-making structures. Political elites evaluate the costs and benefits of their actions and maintain a consistent ordering of preferences. They also assume that through spies, satellites, and other means of information gathering, states have reasonable information regarding one another's capabilities. And, finally, such observers point to the cataclysmic effects of nuclear war. Even as early as 1964, the Congressional Office of Technology Assessment estimated that the number of casualties in a full-scale nuclear exchange might be as high as 100 million American citizens and 80 million Soviets. Given that nuclear war is unwinnable and imposes unacceptable costs, political leaders will act in a risk averse manner and proceed with caution.

While it is true that the superpowers and other major powers occasionally were confronted with crises during the Cold War, these were defused. Even at the height of the Cuban Missile Crisis, both leaders realized the consequences of their actions, and despite the aggressive rhetoric, rational decision-making prevailed. Even as tensions rose between India and Pakistan in 2003, their willingness to compromise might have been partially induced by the fear of a nuclear exchange. In the previous five decades, by contrast, they had gone to war several times.

Thus, some scholars recognize the importance of first and second level perspectives. Individual leaders' decision-making ability is impaired during moments of crisis. Authoritarian states might be more prone to war, or the armed forces might have disproportionate influence on the civilian leadership. However, nuclear weapons have in effect changed the structure of the international system.[26] The use of such weapons is so horrific that this fear will override concerns at the first and second levels of analysis.

The Counter Argument: Nuclear Stability is Ephemeral

By contrast, others view the situation as far more dangerous. They point out that even when states have a monopoly of violence over their territory, decision-making is often driven by standard operation procedures (SOPs) and bureaucratic politics. Instead of an overall, carefully thought-out strategy, parochial interests and narrower perspectives influence political outcomes. For example, at the height of the Cuban Missile Crisis inter-agency squabbles between the Air Force and CIA compromised American intelligence. Inter-service rivalry between the Air Force and the Navy has always influenced American nuclear strategy, and the same is true for the Soviet Union and now for Russia.[27]

Even in the United States, nuclear strategy was seriously influenced by parochial political interests, rather than a strategic assessment of the need for and use of nuclear weapons. To provide one telling example: the number of ICBMs that for decades made up the American arsenal (1,052) was actually the result of political accident and the pursuit of more agency resources. President Kennedy (1961–63) had argued in his election campaign that the previous Republican administration had allowed the Soviets to take the lead in number and quality of missiles. When Kennedy won the election, the Air Force saw a political opportunity to ask for a vastly larger number than originally planned. It urged deployment figures of around 2,000 to 3,000. General Thomas S. Power, then commander of Strategic Air Command, even talked of 10,000. In the end, they settled on a large, but round, number: 1,000 missiles. Hence, the nuclear arsenal ended up consisting of 1,000 new Minutemen missiles (and 52 obsolete Titan missiles).[28]

---

26. Waltz 1990 argues this point, although it seems a deviation from his position that the structure of the system is simply determined by the distribution of power under anarchy, not by the type of weapons.

27. For a compelling narrative of how individual personalities and inter-agency strife influenced American nuclear strategy, see Kaplan 1983.

28. York 1970.

Even with carefully calibrated command and control systems, miscommunications and accidents cannot be ruled out. As Scott Sagan has shown, history is replete with strayed civilian planes being mistaken for enemy aircraft or flights of geese for incoming missiles.[29] If this is true even for the carefully controlled nuclear arsenals of the superpowers, this danger holds even more for less developed and less carefully controlled nuclear command systems.

Moreover, because nuclear deterrence essentially revolves around a game of Chicken, misperceptions about resolve and commitment are likely to occur sooner or later. Indeed, as suggested earlier, there are considerable advantages to maneuvering oneself into a position from which one cannot retreat, thus putting the burden of conflict avoidance on the other actor. But should both actors do so, then the "knot of war," as Khrushchev called it, might be too tight to untangle. The superpowers, through careful management, avoided near misses from escalating even further, but this need not be the case with many more participants engaging in similar games.

Finally, even though we have managed to avoid a nuclear conflict, it cannot be ruled out altogether in the future. Given the horrendous results of such conflict, we must fear the worst, even if the probability is low.

Managing Rogue States

Another source of concern is rogue states, states that violate international agreements on acquiring WMD or that have aggressive intentions. Their governments argue that international actions to prevent them from acquiring WMD are illegitimate. They claim that non-proliferation agreements and their attempted enforcement by organizations such as the UN or the International Atomic Energy Agency (IAEA) are inequitable and unfair, given that they allow the major powers to maintain their own WMD. If the five permanent members of the Security Council are allowed to have nuclear weapons and other WMD, and if other powerful states are acquiring them, why should not mid-range or small states be allowed to have them as well? Moreover, these governments argue that the international system in general is biased towards the interest of the major powers, particularly the West. WMD would allow the disempowered states to redress this inequity.

Among those states that have sought nuclear capability are Iraq, Iran, and North Korea. Iraq's nuclear program started in the late 1970s and early 1980s. North Korea is now thought to have around half a dozen warheads and is trying to develop multi-stage missiles. It already has successfully tested single stage missiles that could hit targets in Japan and other areas. Iran has defied the UN's boycott and has pursued an active nuclear program.

---

29. Sagan 1993.

There are various reasons for concern. One might doubt the strategic rationale of some of these leaders. For example, North Korea's pursuit of nuclear capability has come at considerable suffering to its own population. The decision-making structure is tightly knit with no opportunities for opposition. The personality cults surrounding Kim Il-Song and, after his death, Kim Jong-Il suggest that decisions are likely to conform closely to their perceptions and misperceptions regarding the intentions of the international community. The lack of transparency in turn alarms its neighbors, particularly South Korea and Japan. Mutual miscalculations cannot be ruled out. Similar fears operate when considering virtually all autocratic governments that seek WMD.

From a second level perspective, none of these states—North Korea's government, Iraq's government under Saddam Hussein, and the theocracy in Iran—could be deemed democratic. Popular opinion is either guided without a free flow of external information or outright repressed. Similarly, each of these authoritarian states bases or based its support on a specific set of interest groups which need not have the country's collective good in mind. The armed forces tend to play a considerable role in the ruling coalition.

For these reasons rogue states are a particular concern. The traditional management tools that the superpowers developed during the Cold War seem absent from the newly emerging nuclear powers. Even if such states are less likely to use WMD to challenge the United States, Russia, or one of the other major powers, they might use them to maintain their regimes or against their regional neighbors.

Failed States and Private Groups with WMD

Nuclear proliferation and the development of relatively small nuclear weapons raises further problems, particularly if such weapons escape the purview of government control or if those governments allow non-state actors to acquire the means of violence and even WMD.

If weapons do fall into the hands of private groups or terrorist networks, it might be difficult to discern the perpetrator of a given attack. The entire premise of nuclear deterrence hinges exactly on the ability to strike back at the known attacker. With an unknown sender, retaliation—and thus deterrence—might be impossible. And even if one knew the origins of the attack, would one then retaliate against the country of origin, not knowing whether these actors had operated with their government's sanction?

The very portability of new nuclear weapons makes this scenario possible. At one point the American arsenal included in its inventory the "Davy Crockett" warhead that weighed a mere 51 pounds and could yield the equivalent of 0.01 kiloton explosive (10 tons of TNT). By comparison, the domestic terrorist bomb (a conventional homemade bomb) that was exploded in front of the federal office building in Oklahoma City, killing 168, was around 2 tons TNT equivalent. Other portable nuclear weapons were developed as early as the 1960s. These Special Atomic Demolition Munitions were to be deployed by small teams of special operations forces and weighed around 150 pounds, with a yield between 0.01–1 kiloton.

Terrorist attacks in the first decade of this century in the United States, Indonesia (Bali), Britain, Spain, and many other places have brought renewed concern about the ability of organized networks to inflict harm on civilian populations. Terrorism is, of course, much older than the last few decades, but the ability to inflict harm across the globe and the possibility that such groups might acquire WMD give additional reasons to ponder how this particular type of conflict can be averted or at least controlled.[30]

Despite the horrendous loss of life in the terrorist attacks in the United States on September 11, 2001 (9/11), North America has by and large escaped the frequency of terrorist attacks that were prevalent in Europe in the 1970s when such groups as the German Bader Meinhof, the Italian Red Brigade, the Irish Republican Army, and the Basque group ETA were active. Terrorism was also no stranger to Asian countries. In the past decade, the number of terrorist attacks was highest in Latin America and Asia. Indeed, for most years the number of attacks in the United States was zero; the only attacks occurred in New York in 1993, Oklahoma in 1995, and New York and Washington in 2001, but the number of casualties was comparatively high on average.

So far, no terrorist attacks have been nuclear. There have been biological and chemical attacks, but they have been small in number. Indeed, most have been hoaxes. (The latter are nevertheless deemed terrorist events, given their intent to inflict psychological damage on the target population.) The Monterey Institute has tracked the number of such incidences. While the number of fatalities in 2000 seems high, 778 of the 795 reported fatalities came from one single incident: the poisoning of members of the cult of the Movement for the Restoration of the Ten Commandments of God in Uganda. The institute also keeps track of hoaxes. In 2000 there were 25 hoaxes worldwide, with perpetrators threatening to use or to have used chemical, biological, radiological, and nuclear weapons (CBRN). In 2001 the number jumped to 603, but 566 of these originated in North America in the wake of 9/11 and the sending of anthrax spores in New York and Washington. By 2002 the number of hoaxes had dwindled to 71.

Nevertheless, this relatively low number of incidents does not diminish the reason for concern. First, terrorist networks might be able to use WMD without the fear of retaliation, given their ability to act covertly and the difficulties of assigning responsibility. Moreover, if such individuals

---

30. For one argument about how non-state actors might be deterred, see Auerswald 2006.

Table 4.2 | **Uses, Possession, Attempted Acquisition, Plots, and Threats of Chemical, Biological, Radiological, and Nuclear Weapons (CBRN)**

Region	Year 2000	2001	2002
United States/Canada	7	7	4
Asia	16	5	1
Europe	3	5	3
Middle East	11	1	5 †
Latin America	0	2	3
Russia and NIS*	7	3	4
Other areas	4	2	3
Totals	**48**	**25**	**23**
Fatalities worldwide	795	9	7

* Newly Independent States, i.e., former members of the Soviet Union

† Hamas attempts

Source: Monterey Institute 2003; Wayne Turnbull and Praveen Abhayaratne, "2002 WMD Terrorism Chronology: Incidents Involving Sub-National Actors and Chemical, Biological, Radiological, and Nuclear Materials"; http://cns.miis.edu/reports/pdfs/cbrn2k2.pdf.

do not fear retaliation, either against themselves, their network, or their country of origin, then deterrence might not work. Can one effectively deter a suicide bomber? Consequently, it is useful to briefly discuss the various strategies that have been used to manage this problem.

Strategies to Reduce WMD Threats

International efforts have tried to regulate the development and proliferation of WMD. The IAEA monitors the nuclear proliferation agreements, while the international community has sought to regulate biological and chemical weapons. The Biological Weapons Convention (1972) requires signatories to renounce the development, production, stockpiling, and use of biological weapons. It has been signed by Britain, France, Germany, India, Iran, Iraq, Libya, North Korea, Pakistan, Russia, and the United States.[31] Note the presence of Iraq and North Korea among the signatories. However, both countries (Iraq under Saddam Hussein) were in clear violation of the agreement. Among those that have not signed are Algeria, Egypt, Israel, and Sudan. The Chemical Weapons Convention (1993) requires the same for

---

31. For an overview of the historical development of biological weapons up to the present, see Guillemin 2005.

chemical weapons and has been signed by all the major powers that possess chemical weapons but not by Egypt, Iraq, Israel, Libya, North Korea, Syria, or Taiwan (as of 2002).

A second strategy, and the one currently emphasized by the United States, is to make states accountable and to enforce their monopoly over the means of violence. States that harbor terrorist organizations are deemed directly culpable of terrorist actions. Aiding and abetting terrorist acts is considered equivalent to committing terrorist acts. Thus, by those calculations, the action against the Taliban regime was justified on the grounds that Afghanistan had given sanctuary to the Al Qaeda network that carried out the attacks on 9/11.

Third, countries have implemented a similar strategy with regard to chemical and biological weapons as that used to combat nuclear proliferation. This has involved a three-fold approach. First, all countries are to secure supplies in safe areas, and careful accounting of these supplies has to be carried out. Second, governments should also consolidate these weapons in limited areas rather than spread them geographically. Third, governments should aim to eliminate weapons through multilateral efforts and create alternative financial incentives to suppliers of such weapons. Fourth, governments should work to control the "know-how" of such weapons technology. As part of such a strategy, the United States, for example, actively worked to provide means of employment for the many Soviet experts that had lost their occupations after the Cold War. With a Russian economy in free fall after 1991, such experts were given positions in the United States and the West. Finally, one might use indirect means of limiting the probability of terrorist events by monitoring and controlling delivery systems, that is, by monitoring the movement of people and goods across borders. No doubt such policies will have to be balanced against political rights.

Various elements of these approaches have come together in the Proliferation Security Initiative (2002). This is a broad multilateral effort centered around 15 to 19 core states and politically supported by another 60. So far the results have been mixed. With regard to nuclear materials the initiative has performed well, but with regard chemical and biological weapons there is less room for optimism. For example, the G-8 states[32] pronounced in June 2002 that they would spend $20 billion to prevent terrorists from acquiring CBRNs. But so far little has been devoted to biological weapons. France has committed €5 million, Britain £20,000, and the United States $65 million to fight the expansion of biological weapons.

---

32. Britain, Canada, France, Germany, Italy, Japan, Russia, and the United States.

Conclusion

The development of WMD has altered the human landscape forever. The effects of such weapons cannot be regionally contained, and no longer can we experience them as distant in time and space. The methods of delivery of WMD, whether by intercontinental missiles or by terrorist networks, make the possibility of their use present and direct. Physically, we must live with the reality that missiles can strike any part of the globe in matters of minutes rather than the days or months that used to be involved when states prepared for distant wars. Terrorist networks, which aim to acquire such weapons, operate in our very midst. Psychologically, we cannot turn a blind eye, in the hopes that we can escape unaffected by the use of such weapons in another region. In this sense our global event horizon has expanded. All are now affected by the possible use of WMD, wherever it might take place.

During the Cold War, the two superpowers had tens of thousands of WMD. Besides a vast arsenal of nuclear warheads, both also sought to develop biological and chemical weapons. Our study has tried to identify how they managed to avert disaster and did not end up in a major war.

As our discussion of first level factors showed, political leaders were prone to the same psychological and cognitive pressures as leaders in other eras. Politicians miscalculated, as when Khrushchev thought that Kennedy would not oppose Soviet missiles in Cuba, or when Brezhnev underestimated the Western response to the Soviet incursion into Afghanistan. The difference in regime type, similarly, bode ill for the prospects of peace. Indeed, both states had diametrically opposed economic and political systems. Bureaucratic fights, rivalry in the armed services, and interagency conflict in both superpowers at times threatened to overwhelm central decision-makers. And yet a major war between these powers was avoided. Why was this so?

First, at key moments of crises, some elites were keenly aware that psychological and cognitive barriers might hinder a more sober-minded, rational calculus. From a second image perspective, while it is true that their regimes were vastly different, both the United States and the Soviet Union maintained civilian control over the military. Finally, from a systems level perspective the balance of power, or rather the balance of terror, forestalled aggressive action by either. The prospects of nuclear holocaust for both protagonists, combined with the clarity of a bipolar world, prevented armageddon.

Since the end of the Cold War, the likelihood of such a nuclear exchange has declined dramatically. Nevertheless, its lessons remain highly pertinent today. As more and more states acquire WMD, we must ask whether the same mechanisms that stabilized the superpower relation might be applied to inter-state rivalries. How, for example, might the Indian-Pakistani nuclear relation be managed? We must similarly ask whether the logic of deterrence can be applied to states that aim to overthrow the status quo. Finally, the desire of non-state actors to acquire such weapons raises the question of whether deterrence can even be applied to them. Short of a clear answer to the last question, states for now have tried to minimize the possibility that such groups might indeed acquire WMD.

FIVE

The American Invasion
of Iraq in 2003

*I am afeard there are few die well that die in a battle; for
how can they charitably dispose of anything when blood is
their argument? Now, if these men do not die well, it will
be a black matter for the king that led them to it....*
—*Shakespeare*, Henry V

Prelude to the Iraq War

In 1979 Saddam Hussein, who had already been the *de facto* key leader
within the ruling Ba'ath Party, officially assumed the presidency of Iraq.
Internally, he aimed at consolidating the dominant position of the Ba'ath
Party by controlling ethnic and religious cleavages within the country. In
so doing he occasionally clashed with the Kurds, who are Sunni by faith
but ethnically not Arab, and the Shi'ites, whom he suspected of being
supported by Iran. Externally, Hussein favored secular pan-Arabism and
wanted to make Iraq one of the dominant powers in the Arab world.

In 1980 war broke out between Iraq and Iran. The disputed border
along the Shatt-al-Arab river was one source of contention. The rise to
power of Ayatollah Khomeini was another. Hussein feared that the Shi'ite
religious movement in southeast Iraq, which was supported by the Iranian
religious leaders, threatened his secular regime. Seizing the initiative, he
launched an attack and made initial headway. Western powers, although
nominally neutral, saw Iraq as a potential check on what seemed to have
become a radically religious Iran. The United States was the most ardent
opponent of Khomeini, as his government had toppled the Shah, a long-
standing American ally, and because of the seizure of the American embassy
in Tehran which led to its personnel being taken hostage for well over a
year.

After initial successes, the Iraqi offensive stalled, and a war of attrition
began that would last eight years. Confronted by a highly motivated, but
poorly equipped Iranian military, Hussein opted to use chemical weapons

against it. He also used chemical weapons against the Kurds, whom he suspected of wanting to open a third front to gain greater autonomy.

During this period, Hussein not only could count on tacit support from the West but also received tangible benefits. France had already in 1980 aided Iraq in developing a nuclear reactor, which was destroyed a year later by Israeli bombardment. Germany was implicated in Hussein's chemical weapons development. The United States, while not overtly in favor of Iraq due to its stance on Israel, welcomed its efforts to neutralize Iranian influence in the Middle East.

By the late 1980s, however, after the conclusion of the Iraq-Iranian War, which neither side could claim as a victory, the relationship with the West started to sour. The key issue of contention revolved around Iraq's policy towards Kuwait. Iraqi historiography had long claimed that Kuwait was part of Iraq and that only colonial meddling had led to its independence. Hussein was, furthermore, perturbed by Kuwait's unwillingness to be more flexible in dealing with Iraq's war debt, accumulated during the war with Iran. Finally, Iraq argued that Kuwait engaged in horizontal drilling, thereby siphoning off oil from underneath Iraqi territory.

Based on these grievances, Hussein's government decided to invade Kuwait. It swiftly defeated Kuwaiti forces and occupied the country in the summer of 1990. Fearing that Hussein might have bolder objectives in his sights, such as Saudi Arabia, the United States swiftly deployed a force to contain the Iraqi army in Kuwait alone. This was followed by a multilateral diplomatic initiative that sought to compel Hussein's government to withdraw its forces to the *status quo ante*.

The UN, similarly, took the position that Iraq's invasion was a clear violation of state sovereignty and contravened the UN Charter. When Hussein did not yield to the American threat of force, nor to diplomatic initiatives, the Security Council passed Resolution 678, authorizing any means necessary to force Iraq's withdrawal from Kuwait. The Resolution presented him with an ultimatum. Iraq had to withdraw its forces by January 15, 1991, or suffer the consequences.

With Iraq refusing to yield, the American-led coalition started to amass a vast amount of military personnel and resources. Spearheaded by the American contribution of more than half a million troops, 34 other countries contributed about 150,000 military personnel. Arab states joined as well, with Egypt, Syria, Saudi Arabia, and Kuwait pledging aid and military assistance. In addition, many countries that did not send armed forces into harm's way contributed financially. Thus, Germany and Japan pledged $16 billion to the war effort. Nevertheless, even with this massive coalition, the Iraqi military could not be discounted. By some calculations it was the fifth largest military force in the world. Thus, while military analysts predicted an Allied victory, the expectation was that the number of casualties on both sides would be significant.

These analysts were proven wrong. The Revolution in Military Affairs (RMA) had decisively altered the mode of modern warfare. After the deadline passed, allied aircraft attacked Iraqi positions on 16 January 1991 and delivered precision strikes with great success. Highly advanced technological systems, combined with more conventional war fighting techniques, led to a swift defeat of the Iraqi army. After several weeks of aerial bombardment, which underscored absolute allied air supremacy, the ground war was concluded in a matter of days. The allied forces penetrated deep into Iraq but halted without proceeding to the capital, Baghdad. While the allied deaths numbered in the several hundreds, the Iraqi numbers were in the tens of thousands. Even though the Republican Guard, the key units on which Hussein depended, had escaped annihilation, the defeat was clear and the Iraqi government conceded defeat.[1]

Shortly thereafter, the Shi'ite and Kurdish regions erupted in revolt against Hussein's brutal repression. Although defeated, the Iraqi military still was powerful enough to suppress them. The United States now found itself in a quandary; while President Bush had called on the population to bring down Hussein's government, many of its allies opposed territorial partition of Iraq. Turkey feared that an independent Kurdish state at its borders would embolden secessionist demands from the sizeable Kurdish population within Turkey itself. Arab states feared that a *de facto* partitioned Iraq would expand the influence of Iran in the region. Moreover, the coalition was authorized by the UN Resolution to extricate Iraq from Kuwait, which had been achieved. It said nothing about domestic government reform.

Consequently, the United States and Britain established no-fly zones over the Kurdish and Shi'ite areas to limit Hussein's means of repression. The Security Council also imposed further restrictions on Iraq's WMD program. Iraq had used chemical weapons, and, as the allied forces found out after their victory, it had made inroads into the development of nuclear weapons—but with little success. The Resolution called on two international agencies, the UN Special Commission (UNSCOM) and the IAEA, to verify Iraq's compliance and destroy any WMD that they might find.

Iraq's compliance became a continuous source of controversy. In the decade after the initial victory, the allies enforced economic sanctions, while Britain and the United States also used air and cruise missile strikes against Iraqi sites to enforce agreement. By 1998, neither UNSCOM nor the IAEA were yet satisfied with Iraqi compliance. After being refused entry into some key sites, the agencies withdrew from Iraq altogether. Thus, from 1998 until just before the Iraq War of 2003, international agencies lacked access to information on Iraq's weapons programs.

Shortly after 9/11, President George W. Bush's administration decided to invade Afghanistan because the Taliban regime had aided and

---

1. For an overview of the campaign, see Freedman and Karsh 1991.

abetted the Al Qaeda terrorist group that carried out the attacks. As we saw in the last chapter, the American government explicitly stated it would not differentiate between the non-government perpetrators of terrorist acts and the governments that supported them. The initial military campaign aimed to bring down the Taliban regime and capture Osama bin-Laden, the mastermind behind the Al Qaeda network. After a short offensive by the American military, allied troops, and Afghan allies, the Taliban government indeed fell. Subsequently, however, Taliban forces regrouped. Shielded by the inhospitable terrain and the support of warlords and clans in the Afghan-Pakistan border region, they continue to harass the Afghan government. By late 2008 Osama bin-Laden remained at large, and the Taliban were rebuilding their strength.

The connection between the already unpopular Taliban regime and terrorism was clear to the international community. Indeed, a broad coalition of countries supported the United States in its endeavors. Shortly after 9/11 the NATO alliance invoked Article 5 for the first time:

> The Parties agree that an armed attack against one or more of them in Europe or North America shall be considered an attack against them all and consequently they agree that, if such an armed attack occurs, each of them, in exercise of the right of individual or collective self-defence recognised by Article 51 of the Charter of the United Nations, will assist the Party or Parties so attacked by taking forthwith, individually and in concert with the other Parties, such action as it deems necessary, including the use of armed force.

Far more controversial, however, was the American decision to invade Iraq. The Bush administration, together with British Prime Minister Tony Blair's government, argued that their intelligence indicated that Iraq possessed WMD and stood poised to use these against Western powers. Moreover, the American executive argued that there were clear links between Al Qaeda, the Iraqi government, and related networks. Given that Hussein had demonstrated his aggressive intentions both by attacking neighboring states such as Iran and Kuwait and by his use of chemical weapons against Iran and his own Kurdish population, the Bush administration declared it would pursue a policy of preemptive war rather than wait for an attack on American soil.

The administration had woven a seamless web between preemptive war and preventive war: "Preemption is not controversial; legally, morally, or strategically ... To preempt means to strike first ... in the face of an attack that is either already underway or is very credibly imminent."[2] A preventive

---

2. Gray 2007, v–vi. Jervis 2003b similarly notes the distinction between the two types of war.

war is waged in order to forestall the menace getting larger. The United States had decided to wage a preventive war but couched it in terms of the legally more justifiable language of a preemptive war, declaring that:

It is an enduring American principle that this duty obligates the government to anticipate and counter threats ... before the threats can do grave damage. The greater the threat, the greater is the risk of inaction—and the more compelling the case for taking anticipatory action to defend ourselves, even if uncertainty remains as to the time and place of the enemy's attack. There are few greater threats than a terrorist attack with WMD. To forestall or prevent such hostile acts by our adversaries, the United States will, if necessary, act preemptively in exercising our inherent right of self-defense.[3]

The Republican administration further asserted that the war would be short and would meet with widespread Iraqi support, given the domestic opposition to Hussein's tyrannical reign. Shi'ites and Kurds, who were previously oppressed by the Sunni minority, were expected to rally to help the allied invading forces. The costs of the war would be minimal, and indeed much of it would be financed by oil revenues after Hussein was ousted.

After a short military campaign, with no more than a few hundred allied military killed (but with thousands of Iraqi casualties), President Bush declared in May 2003 that hostilities had ceased and that the Hussein government had been brought down. Allied forces were expected to be withdrawn in short order.

Five years later, however, more than 100,000 allied troops are still stationed in Iraq. Thousands have died.[4] The costs of the war have been calculated in the hundreds of billions of dollars, and one estimate indicates that total costs might even exceed US$3 trillion, if one takes the long-term medical expenses for the wounded and forgone income into account.[5]

It has become readily apparent that the American decision to invade Iraq was built on faulty evidence, poor strategy, and even outright deceit. No WMD were found. And no connection to Al Qaeda has been unearthed, as the Bush administration itself had to concede. Furthermore, Washington's unilateralism jeopardized its relations with its European allies and provoked other governments to outright opposition. France had been one of the first countries to send troops to Afghanistan but emerged

---

3. White House, National Security Strategy 2002, section V; http://www.whitehouse.gov/nsc/nss/2006/sectionV.html.

4. By the fall of 2008, the number of allied casualties had approached 4,500, with more than 4,000 American dead.

5. Stiglitz and Bilmes 2008.

with Germany as staunch opponents of the Bush Doctrine and the Iraq War.[6] Similarly, despite the close Canadian-American relationship in security and economic affairs (with Canadians fighting in some of the most dangerous areas of Afghanistan), Prime Minister Jean Chrétien's government distanced itself from Washington's policy in Iraq.

Given the magnitude of the American effort in terms of lives lost, the economic expenditures, and the diplomatic costs, only time can tell whether this marks the end of American standing in the global arena. So what led the American government to attack Iraq?

First Level Analysis

Cognitive and psychological factors influenced decision-making in various ways and contributed significantly to the decision to go to war with Iraq. First, the Bush administration was oblivious to inconsistencies in its own belief system.[7] On the one hand it believed that Hussein could not be deterred by the allied control of nuclear weapons even though the allied coalition's WMD vastly outnumbered any such weapons that he might have. As we have seen, even after the Cold War, the nuclear arsenal in the hands of the United States, Britain, and France remained vast. And even if the United States did not wish to respond with a nuclear strike to possible aggression by Hussein's government, its conventional forces were more than capable of destroying the Iraqi forces in 2003, as they had vanquished the far more powerful Iraqi army a decade earlier.

At the same time, however, Washington believed that Baghdad's possession of nuclear weapons would deter the United States from confronting Hussein either conventionally or with nuclear weapons, should he threaten vital American interests. Thus, the Bush administration believed that deterrence would not work to contain Iraq, but it would work to prevent American military action against Iraq, should Hussein engage in the expansionist policies of years past. The inconsistency in this position regarding the effectiveness of deterrence escaped the White House.

Second, highly placed neo-conservatives in Bush's cabinet, such as Vice-President Dick Cheney, Secretary of Defense Donald Rumsfeld, and Deputy Secretary of Defense Paul Wolfowitz, dispelled and ignored evidence that contradicted their preferred policy. When intelligence circles questioned their claim that Iraq was involved in 9/11 and other terrorist activities against the United States, Wolfowitz responded, "just because the FBI and the CIA have failed to find the linkages doesn't mean they don't exist."[8] General Eric Shinseki, chief of the Army, noted, contrary to the

---

6. On the confrontations between the United States and France in the Security Council, see Marfleet and Miller 2005.

7. Jervis 2003a.

8. Kinzer 2007, 286.

argument made by the White House, that at least 250,000 troops were needed to carry out the postwar mission and that long-term stability in Iraq could not be taken for granted. General Jack Keane, the Army's vice-chief of staff, believed that invasion of Iraq would detract from the yet in-complete mission in Afghanistan. He recommended that the United States maintain two divisions on the border with Pakistan.[9] Wolfowitz publicly denounced Shinseki. He claimed instead that the American troop level shortly after the invasion would be no more than 30,000–34,000. Marine Corps General Anthony Zinni, who had been chief of Central Command (the military headquarters for the Middle East), criticized the Bush plans from the start and commented that his plans were ignored altogether. Interviewed several months after Bush had declared an end to fighting, he opined, "I think the American people were conned into this."[10]

Contrary to the estimates that the war would be costly, Wolfowitz argued that oil exports would pay for the costs of reconstructing Iraq. He dismissed those who claimed that the war might cost as much as $95 billion by stating, "I don't think he or she knows what he is talking about."[11] Lawrence Lindsay, Bush's economic adviser at the time, was ousted because he thought the war might cost as much as $100–$200 billion.[12] (By 2008 Congress had already allocated $600 billion, which undoubtedly is going to rise in the years ahead.) Cognitive dissonance in the White House inner circle led to cavalier dismissal of evidence that contradicted their pre-existing mindset.

Third, best-case scenarios were eagerly adopted. Rather than fret about the difficulties of controlling the various religious and ethnic tensions of a post-Hussein Iraq, the administration expected social harmony, that Sunnis, Shi'ites, and Kurds would embrace the American liberators. Other cleavages—family, clan or tribal rivalries—were not considered to be important. Pessimistic—that is, realistic—military planning was discouraged. Instead, plans that foresaw a quick reduction in troops after the initial phase of the war were readily adopted. In August 2002, Tommy Franks, who went on to command the invasion forces, participated in a planning session that envisioned a short stabilization phase, followed by a recovery phase, and then a transition phase, which estimated that roughly three to three and a half years after the initial invasion, the American military presence in Iraq would be no more than 5,000 troops.[13] Shortly after Baghdad was taken, Franks told senior officers that the first

9. Ricks 2007, 33.

10. Thomas Ricks, "Americans 'Conned' into Backing War, Ex-general Asserts," *Chicago Tribune*, 31 December 2003.

11. Ricks 2007, 98.

12. David Herszenhorn, "Estimates of Iraq War Cost Were Not Close to Ballpark," *New York Times*, 19 March 2008.

13. Michael Gordon, "A Prewar Slide Show Cast Iraq in Rosy Hues." *New York Times*, 15 February 2007.

units would be withdrawn in 60 days and that by September of 2003 the military presence would be less than 30,000 troops.[14] As the army's own internal report later revealed, the occupation was based on faulty assumptions, such as the belief that Iraq's ministries and institutions would continue to operate after Hussein's government was brought down as they had before.[15] British documents confirm this picture of rigid beliefs in the neo-conservative camp. One of the most damning critiques emerged from within Tony Blair's own cabinet and discussions with his advisors:

> C [Sir Richard Dearlove] reported on his recent talks in Washington ... Bush wanted to remove Saddam, through military action, justified by the conjunction of terrorism and WMD. But the intelligence and facts were being fixed around the policy.... There was little discussion in Washington of the aftermath after military action.[16]

Second Level Perspectives

The conflict between the United States and Iraq reflected the classic antagonism between democratic and authoritarian states. The Bush administration expanded its initial objectives—bringing down Hussein and eliminating any potential threat to the United States or American allies in the Middle East—to establishing an incipient democratic state in Iraq. It thought that this would propel democratic movements throughout the region and diminish the likelihood of conflict in general. Thus, American policy seemed at least partially driven by the premise that democratic states do not fight each other. President Bush said, "We fight, as we always fight, for a just peace—a peace that favors liberty.... And we will extend the peace by encouraging free and open societies on every continent."[17] Iraq was simply one component of an "axis of evil"—along with Iran and North Korea—and had to be defeated.

Other second level factors played a role as well. Rivalry between the various services, agencies, and bureaucracies impeded intelligence gathering and planning. The Department of Defense (DoD), headed by Secretary Rumsfeld, and the State Department, under Secretary of State

---

14. Kinzer 2007, 285.

15. The report "On Point II: Transition to the New Campaign" also indicated that the number of troops for the Phase IV (state-building phase) was far too small. Michael Gordon, "Occupation Plan for Iraq Faulted in Army History," *New York Times*, 29 June 2008.

16. The memo originated from Matthew Rycroft for a meeting on 23 July 2002. See also Kinzer 2007, 291. The memo was leaked and published in the *Sunday Times* in the summer of 2005; see http://www.downingstreetmemo.com/docs/memotext.pdf.

17. George W. Bush, West Point Speech, 1 June 2002. This speech forms the very first part of the National Security Strategy; see http://www.whitehouse.gov/nsc/nss/2002/nss1. html. See also Flibbert 2006, 341.

Colin Powell, clashed on many occasions. As a former general, Powell was more skeptical of the optimistic war plans that the White House and DoD seemed to endorse. The military also doubted the optimistic estimates pushed by top civilians at the DoD, although it was divided itself, with some high-ranking officers, such as Chief of Central Command Tommy Franks, siding with Vice-President Cheney, Rumsfeld, and other neo-conservatives. By contrast, Marine Corps General Zinni, who earlier had been Chief of Central Command, and others opposed the war plan.

In this sense, civil-military relations evolved differently than in other cases of conflict, such as World War I. As we saw in our discussion of that conflict, weak oversight of the military, combined with a military that favored an offensive strategy, presented some civilian leaders with a fait accompli. Civilians had little room for maneuver as military timetables dictated the need to pursue a first strike. This was not the case with Iraq. Many members of the armed forces favored concentrating on Afghanistan rather than Iraq. However, civilian politicians who had early on decided that Iraq should be included with Afghanistan as a target for military intervention dictated military policy. Risa Brooks concluded in her study of this conflict that American civilian leadership maintained control in spite of the military's different preferences. The result was poor strategic assessment, particularly regarding what would happen after Iraq's military had been defeated: "The United States had critical flaws in how military and political officials were coordinating with each other."[18] Strategic coordination—the coordination of military activities with political objectives—was fundamentally unsound.

Finally, the unified political system stifled opposing views and dissent. Whereas the division of powers in American government can often lend itself to diverse positions, this was not the case in the prelude to the invasion. Republicans controlled the executive as well as both Houses of Congress in 2003. By contrast, in the prelude to the Iraq war of 1991, President George H.W. Bush faced a Democratic Senate and House. His son could count on legislative support to a greater extent than he could. The events of 9/11 also gave the executive considerable means to frame the discussion.[19] By suggesting that Iraq was connected to those events, Democrats who opposed the war feared being labeled as "soft" on terrorism.

---

18. Brooks 2008, 255. Her overall assessment of strategic assessment as "mixed" is based on the fact that some other components of strategic assessment, such as information sharing among civilians and military and the clarity of the chain of command, performed reasonably well.

19. See Flibbert 2006. For an interesting discussion of how the neo-conservative political community could use 9/11 as a focusing event to justify intervention in Iraq, see Mazarr 2007.

Third Level Views

At almost the same time that Iraq engaged in its military adventures, first in Iran and then in Kuwait, the Soviet Union was disintegrating. Gorbachev's reforms had unleashed a pent-up demand for individual and state rights, and even Russia itself disavowed the Union. The Warsaw Pact started to unravel, with Germany eventually unifying and the East European countries turning away from communism. All this culminated by the end of 1991 in the break-up of the Soviet Union and the fall of communist regimes everywhere. In brief, in a few short years, the system had transformed from a clearly bipolar world to unipolarity. The United States was unquestionably the sole military superpower.

At one time an ally of Iraq, Moscow had distanced itself from Hussein when he clamped down on communist opponents in the country. Thus, throughout the 1980s, Iraq sought the support of the West and purchased many of its weapons systems from France, although the Soviet Union also remained a major arms supplier. By the time of the Kuwait invasion, however, the Union was split by internal turmoil. Iraq could not ally with a superpower in crisis to stifle American and British demands.

The balance of power between the allied forces and Iraq prior to the invasion in 2003 was even more lopsided than in 1991, even though the United States and Britain failed to secure broad support from the members of the UN, as it had in 1991. Although the number of troops on the American-British side was significantly smaller than in the first Gulf War, the decade-long embargo had left the Iraqi standing military forces much weaker than they appeared. On paper, it still seemed formidable, with an army numbering 350,000 strong.[20] The American and British armies combined numbered around 600,000 troops, with many of them not being deployable to Iraq and needed in other areas. The allied forces had roughly 8,200 main battle tanks, while Iraq could field 2,600. Moreover, the allied air forces had more than 400,000 men under arms (but of course not all in the Iraqi theater) while Iraq had only 20,000. The allies had more than 10 times the number of combat aircraft. Thus, they had clear air supremacy and a lead in every high-tech category. Simply put, the balance of forces created a permissive cause for the American-British invasion.

The coalition dynamics in 2003 shaped up quite differently than in 1991. True, the "coalition of the willing" counted several dozen members, but the only real military contributions came from Britain and the United States, with far smaller forces from Poland, Australia, and Denmark. Even a stalwart ally such as Turkey refused the United States permission to use its territory as the launching platform for a northern front. The coalition had to rely on its bases in friendly Gulf States. All in all, the United States

---

20. Figures from the International Institute for Strategic Studies, *Military Balance 2002–2003* (London: Oxford University Press, 2002–03).

and Britain had approximately 300,000 service men and women in the regional theater, with small contributions of its allies. Ultimately, the ground war involved 170,000 troops.[21]

However, although the allied "coalition of the willing" was far less impressive than the Bush administration made it out to be, Iraq's situation was far worse. While several countries denounced the Bush-Blair actions, they were hardly inclined to come to Hussein's aid. Iraq stood alone.

Moreover, the lessons from the 1991 war seemed to validate several assumptions of an emerging doctrine. First, the Revolution in Military Affairs (RMA) had given any country that possessed precision-guided weapons systems the upper hand against a foe that lacked such technology. A military that had mastered the complicated communications and logistics challenges associated with the RMA could hope to knock out radar and other air defense systems and thus paralyze a possible counterattack. The lopsided victory of 1991 proved that even a vaunted military such as Iraq's, strong in numbers but less technically advanced, could be overwhelmed in short order. In other words, a country that mastered the RMA had an offensive advantage. Second, calculations before the invasion suggested that relatively small numbers of troops might be able to achieve significant successes, as American special operations had done in Afghanistan. Even the higher estimates of the military, which were significantly larger than the estimates of Cheney and Rumsfeld, were modest compared to the 1991 buildup. These calculations conformed with Rumsfeld's objectives of transforming the military into rapidly mobile forces with a "lighter footprint," that is, into forces that required less infrastructural support than the previous heavy divisions of the Cold War period.

Thus, neither the alliance structure, nor the balance of power, nor a countervailing opposite superpower stood in the way of the American-British invasion.[22] The structural opportunity provided by preponderant power and the preferences of the Bush and Blair administrations, which can be well understood by analyses at the first and second levels, clarify why Britain, the United States, and several of their allies entered into the war with Iraq.

Conclusion

Unlike our study of World War I and the Cold War, the analysis of the Iraq War shows that there was no confrontation of great powers. Nevertheless, it does indicate the problems that result from the proliferation of WMD. In the past, regional powers might threaten a great power's interests, but they rarely threatened the security of the stronger state. WMD change the

21. Brooks 2008, 228.

22. Jervis 2003b also notes how the American hegemonic position allowed it to act; indeed, Jervis believes that American policy shades into imperialism.

equation by providing weaker states with the means of inflicting considerable casualties and damage. Moreover, in this first decade of the new millennium, terrorist attacks against the United States, Spain, Britain, Indonesia, Pakistan, India, and elsewhere suggest that the danger of proliferation and the possible use of WMD by non-state actors cannot be discounted altogether.

Using the public dread of WMD and terrorism, the Bush administration tried to justify its decision to invade Iraq, even though Iraq's WMD capability had been severely degraded by the air strikes carried out under Operation Desert Fox in 1998 and by UNSCOM and IAEA inspections. Nor was the Iraq government involved with Al Qaeda operations. American preponderant power, however, provided it with the structural opportunity to fight distant preventive wars. With the world no longer demarcated in two rival camps, the end of the Cold War left American ambitions largely unchecked. However, while unipolarity made war with Iraq possible, the particular belief system of the White House inner circle was the precipitating cause. No doubt Hussein inflamed the situation by his tyrannical actions, but it was the Bush administration's choice to opt for invasion and regime change rather than pursue another option, such as containment or deterrence. Without substantial congressional opposition, and by overruling recalcitrant military leaders, the White House was free to make the invasion part of its overall War on Terror.

RESOURCES

Useful Links and Core Resources for the Study of International Relations[1]

Some of these resources are freely available on the Internet. Others require subscriptions. Check with your library to find out if you have access to the subscription-based resources.

America: History & Life
By subscription
This is the definitive resource for scholarly material related to all aspects of the history of Canada and the United States, from prehistory to the present, from economics to war. It includes indexing of over 1,700 journals. In addition, it provides an international perspective with English-language abstracts to articles in 40 different languages. For coverage of other countries, see *Historical Abstracts* below.

Center for Strategic and International Studies
http://csis.org/
A bipartisan, nonprofit organization headquartered in Washington, DC, CSIS conducts research and analysis and develops policy initiatives that look into the future and anticipate change. The site includes available reports on current global security and governance issues.

Cold War International History Project
http://www.wilsoncenter.org/index.cfm?topic_id=1409&fuseaction=topics.home
The Wilson International Center for Scholars provides this project's reports on historically significant archived materials related to the Cold War. The goal of the project is to continuously uncover and make available sources from the former Communist bloc in an effort to analyze the issues from a non-Western perspective. The other two contributors to

---

1. I gratefully acknowledge the assistance of Lucy E. Lyons, the librarian responsible for political science at the Northwestern University Library.

these efforts are the National Security Archive in the United States and the Harvard Project on Cold War Studies, both listed below.

Declassified Documents Reference System, United States
By subscription

This database makes accessible the texts and images of select declassified American documents from diverse sources, including the CIA, Department of State, National Security Council, Department of Defense, and the FBI. It is a good source of primary documents related to the Cold War.

FIRST: Facts on International Relations and Security Trends
http://first.sipri.org/

FIRST provides access to statistics and documents prepared by over 15 centers, agencies, and programs, including Human Rights Watch, the International Energy Agency, Transparency International, and the World Bank Group. This extensive and integrated database includes works on topics such as armed conflicts and provides facts, figures, and chronologies.

Harvard Project on Cold War Studies
http://www.fas.harvard.edu/~hpcws/

With the National Security Archive and Cold War International History Project, this site promotes research and analysis of recently released East-bloc archives.

Historical Abstracts
By subscription

This is the definitive, authoritative source on all aspects of world history (excluding Canada and the United States) from 1450 to the present. Subjects include military, cultural, and economic history. For Canadian and American history, see *America: History & Life* above.

Human Security Gateway
http://www.hsrgroup.org/

This very rich collection of documents from the Human Security Report Project incorporates a powerful search structure and daily updates. It is international in scope and covers such topics as natural resources and armed conflict, as well as gender and security.

International Bibliography of the Social Sciences
By subscription

Compiled by the Library of the London School of Economics and Political Science, this important resource provides information on publications from over 2,600 journals and books in the fields of economics, sociology, and political science.

International Crisis Group
http://www.crisisweb.org/home/index.cfm
This non-governmental organization offers numerous reports online that analyze local conditions in countries at risk. Search by country or thematic issue such as international terrorism, climate change, or energy.

International Data Base: World Statistics
http://www.census.gov/ipc/www/idb/
The American Census Bureau maintains the IDB as a simple and quick reference tool to locate demographic and socio-economic statistics for 227 countries.

International Political Science Abstracts
By subscription
Produced by the International Political Science Association since 1951, this work indexes and abstracts articles on global issues from serials published throughout the world.

International Relations and Security Network
http://www.isn.ethz.ch/
ISN is an open-access information service that provides timely and historical analyses of world events related to international security issues, such as peacekeeping and arms control.

National Security Archive
http://www.gwu.edu/~nsarchiv/
This independent non-governmental research institute collects and manages declassified documents of the United States, thereby providing evidence of the Western perspective of the Cold War. These documents complement the projects of the *Cold War International History Project* and the *Harvard Project on Cold War Studies*, both listed above.

PAIS International
By subscription
This is a core publication of social sciences literature from all over the world. It provides citations to articles and books; government documents; statistical compilations; and reports of public, intergovernmental, and private organizations, as well as other materials published between 1937 and the present.

Peace Research Abstracts
By subscription
The database of PRA includes many links to full texts, as well as abstracts and citations, from top journals, referring to articles on subjects such as conflict resolution, international affairs, peace psychology, security, and others.

World War I Document Archive
http://wwi.lib.byu.edu/index.php/Main_Page
From telegrams to treaties, this is an extensive archive of primary documents related to World War I. The archive is constructed of materials gathered throughout the world.

Worldwide Political Science Abstracts
By subscription
This is a key resource for the study of international relations. It covers more than 1,500 journals in political science and its complementary fields. Coverage is international in scope.

WWWVL: International Affairs
http://www2.etown.edu/vl/
The Virtual Library project has vetted all of the links in this very comprehensive gateway to research in peace studies, global security, and related topics.

Case Studies

Bennett, Paul, and Jack Snyder. 1993. *Salt II and the Soviet First-Strike Threat*. Pew Case 330. Washington, DC: GUISD Pew Case Study Center.
Martin, Curtis. 2005. *Going to the United Nations: George W. Bush and Iraq*. Pew Case 278. Washington, DC: GUISD Pew Case Study Center.

PART II
THE GLOBAL ECONOMY

SIX

Tools of the Trade:
Comparative Case Strategy and
Hegemonic Stability Theory

Research Strategies with One or Many Cases

Causal Explanations versus Descriptions

All social and political phenomena are highly complex end results of individual and group interaction. As we saw from our discussions of World
War I, the nuclear predicament, and the Iraq war, many factors play a role
in explaining why these events happened. Nevertheless, social scientists
seek to discern patterns among this complexity. Although we know that
complex events rarely lend themselves to simple explanations, as theorists
we try to reduce this complexity in order to understand whether some
causes are more significant than others. Do some causes perhaps appear
with greater frequency? Moreover, if we are able to understand seemingly
diverse events across time and across different geographical areas, we will
reach a deeper understanding of the events in question, because they are
recognized as elements of a pattern rather than ad hoc occurrences. In so
doing we might also be able to influence outcomes.

This is the difference between social scientists and humanists, particularly historians. The latter are less inclined to seek generalizations but
try to produce a rich narrative of events. Description rather than explanation drives most historical research. As sociologists or political scientists,
we seek instead to order disparate narratives to explain why events took
the course they did.

Explanations include an account of the key factors that cause a
particular outcome to occur. The explanatory causes of the phenomenon
are deemed independent variables (or *explanans*). The outcome to be
explained constitutes the dependent variable (the *explanandum*). These
causal factors can be measured (or operationalized) in some form either
mathematically or descriptively, and they can take on various dimensions
and strength. They are independent in the sense that we use them to explain
an outcome, but they are themselves not determined by that outcome; if

they were, our explanation would become circular. We should be able to measure the causal variable independently from the event to be explained. For example, it would be incorrect to argue that "wars are caused by the inherently violent nature of human beings" and then operationalize the causal variable, the nature of human beings, by noting that we know that human beings are violent because they wage war.

A theory links causal statements in a comprehensive order. When a given causal variable is in turn determined by other causal factors, it constitutes an intervening variable and forms part of a larger set of causal claims. A theoretical account specifies *how* the particular value of the independent variable determines the particular values of subsequent intervening and dependent variables. Schematically, a causal argument proceeds in this form:

Independent variable → Intervening variable → Dependent variable

and it consists of three elements: "… the idea of a causal mechanism connecting cause and effect, the idea of a correlation between two or more variables, and the idea that one event is a necessary or sufficient condition for another."[1] It is the task of the theorist to show how a state of affairs at one point in time influences the subsequent state of affairs.

Suppose, for example, that we are trying to understand why Germany in the interwar years turned to totalitarianism. What led to the rise of the Nazi Party? We might conjecture that hard economic circumstances make people willing to choose desperate measures. So we expect that poverty (a variable since society can also be wealthy) correlates with regime type (also a variable since a regime can be democratic or authoritarian). If poverty is high, then we expect that authoritarianism is more likely to emerge. If a country is wealthy, we expect the regime to be democratic. This provides the skeleton of our causal connection between poverty and authoritarianism in interwar Germany.

However, we also need to specify the mechanism of how this came about. We might, for example, note the rise of a politician who promised an end to this economic crisis provided he be given power. Hitler promised to pull Germany out of poverty and revive Germany's strength, and people flocked to his side. In other words, we require a theory of agency to connect the structural condition to the political outcome. Why did individuals in this particular structural situation choose authoritarianism? They might have opted for something else—emigration, social welfare policies, etc. It is the structural condition mediated by the particular rise of a skillful and ruthless politician that ended up producing the result.

---

1. Little 1991, 14.

However, we could also ask ourselves whether the rise of poverty in Germany really constituted an independent variable. What in turn caused Germany to slide from relative welfare (it was after all one of the leading economies of the world prior to World War I) into depression? It seems possible that the harsh repayments that the allied powers imposed after 1918 contributed to the economic decline of Germany. Thus, we hypothesize the following causal sequence: harsh postwar repayments by the defeated led to economic depression, which in turn caused the rise of the Nazi Party. We might then wonder whether this is a causal sequence that might occur in other instances by looking at other postwar settlements. One could, for example, examine whether the treatment of Austria and Turkey (allies of Germany in World War I) differed from that of Germany and observe whether that led to a different outcome. This would constitute cross-case comparison. Conversely, we could also examine Germany history more closely to see whether the treatment of Germany after World War II resulted in a different outcome. This would constitute single case analysis over time. And, indeed, the allies after 1945 refrained from punishing Germany in the same manner. West Germany went through dramatic economic growth in the 1950s, and a vibrant democratic system emerged.

Measuring independent and dependent variables is not always easy. How do we measure and code "economic depression" or "regime type"? This requires the researcher to be specific on how she operationalizes the variables of the research design. We need to develop clear methods for measuring the theoretical concept that we are using, and we need to do so in such a way that other researchers both understand the measurement system and can use our operationalization of variables in their own research. For example, if we want to know whether a regime is authoritarian or democratic, we will have to develop tools through which we can make such judgments across different cases. Other researchers should be able to use the same methods of variable operationalization to falsify or corroborate our findings.

In sum, causal explanation seeks to identify key causal mechanisms rather than to describe all the historical nuances of the situation. One should not reject a social scientific account because it is incomplete: *every theoretical representation of a complex event is incomplete because it does not seek to provide a full description of everything that was related to the phenomenon in question*. Instead, a social scientific account should be rejected if it is proven incorrect in its causal claim.

The Scientific Method

How do we know if a causal explanation is valid or incorrect? The philosopher of science Karl Popper argued that theories are scientific if they are potentially open to falsification or corroboration.[2] A theory is falsified if it fails to explain or predict what it *should* be able to explain or predict. This occurs when a theory fails an important test. For example, if I argue that poverty leads to authoritarianism, and I find a country where poverty does not correlate with authoritarianism—say, India—then my theory is falsified. It is not valid. A theory is corroborated if the causal explanation for a given country does conform to my expectations. If I predict that economic decline will lead to authoritarianism, and if I subsequently observe such a sequence of events in a given country, then my theory is corroborated. It has been validated.

If arguments cannot *in principle* be falsified or corroborated, they are not scientific theories but matters of ideology or normative beliefs. Popper's statement that theories should be falsifiable in principle means that they can be considered scientific statements, even if they have yet to be subjected to actual tests. It should be possible to test the validity of the argument. Consequently, Popper argued that Marxism, which predicted that socialism would be the end stage of history, was an unscientific argument as it could not be proven correct or incorrect.

It is important to recognize that most philosophers of science who ascribe to this logic of inquiry primarily focus on the natural sciences. But social phenomena are not subject to the strict law-like generalizations that occur in the natural world. In the confines of this book, we cannot delve into the complex discussions of how the natural sciences and social sciences should use distinct methods.[3] However, part of the reason why they do so is the matter of the individual volition of human subjects as compared to inanimate natural objects. Moreover, the interaction of human groups—and of entire countries—is, as already indicated, highly complex. Given individual agency and the complexity of human interaction, political events rarely lend themselves to the type of mechanistic explanations common in the natural sciences.

Nevertheless, without suggesting that the social world should be studied and treated as similar to the natural world, it is possible to examine whether some causal statements are more powerful than others. Even if we do not arrive at law-like generalizations, it might be possible to discern certain patterns that tend to produce certain results with some degree of probability. Thus, the statement that harsh postwar settlements lead to poverty and subsequently to authoritarianism might not always be true, but that is no reason to disregard it entirely. It might occur in the majority of cases. We would then examine in greater detail why this relation did not occur in the other cases. What led to the emergence of a

2. For a brief discussion of Popper and the naturalist approach to social science, see Little 1991, 222–27.

3. For an overview of some of these arguments, see Ryan 1973.

robust democracy even if harsh settlements led to poverty? Were previous political institutions or culture perhaps intervening variables?

Research Designs Using Experimental Strategies

There are various ways of examining whether a particular cause is more salient than others, or whether a given factor dramatically changes the outcome. In the natural sciences and in medical analysis, researchers try to control all variables, that is, keep them constant and manipulate the key variable of investigation. For example, if I want to know whether a particular medical treatment has a beneficial effect, I might create two very similar groups (similar in age, general physical condition, etc.) and give one group the treatment while the other gets a placebo. The variation in the hypothesized causal variable should produce a variation in the outcome while other variables remain the same.

With regard to political events, it is usually impossible to hold many variables artificially constant. Rarely will two cases be exactly similar. Nevertheless, we do try to approximate the logic of experimental research by comparing across different cases while trying to neutralize the effect of rival causal explanations. There are a variety of ways for doing causal research with a single case, with only a few cases, and with many cases.

1. Research Designs Using Single Case Analysis

It is possible to examine causal arguments even by looking at only one case.[4] Single case analysis can be used to test theories. If a particular theory should hold for a given case, but proves not to provide a satisfactory explanation, then the theory is false. This might be regarded as a "crucial test approach." For example, if one held a relatively simple theoretical perspective that poverty leads to authoritarianism, then this thesis should hold in countries that are clearly less developed. If one examined India prior to its recent economic growth, one would expect to find that the Indian government was authoritarian. However, our empirical finding that India has a long-standing democratic system serves to falsify the theoretical claim.

As a rule of thumb, one should pick an "easy case" for the argument one is trying to test. That is, one should pick a test case that should be explained easily by the theory. It should be a fair test. Moreover, if the theory fails to explain even this easy case, then it will likely fail to explain cases that are more complicated. In other words, the failure to pass an easy test will constitute a powerful refutation of the argument.

Conversely, if one is trying to advance a theoretical argument of one's own, one should pick a "tough case." For example, if I wanted to

---

4. For a discussion of various research strategies, see Eckstein 1975.

argue that the timing of industrialization affected the type of regime (the late industrialization thesis that we will discuss later), I would pick a case that in all aspects would lead one to expect a democratic regime, except that it had industrialized at a late date. If I found that this country had an authoritarian system, then my argument would not only be validated, but it would likely hold in many other cases. I would have passed a tough test. That is, if my theoretical claim holds even in that case, then it has proven to be a powerful theory given its likely broad applicability.

Single case analysis also lends itself to causal analysis if one observes variation in the outcome over time. This constitutes diachronic (across time) analysis. For example, say one observes at a particular point in time (t = 1) that in a given country poverty and authoritarianism coincide. However, at a later date (t = 2) the country has gone through economic development. If we now observe that economic well-being and democracy are present, then this would corroborate the argument that economic depression correlates with authoritarianism. Conversely, if we observe that the regime is still authoritarian despite economic prosperity, then we would conclude that economic well-being and regime type are unrelated.

2. Research Designs Using (Large N) Statistical Analysis

On the other end of the spectrum, one can draw inferences by examining large numbers of cases. In this inductive approach, one collects extensive data over many cases and then tries to examine through statistical analysis whether there are common elements among them.

For example, if we expected that war prone states shared a common characteristic but we had many possible variables to consider, we might create a data set based on as many cases as we could calculate. Thus, researchers have compiled collections of data on virtually every war in the past centuries and then examined whether a common trait emerged among these very disparate cases (as the Correlates of War Project tried to do).

This is in essence a many-case comparative strategy. We might code our cases in the following manner.

Country	Presence of Independent Variables	Dependent Variable
Germany 1914	x, y, z	war
France 1815	x, y, b	war
Netherlands 1672	x, f, d	war
Spain 1588	w, y, c	war
Germany 1939	g, y, q	war

And so on. We would then conclude from this relatively small data set that factor y seems to occur in four out of five cases and must be deemed an important factor that could lead to the outbreak of war. The more observations we have, the stronger the probabilistic assertion that variable y was a key factor. This would remain a probabilistic assertion, as we would rarely have the complete universe of cases, nor would it be easy to code the various factors, given the lack of historical records and the difficulties in coding variables. However, we might be able to find whether or not there is a relatively close fit between the frequency of independent and dependent variables.

3. Research Designs Using (Small N) Comparative Case Strategy

In many instances, however, it will be difficult to create a large data set, or we might lack confidence in grouping cases together because we do not know enough about them, or because we do not know how to code a particular variable. Detailed knowledge of cases might be necessary to fully specify the causal mechanisms behind the observed correlations. Consequently, international relations research often revolves around comparisons among a limited number of cases. There are various ways through which one can still make causal inferences with only a limited number of cases.

First, we might examine why two seemingly similar cases produced different outcomes. For instance, if one observes that two countries are economically underdeveloped but show variation in regime type, one will want to know what caused this variation. In this research design, we pick similar cases that vary along the one key dimension that we expect to be of causal significance and try to control for alternative possible explanations.

In this comparative case strategy—the Method of Difference—we focus on explaining different outcomes among cases that are similar in many other respects.[5] What is the key variable that causes relatively similar cases to vary in outcome?

The research design looks as follows:

Cases	Independent Variables	Dependent Variable
Case 1	X present, Y present, Z present	outcome C
Case 2	X present, Y present, Z not present	outcome D
Case 3	X present, Y present, Z weakly present	outcome C (but marginally so)

From this, we can conclude that Z is the key causal factor. We might even be able to conclude that the higher the score on Z, the more likely is a high score producing outcome C.

We might proceed through a second strategy as well. In this comparative case approach, we ask why dissimilar cases produce a similar outcome. This is the Method of Agreement. How is it that two cases that are different in so many respects produce a similar outcome?

---

5. Lijphart 1971.

Cases	Variables		
Case 1	W present, X present, Y present	→	outcome: Z
Case 2	W present, X not present, Y not present	→	outcome: Z

The similar score on the independent variable W is the key factor that produces the similarity in outcome.

The examples above are based on comparisons at the same moment in time— synchronic analysis as opposed to diachronic comparison. However, one can combine the two by comparing Case 1 at two or three different points in time with Case 2 at several distinct points in time. This would allow us to expand the number of observations, thus making our causal inferences more robust.

4. Which Strategy to Use?

As I suggested above, experimental design is rarely feasible for students of international relations. It has, however, been used to produce interesting results in the studies of individual decision-making, that is, the kind of first level analysis discussed in Part I of this book. Consequently, scholarship in international relations tends to rely on single case analysis, small N comparisons, and large N statistical inference. Each of these has its advantages and disadvantages. The choice among these strategies might be dictated by the objective of the particular scholar, the evidence available, and the abilities of the researcher in question (such as, for example, command of foreign languages).

Single case analysis is useful for testing theories but not very useful for suggesting generalizable theories of one's own. Because one is only examining one case, any extrapolations to other cases must be made with caution. We have relatively few observations, and we do not know if other cases would be similar or dissimilar along many of the independent variables. It is useful as a crucial test approach to existing theories but less useful for the generation of new theories.

Examining one case has one great advantage in that a scholar can deeply immerse herself into the material at hand. Hence, studies in comparative politics require that the researcher become proficient in the language and history of a given country. Field work in that area would be helpful as well. Thus, single case analysis can provide the researcher with the chance of acquiring great in-depth knowledge of a given case but at the cost of generalizability.

Large N statistical analysis presents the other side of the coin. Given that one works with many observations, statistical analysis might yield quite robust probabilistic statements. Generalizability of the argument is enhanced, and hence this kind of analysis is well suited for generating new theoretical insights and causal claims. Nevertheless, it also has drawbacks.

First, it requires us to aggregate and code data across many cases. It is impossible for any researcher to acquire great in-depth knowledge of each case, and so she runs the danger that the operationalization of variables is incorrect. For example, if we regard party competition as one of the key traits of a democratic system, we might code single party dominance as characteristic of an authoritarian regime. Thus, we would code the Soviet Union as an authoritarian system, given the dominance of the Communist Party. But by that logic Japan could be classified as authoritarian as well, given the dominance of the Liberal Democratic Party there since the mid-1950s. Yet, our contextual knowledge of Japan clearly indicates it is a democratic system.

Second, the researcher will not always have a large number of cases at her disposal. The number of cases might be reduced by the lack of evidence or because one wants to control for particular variables. For example, if the researcher is examining crisis decision-making by the governments of the superpowers during the Cold War, she might have only a limited set of cases to work with—the Cuban Missile Crisis, the Berlin crises, etc.

Third, even if data are apparently available across many cases, one must proceed with caution. Many countries do not have the means to generate complicated and reliable data on growth rates, demographics, inflation, and other key indicators that might inform analysis.

The comparative case method provides several advantages. First, the limited number of cases allows the researcher to acquire a reasonable in-depth knowledge of each. Consequently, she can be relatively confident that the operationalization of variables can be trusted. Second, this knowledge of cases also allows the researcher to focus on key variables based on expected results. For example, our historical knowledge of the various authoritarian countries in Europe might lead us to expect that the military played a role in determining foreign policy prior to World War I. We can subsequently test our hypothesis to see whether this was indeed the case in Germany and other countries by carefully tracing the sequence of decisions by looking at historical records, biographies, etc.

Here again, though, there are drawbacks. When focusing on a few cases, there is the danger of selecting according to the dependent variable. That is, the researcher has selected cases based on their score on the dependent variable. This might bias estimates of causal effects. Particularly troublesome, according to some scholars, is the situation where there is no variation on the dependent variable at all. However, a rival perspective suggests that this problem can be overcome.[6]

---

6. King, Keohane, and Verba (1994, 124–32) are particularly concerned about selection on the dependent variable. For the alternative view, see George and Bennett 2004, 22–25.

The small number of cases might also make it difficult to control for the number of alternative explanations and might lead the researcher to derive incorrect conclusions. The problem is magnified if one chooses only two cases.[7] It is thus critical that the researcher chooses as many relevant cases as feasible to examine the causal argument while at the same time trying to maintain in-depth knowledge of the cases at hand.

In a research environment, where the number of cases is vast, one might use statistical methods and large N analysis to discern causal sequences with a reasonable probability. However, a large number of cases does not necessarily indicate causality but merely the correlation of independent and dependent variables. We still need to figure out how the particular causal chain develops leading factor x to produce y.

Moreover, even with a large number of cases, it will be impossible to control for all independent variables. Hence, our conclusions must be probabilistic rather than law-like. The non-mechanistic, social world in which political actors operate seldom lends itself to a simple encompassing explanation. We study clouds, not clocks.[8]

Given the multiple causes that are at work, the indeterminacy of correlations, and historical contingencies, it is critical that the researcher chart the sequence along which causal chains unfold. Consequently, whichever strategy one pursues, small N or large N, it is useful to apply structured, focused comparison to at least some of the cases. This method consists of applying "standardized, general questions" to each historical case: "The investigator ... seeks to identify the variety of different causal patterns that can occur for the phenomenon in question."[9]

Structured focused comparison is especially appropriate when the number of cases is limited and many possible explanations seem to be at work. Moreover, as Alex George, one of the key proponents of this method, argues, the combination of historical analysis with a given set of questions about each case "enables the development of ... differentiated, policy-relevant theory."[10] The researcher remains sensitive to the historical nuances of each case but examines each by applying the same set of hypotheses. When noticing the variation between these cases, the researcher also tries to explain why hypotheses might or might not be confirmed in that particular instance.

Structured focused comparison should proceed side by side with process tracing. Process tracing examines the data and searches for the underlying causal mechanisms, processes, and intervening variables that

7. Lieberson 1992.
8. Almond and Genco 1977.
9. George 1979, 60.
10. For theoretical discussions of this methodology and examples of the policy relevant work that it yields, see, for example, Jentleson, Levite, and Berman 1993; George and Smoke 1974; King, Keohane, and Verba 1994, 45.

link putative causes to observed effects. In doing this, the researcher tries to deal with the problem of "equifinality"—the problem that a similar outcome might have resulted from myriad different causal sequences. By tracing each causal step, checking against the historical evidence, interviewing possible participants, and looking for confirming or disconfirming evidence of rival causal patterns, the researcher tries to demonstrate how each step of the sequence unfolded. Process tracing thus examines "... whether the causal process a theory hypothesizes or implies in a case is in fact evident in the sequence and values of the intervening variables in that case."[11]

Similarly, the theorist Jon Elster argues that social science should proceed by examining mechanisms rather than by pursuing social scientific laws that aim for prediction and hold in all cases. Instead, he says, "... for explanatory purposes the mechanism is what matters. It provides understanding whereas prediction at most offers control."[12]

The Logic of Collective Action

In the section above, we discussed how one might compare different cases by using various methodologies for doing research. In this section, I advance a substantive theory that we can use to good effect in analyzing economic affairs as well as environmental issues (which we will discuss in Part III). This is the theory of collective action, which economists have long recognized and which was popularized in the study of politics by Mancur Olson.[13]

Collective goods, or public goods, have two features. First, they are non-exclusive. One cannot exclude someone else from enjoying the benefits of that good, once at least one actor has provided for such good. For example, if I plant a beautiful tree in my front yard, then not only do I enjoy that good myself, but every passerby who similarly enjoys trees benefits from my action. In so doing, I have provided a public good to the neighborhood. Second, public goods are non-rival, that is, one's enjoyment of the good does not diminish someone else's enjoyment of that good. This is also called jointness of supply. Sticking with the metaphor above, if I beautify my garden, I enjoy the garden myself. However, my enjoyment does not diminish the ability of others who walk by my house to enjoy that good as well.

The problem with public goods is the danger of free riding. If goods are fully non-exclusive and non-rival, then the danger exists that no one will provide for the good in question, or at the very least they will tend to

---

11. George and Bennett 2004, 6.
12. Elster 1989, 10.
13. Olson 1965.

contribute as little as possible.[14] In the above example, we might recognize that the private garden, while providing benefits, does not fully constitute a collective good. I will most likely benefit more than others. I can sit in my garden and plant the flowers and trees that I want. I could even try to shield the garden from my neighbors by putting up hedges and fences.

Now imagine that I did not live in a house but in a large apartment building and that I and my neighbors had a communal garden to which all had equal access. If I took it upon myself to beautify this garden, all my neighbors could enjoy that good as much as myself. The benefits, in other words, accrue to each occupant of the apartment building. However, the costs—purchasing plants; the work involved in planting, watering, weeding, and fertilizing—accrue to me directly. Collective goods thus impose private costs but collective benefits. Under such circumstances, each individual will rationally hope for the other person to provide for that good.

In this sense, collective action problems are in essence multi-person Prisoner's Dilemmas.[15] While each individual would benefit from mutual cooperation, no one does anything to provide for the good; each individual's first preference is to defect while the other cooperates. The individual's strategy is thus to opt for DC. Each person will choose to free ride. With each member choosing that option, the outcome will be mutual defection (DD). The good will not be provided at all, or it will be under-provided.

In order to prevent this outcome, the group will require at least one actor who is willing to bear the costs. This leader will provide for the good and incur the costs of doing so. Indeed, the leader will likely force the other members of the collective to contribute their fair share through coercion and incentives. In international politics this means that hierarchy is necessary to overcome the strategic incentive for states to free ride when it comes to collective goods that might benefit many states.

With regard to domestic politics, we might imagine that most individuals believe that government provides for critical functions such as military defense, roads, public education, etc. We will thus support taxation as a means to raise revenue for those key functions. However, if paying one's taxes were purely a voluntary process, then individuals would shirk their load. One would hope that others would pay their share while attempting to free ride oneself. Moreover, without a guarantee that others are not free riding, one would be irrational to pay oneself. In short, government plays a critical role in enforcing compliance to the tax codes.

Similarly in international economic affairs and environmental issues, states will attempt to free ride where collective goods are involved—given the condition of international anarchy (the absence of a world government). Short of a dominant actor, the hegemon, who enforces rules of

---

14. Olson focused particularly on non-exclusiveness to make his argument, but the logic of the argument remains the same.

15. Hardin 1982, ch. 2.

conduct and behavior, the provision of the collective good will suffer. As we will see, international leadership can be critical to international economic stability.

SEVEN

Three Views of
Economics and Politics

Mercantilism

Mercantilism, or economic nationalism, refers to both the economic theory regarding the role of the state in the economy and to the actual practices of the European states from the fifteenth century on.[1] Both the practice and this early economic theory are closely related to the emergence of capitalism and integrated territorial states. Thus, part of the account of mercantilism will resonate with our earlier discussion of the changes in the mode of warfare from the fourteenth century onward.

As we saw in Part I, mercantilism, liberalism, and Marxism advanced quite distinct views regarding the relation of economics to politics and how economic relations either precipitate or prevent international war. Liberals see economic relations as relatively benign and conducive to peace, whereas mercantilists and Marxists see economics as intertwined with conflict. However, warfare and economic development have also interacted in other ways.

Mercantilism is closely connected to the transition from the feudal system to early forms of capitalism. As a logic of organization, feudalism had military, political, and economic elements. Militarily, feudalism was based on warfare by mounted knights (lords, aristocrats). Warfare was conducted by a highly skilled and small group. The lord owned the means of warfare (his armor, his horse), and armored servants and lesser lords were required to serve at his command. Given that the means were privately owned, this meant that military power was localized and centered on regional strongholds. Politically, feudalism entailed fragmented political authority. Lords, dukes, and counts held governmental and judicial power within their domain. Lower and higher ranks were bound to each other by a system of personal ties—serfs to lords, lords to higher nobles, and higher nobles to the king. One gained such authority by birth and lineage, not because of particular merit. Economically, this system meant that the

---

1. For a fuller description with a discussion of some of mercantilism's proponents, see Perlman and McCann 1998, ch. 3.

aristocracy owned the land. Lords had the land tilled and worked by peasants tied to the land as serfs. These serfs owed the lord service as well as goods-in-kind. They were obliged to hand over a particular amount of grain or animal stock at specified periods. In exchange, the lord provided them military protection. The economic system as a whole relied largely on barter exchange, given the lack of reliable coinage (paper money was unknown). Many lords issued their own coin and used their own weights and measures. Thus, even in England, which was more centralized than many other parts of Europe, there were thousands of different weights and measures in use.[2]

At the peak of this order stood the mounted knights—those who ruled by the force of arms. Commoners who earned their money in trade and commerce were considered inferior. Consequently, the interests of the townsfolk (the commoners) often stood in tension with those of the aristocracy. Indeed, the inhabitants of the urban centers (the burgh, hence burghers) came to denote a completely different class from the aristocracy and were called the bourgeoisie. (Marx later used the term to describe capitalists in general.)

By the fourteenth century, the feudal order started to crack. New technologies and modes of warfare emerged. These required the use of gunpowder, more elaborate fortification, and larger armies. This in turn favored greater centralization and rational administration, as well as the creation of a monetary economy. Rulers who could coordinate these military, economic, and political changes could control much larger territories, mobilize their inhabitants, and thus field larger armies for warfare. Larger territories and better administration also allowed the ruler to raise more taxes. Gradually, this required rulers not only to develop more coherent national economies through standardized coinage, weights and measures, and systematized legal systems, but also to reduce internal barriers to trade and support key industries. Simply put, rulers started to take an active role in centralizing administration, expanding the realm, and creating a more efficient economic system. State making, economic development, and success in war—all went hand in hand.[3] Kings and high lords needed to take an active role in all three. Domestic development accompanied the view that the international system was competitive; indeed, it was seen as a zero sum game: one state's gain was considered to come at another's loss.

From the fifteenth century on, virtually every state in Europe followed mercantilist policies. Even England and the Netherlands, who would later be touted as free trading and non-interventionist states, used mercantilist practices. France in the sixteenth century did so very explicitly under Colbert

---

2. A fascinating account of the importance of standardizing weights and measure is Kula 1986.

3. The emergence of the state and the beginnings of national economies are discussed in Spruyt 1994.

in order to meet external challenges from England and Spain. Germany, in trying to catch up to other states, adopted mercantilism in the nineteenth century, with Gustav Schmoller as one of its theoretical proponents. In his view, mercantilism constituted "the total transformation of society and its organization, as well as of the state and its institutions, in the replacing of a local and territorial economic policy by that of the national state."[4] Even the United States had thinkers who were influenced by mercantilist doctrine. Among the founding fathers of the Republic, Alexander Hamilton argued for protection to enhance American manufacturing.

Elements of mercantilist doctrine are alive and well even today. However, in its current connotation, it has severed the connection between economic development and war, which is no longer perceived to be beneficial for the state's economy. This *neo-mercantilism* maintains that governments have an important role to play in creating efficient markets and in facilitating domestic economic activity, that political rulers should intervene in the economy, and that government can aid important economic sectors and create competitive advantage internationally. For example, during the 1960s and 1970s, the French supported "champions of industry" with public funds, because they believed those sectors or firms were critical for economic success as a whole. As one French official stated in 1962, "French planning ... is essentially the extension to the national level of the kind of planning effort made by any private business with thought for the future."[5] Business and the state had similar objectives, and it was up to the state to coordinate the private sector to best achieve its goals. Similarly, in the very recent past, the Japanese Ministry of International Trade and Industry (MITI) actively engaged in supporting favored economic sectors and groups.

Neo-mercantilist governments also favor protectionism through tariffs, import quotas, or other means to limit imports. They seek to defend domestic markets from external competitors by making the goods of foreign firms artificially more expensive.

Liberalism

In the seventeenth and eighteenth centuries, different ideas emerged about how politics and economics hinge together. David Hume argued that international monetary flows and trade trended towards an equilibrium over a period of time. Most importantly, Adam Smith argued explicitly against the mercantilist doctrine in his book *The Wealth of Nations* (1776). Even in France, which had a strong mercantilist policy, thinkers such as Turgot started to argue for a policy of limited intervention and letting the market

---

4. As cited in Perlman and McCann 1998, 79.
5. Cohen 1977, 7.

run its own course—a system christened *laissez-faire* from the French, to let act.

Smith assumed that individuals would pursue their own interest by specializing in activities that maximized their gains. In so doing, they would produce more goods and offer the surplus of their production for sale; their self-interested activity would benefit society as a whole. The pursuit of individual interest would be mutually beneficial, and this would occur without government intervention. "The invisible hand" of self-interest would lead to a division of labor within society with individuals specializing in what they did best. Smith then extrapolated from specialization at the level of individuals within a society to the level of the state. If a country specialized in an area in which it had an advantage, and then engaged in international trade, this would not only benefit that country but would also maximize global production. David Ricardo in 1817 (see below) subsequently expanded on these ideas and clarified how a state could specialize in those sectors in which it enjoyed a relative advantage and trade for other goods. Both trading states would gain.[6] Ricardo's key insight was that a country would always benefit from specialization and trade, even if it was less efficient than its trading partner.

Consequently, liberal doctrine argues for limited government intervention in the economic sphere. It explicitly counsels against protectionist measures that hinder competition and diminish international trade. Subsidies and tariffs are to be avoided. However, liberal theorists do not argue that government has no role to play at all in the economics of the state. Indeed, there are important areas in which it should perform key functions. In today's modern economy, government plays a critical role in affecting economic behavior in multiple ways.

First, it sets legal parameters for economic interaction and punishes violators who do not follow existing laws. It thus enforces contracts, a critical feature of exchange. Government, furthermore, defines property rights: what entitles someone to ownership of a commodity or good and under which conditions someone can claim a patent on an invention, thus allowing that person to reap gains from her own skill. Clearly, such conditions are critical to how individuals and firms engage in research and development. National regulations and laws also provide information to consumers and producers. In order for market exchange to work well, individuals need to be informed about the contracting parties and the goods that are exchanged. Is this producer reliable, or has this firm violated contracts before? Are the goods being produced safe for consumers?

Second, government is critical in the provision of public goods. As noted earlier, the problem with collective goods is that they often lead to free riding. Given that benefits will accrue to all if a good is provided, but the costs of provision are concentrated, there is a danger that self-

---

6. Ricardo 1973.

interest will lead to the under-provision or non-provision of that good. For example, while we might not agree on the level of taxation, we probably agree that taxation overall is beneficial. We want government to build roads, support public education, and so on. But if I could get away with it, I would avoid paying taxes or engage in tax evasion, while everyone else pays their taxes. I would still get to enjoy the goods provided by government (I would drive on the road and so on), but I would incur no costs or less costs than you. If all people engaged in that behavior, the government would not be able to collect taxes. Thus, we need government to enforce the tax code. To give one recent example, when the Soviet Union broke apart, its central government effectively ceased to function and public revenue dropped precipitously.

Moreover, government also has an important role to play when market failure occurs. In situations of monopoly and oligopoly, one firm or a few firms acting together can set the price of a good above where it would otherwise be if supply and demand could work freely. For example, if there were only one phone company in a given country, such a company could charge prices well above the price that would emerge if competition existed. This is exactly how the telecommunications industry worked on a global level till the breakup of AT&T in the United States and the Post Telegraph and Telephone systems in Europe and Japan in the 1980s and 1990s. The state, consequently, needs to break up monopolies or oligopolies to prevent such market failure.

Finally, the state also might have preponderant interests and moral concerns about market exchange in some spheres. Slavery, of course, has been long outlawed, although it continues to exist in some areas of the world. More recently, governments have had to decide on the use of stem cell research, whether or not the use of certain drugs is legal, whether one can contractually agree to have someone else's child (i.e., surrogate motherhood), and so on.

To conclude, liberals do not see economic relations as a zero sum game but recognize that cooperation can provide mutual gain. Moreover, they are primarily concerned with *absolute* gains not *relative* gains. Thus, although one country might gain more than another from trade, the key point to remember is that both countries come out ahead. Moreover, liberals believe that while governments have important functions to play in the economic sphere, they should act with caution. Often they are unable to pick winners, and thus they should refrain from subsidies and other means of direct support of interests that might fail. More often than not, when governments choose "champions of industry," they tend to pick the wrong firm or sector. Similarly, governments should refrain from tariffs and other protectionist measures, which distort the division of labor and hence inflate prices to the consumer. Also, such means of protection are often driven by special interests capturing government power, as Adam Smith observed.

Ricardo's Law of Comparative Advantage

Ricardo's argument that a country does well to specialize and trade with another country, even if it is more efficient in every sector, is best explained by an example. Say that in Country A the workforce of 10 million workers can produce within one year 100,000 cars *or* 400 aircraft. Consequently, if it allocated its workforce to both sectors, it could produce over two years 100,000 cars *and* 400 aircraft. Or it could produce 200,000 cars or 800 aircraft if it specialized in one of these two sectors.

With a similar size of workforce, Country B can produce in one year 20,000 cars *or* 200 aircraft. Consequently, if it allocated its workforce to both sectors, it could produce 20,000 cars *and* 200 aircraft over two years, or it could produce 40,000 cars *or* 400 aircraft if it specialized in one of the two.

Note that A is more efficient than B in both car and aircraft production. However, in car production, A is five times more efficient than B, while in aircraft production it is only twice as efficient. Ricardo's key point is that it pays A to specialize in that area in which its comparative advantage is greatest (car production) leaving B to specialize in the sector in which its disadvantage was the least (aircraft).

If they so specialized, then A could produce 200,000 cars in two years. In those same two years, B could produce 400 aircraft. This sets up terms for trade. A could offer B 60,000 cars in exchange for all of B's aircraft, resulting in A having 140,000 cars and 400 aircraft and B having 60,000 cars. A is now better off than it would have been if it had chosen to produce both cars and aircraft—it has 40,000 more cars. B has 60,000 cars instead of the 40,000 that it otherwise would have if had allocated two years of its labor force to making them. In other words, specialization and division of labor, combined with trade, makes both parties better off, even if one of the countries is more efficient in each of the sectors in which trade is conducted.

Marxism

Karl Marx (1818–83) provided yet another perspective on how economics and politics interact. He advanced an evolutionary theory of history, which subsequent Marxists have termed "historical materialism." In this view, history proceeds in various stages, each of which is characterized by a dominant form of economic organization. Examining European history, Marx observed that in ancient times production of goods and agriculture was performed by slave labor. In the Middle Ages feudalism supplanted slave labor with nominally free but indentured serfs performing the primary production. Serfs held some lands from their lord in exchange for which they were required to perform certain services and provide the lord

Figure 7.1 | **The Socialist Evolutionary Theory of History (Historical Materialism)**

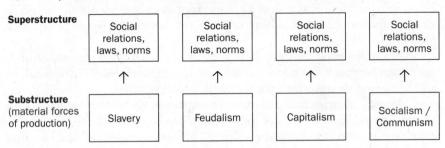

with in-kind goods. Subsequently, in the capitalist stage, workers (the proletariat) performed services for the capitalist owners of factories, capital, and land (the bourgeoisie). The workers themselves owned no means of production, but in exchange for selling their labor they were paid in money. In the final stage of history, the proletariat would seize power from the capitalists, and all means of production would be owned collectively by all members of society.

The theory is historically materialist in that Marx argued that the material means of production—that is, the manner in which goods were produced—determined social organization, laws, and even ideas—what Marx termed the superstructure. Thus, the material mode of economic organization formed the substructure that determined the superstructure.

Marx was particularly interested in capitalism. This stage was characterized by a class division between the bourgeoisie and the proletariat. While the bourgeoisie owned the means of production, the proletariat possessed only the ability to work for wages; that is, they could only sell their labor. These class divisions, Marx believed, would lead to class conflict, where the state (government) would act as the instrument of the ruling class. Government was inherently repressive in his view.

Marx further concluded that the capitalist system was logically flawed, as it would result inevitably in a tension between over-production and under-consumption. He noted that it would be rational for capitalists to produce more and more goods and to try to sell those goods. Because they competed with other producers, any rational capitalists would try to lower prices—since consumers wish to pay the lowest price possible—and thus sell more goods. Consequently, because of competitive pressures, capitalists would continuously seek to repress their labor force and push wages down, making products cheaper. Producers might also employ more women, children, and foreign workers who could be paid less. This would reduce the costs of producing items by cutting wages. However, by doing so, the capitalists would impoverish their own consumers. The workers themselves would not be able to pay for the products they were manufacturing.[7] In the end, class conflict would lead the impoverished workers to seize the state and appropriate the resources for the working class. Goods would be held in common by the state during the socialist phase.

Marx believed that conflicts among countries were due to capitalism. Wars originated because capitalist states fight each other for markets and resources or come into conflict with socialist states.

Marx's theories had a significant impact in several areas. First, they laid the foundation of the centrally planned economies of the communist countries. Indeed, by the mid-twentieth century, the most advanced states consisted of a camp of capitalist states and a camp of socialist states at loggerheads with each other, as we saw in the discussion of the Cold War. Only the breakup of the Soviet Union and the ousting of communist regimes in its satellite countries brought these policies to a halt. The Soviet Union, as the most advanced socialist state, provides a stark example of how the state appropriated the means of production to itself. Ten years after the October Revolution (1917) the regime had already seized more than two-thirds of industrial production. Prior to the Gorbachev reforms, which started around 1986, the communist regime maintained an iron grip on all industrial sectors. Given the stark differences between capitalist production and socialist planning, it is worth examining this case in some detail.

The Soviet Model: Collective and State Ownership of the Means of Production

Most notably, the Soviet state itself appropriated the means of production, particularly in industrial production (in agriculture it tolerated a larger degree of collective management and even some privately administered lands).[8] The government acted as the main supplier of goods to the consumer, and it set prices and wages. Allocation did not occur through market dynamics but through the state by means of central planning that used complicated input-output models. Five- and ten-year plans were drafted showing how the economy should develop. Prices did not reflect market supply and demand but were accounting devices to reflect the ratios of input and output. For example, the price of oil in the Soviet Union was not a reflection of what the world market might pay for it but reflected the calculated amount of labor time and goods it took to discover oil, bring it to the surface, refine it, and bring it to the Soviet citizen.

---

7. Hardly a Marxist himself, Henry Ford believed that decently remunerated workers were indeed the consumers of their own products. While he primarily had absenteeism and job turnover in mind, his raising of the minimum wage to $5 a day in 1914 (double the sector average) in essence created the consumer market for his mass-produced automobiles.

8. For an overview of how the Soviet economic system worked, see Zimbalist and Sherman 1984, particularly chapters 7–8.

Table 7.1 | **Ownership of Means of Industrial Production in the Soviet Union (by %)**

	1928	1950	1980
Public organizations (state)	69	92	98
Cooperatives	13	8	2
Private	18	0	0

Source: Central Statistical Agency of the Soviet Union. Cited in Zimbalist and Sherman 1984, 207.

However, the problems with this system became worse and worse over time, and they proved themselves endemic to any centrally planned economy. First, collective ownership diminished incentives for individuals to work harder. If one had to share one's profits and fruits of one's labor, then rational self-interest dictated that one should put in less effort. Moreover, individuals had an incentive not to tell higher authorities how many inputs they might need to produce a certain good, while at the same time they would inflate their own contributions. Information distortions were rampant. Managers would request more input resources from the Central Planning Bureau than they actually needed, thus giving themselves a cushion. The Central Planning Bureau in turn knew that it was getting disinformation and inaccurate estimates, and tried to counter them by providing unrealistic targets and disinformation of its own. Second, the technical complexity of input-output models proved bewildering and became ever more so as production processes became more complicated. It proved impossible to get the amounts exactly right, to get goods shipped on time, and to predict how external events (such as the weather) might affect production. Third, given that prices did not reflect what the world market would pay, there were serious price distortions. Thus, the Soviet Union ended up selling vastly under-priced energy supplies to its member republics and Warsaw Pact allies.[9]

Marxist Influences in the Less Developed Countries

Marxist theory also had a profound effect on the economic policies of less developed countries (LDCs) and newly independent states after World War II.[10] Scholars and decision-makers in these countries believed that the international system was biased in favor of the economically more developed

---

9. Bunce 1985 describes how the Soviet external empire became a financial burden. Aslund 1995 gives an account of the economic challenges facing the Soviet Union and the transition to a capitalist economy following 1991.

10. As a consequence of this evolutionary theory, Marxism is ambivalent about the benefits of capitalism in pre-capitalist states. For instance, Marx believed that there were positive aspects to British rule in India as it propelled the latter to a more advanced stage of

capitalist countries. Some thinkers, such as world-systems theorists, argued that international trade could be understood by a center-periphery model: the capitalist countries in the center profited from the capitalist world-system while the less developed countries on their periphery remained less developed and largely operated as suppliers of raw materials and less valuable goods for the advanced countries.

Dependency theorists noted how the capitalist class in the center countries gained acquiescence from their workers by sharing some of the gains of this system.[11] For example, they might grant certain welfare benefits to the working class. Similarly the capitalists of the center allowed the ruling elites in the periphery to profit from the exploitation of the workers in these less developed countries. Privileged families in the periphery were supported by economic and military means to prevent a socialist revolution. The big losers in this arrangement were the populations in the periphery. Thus, an alliance between ruling elites in the advanced countries and the few privileged elites in the developing countries combined to thwart true development of the overall population in the poorer countries.[12] Moreover, dependency theorists such as Raoul Prebisch noted in the 1960s that manufactured goods in the developed countries continued to increase in value, whereas the LDCs' agricultural and natural resource products did not. Thus, the LDCs fell further and further behind.[13]

Some of these theorists advocated Marxist mobilization as a solution and favored nationalization of foreign-owned resources in the periphery. And, indeed, in many former colonies governments seized foreign plantations, mines, and factories and brought them under state control. Other LDCs, while recognizing the constraints imposed by capitalism, also understood the problems associated with communism, and they opted for a blend of neo-mercantilism and Marxism. This was the option chosen by most Latin American states, which chose indigenous creation of an industrial base by import substitution and protectionism. Within a capitalist world system, a reasonable level of development could thus be obtained, and dependent development was possible.

---

historical development. Capitalism was considered a necessary stage in historical evolution without which progress to socialism could not occur.

11. A good overview of various theories of dependency and dependent development is provided by Evans 1979.

12. Given the close relations between some of the former imperial powers within their erstwhile colonies, and given the interference of the United States with domestic politics in Africa, Asia, and Latin America, this claim seems quite plausible to many. Thus, the links between France and Belgium and Zaire's President Mobutu and their ties to other African dictators could be attributed to neo-colonial domination. American destabilization of governments in Nicaragua, Chile, and other places could similarly be adduced as evidence of the capitalist alliance. American support for Iran's Shah and President Marcos in the Philippines gave the Marxists additional credence.

13. On Prebisch, see Evans 1979, 26.

EIGHT

Paradigmatic Legacies: Variations in Capitalism

Liberalism, mercantilism, and Marxism have all influenced contemporary economic policies. None of these ideal types was ever fully adopted in practice. As noted before, even in the Soviet Union, despite heavy-handed government intervention along Marxist precepts, almost one-third of agricultural production came from privately owned small plots of land. People were far more eager to grow crops in their backyards than to toil on state-owned enterprises.

While Marxist theory exercised a profound effect throughout the twentieth century by influencing the policies and actions of the socialist states, by the end of the century its appeal had diminished dramatically. The reform process which started under Mikhail Gorbachev in 1985 ended with the collapse of the communist regime, the demise of the Warsaw Pact, and the disintegration of the Soviet Union itself. Its successor states disavowed Marxist principles to varying degrees and sought to join the capitalist international order. The Baltics led the way and were rapidly integrated with Western Europe. Russia itself tried to transform the stagnant centrally planned economy into a competitive capitalist state through shock therapy.[1] More than a decade and a half later, the economy has no doubt taken on capitalist characteristics, albeit still with burdensome political interference. China, the other communist superpower, went through its own transformation. Starting with reforms in the late 1970s and picking up in earnest in the 1990s, the Chinese economy has shed most of the key tenets of socialism. Although the Communist Party continues to hold on to power, the economy is for all intents and purposes indistinguishable from other rapidly developing East Asian countries. In short, Marxism in its pure form has almost disappeared as a key economic strategy. Nevertheless, in influencing some of the features of the welfare state in earlier decades, it continues to play an indirect role in modern capitalist economies today.

Overall we can distinguish three styles of economic management across the most advanced capitalist countries in the postwar era. The

---

1. For a comprehensive description of these events, see Aslund 1995.

United States and Britain, particularly after the government of Margaret Thatcher, come closest to the liberal ideal type. In this model of government, intervention is eschewed and international trade restrictions are rolled back. By contrast, quite a few countries in East Asia have exemplified a more interventionist, neo-mercantilist model, finding that government activism combined with protection creates comparative advantages. Western Europe has developed a hybrid version, based on a moderate degree of interventionism and liberal ideas, but it has also been influenced by the egalitarian aspects that accompanied the labor movement and socialism. We might call this social-democratic capitalism or the European corporatist model.

It is, however, important to recognize that these differences are matters of degree. All three modes of economic organization are capitalist. This means that property is privately owned and prices are set by the market, not by government planning. Thus, while the state may own considerable resources and firms in some countries in Europe or East Asia, the government acts like a private firm. For example, when the French government owned car manufacturer Renault, the company competed just as a privately held firm would compete in terms of prices and models. Resource allocation and prices are set by supply and demand of producers and consumers, not by central government planning as in communist systems.

The differences between the three come from the degree to which government intermeshes with the private sphere and the nature of the social bargain between government, employers, and labor. In the United States this has entailed closer adherence to liberal tenets. But even there government plays an important role. As we saw from the earlier discussion, government sets market conditions through legislation, contract enforcement, and the provision of public goods. The government also has a large impact on the economy in its expenditure on defense, Medicaid, and social security.

The East Asian developmental model has traditionally used a combination of explicit government and firm cooperation to compete internationally. Trailing the United States and Western Europe, the East Asian states after World War II borrowed insights from the mercantilist view that state-building and economic development went hand in hand. Catching up with the West required more government intervention than the liberal model indicated. Despite the relatively high degree of government planning and coordination, this was decidedly not socialism but the regulation of competition at home and the pursuit of export-led growth abroad. Government helped planning by funding research and development and by indicating in which sectors the country's firms might succeed. Firms competed with each other by using a real price mechanism and with the market indicating how resources should be allocated. Labor was largely excluded from decision-making.

In continental Europe, the social bargain worked out differently. Unlike Japan and other East Asian countries, government did not intervene to suggest which sectors might be competitive or not. France perhaps came closest to the East Asian model. Germany and the other social welfare states, however, chose a different path. They blended liberalism and elements of neo-mercantilism in a unique way, with government playing an important role in facilitating a social compromise among firms, labor, and itself. Indeed, Marxist ideas had had an indirect influence on governments in the nineteenth century, propelling even conservative ones to adopt social welfare measures to stave off socialism. Thus, the conservative government of Otto von Bismarck, who was adamantly opposed to socialism, nevertheless created the early foundations of the welfare state in Germany to prevent the appeal of socialist principles among the workforce. This mode of economic organization is described as corporatism, which does not refer to companies (corporations) but to the idea that economic society forms an integrated whole, similar to the interaction of organs in the human body.[2]

These three models—liberal capitalism (sometimes also called Anglo-Saxon liberalism), the East Asian development model, and the European corporatist welfare state—typified the capitalist world in the second half of the twentieth century. China, which still professes to be a Marxist state, has adopted many policies that look similar to the East Asian developmental model that Japan, South Korea, and Taiwan followed with startling success.

In the following sections, we will examine two main questions. First, we will study how these three different forms of economic policy operate in practice and how states ended up gravitating towards one of these types. We will then consider whether globalization and increasing interactions have led to convergence among these different types of states. In other words, do we still see such differences in economic styles as we progress into the twenty-first century, or are we trending towards one similar style?

Analyzing Varieties of Capitalism

How can we distinguish liberal capitalist states from neo-mercantilist or corporatist countries? And what determines whether a country is largely liberal, corporatist, or neo-mercantilist? Peter Katzenstein has suggested a useful method to guide our analysis.[3]

In the 1970s, the world was hit by a severe economic crisis, partially driven by the spike in oil prices. At the beginning of the decade a barrel of

---

2. The etymology of the term clarifies the thought behind the concept. The Latin term for the human body is *corpus*, but corpus also denotes a collection or organized whole.
3. Katzenstein 1978.

oil cost roughly $2; by the end it had risen as high as $40. As a consequence, many capitalist states experienced double digit inflation and double digit unemployment. Given that all capitalist countries were affected by this problem, this poses an interesting question: how did countries respond to this shared external environmental challenge?

Katzenstein's research design was a form of comparison by method of difference. Some countries, such as the United States, largely let the market run its course—the liberal solution. Other countries, such as France, used far more government intervention to combat the problem—a neo-mercantilist strategy. (Among other things France opted for government support for more production of nuclear energy.) How could one explain the variation in state responses? Two possible causal explanations came to mind. The differences might be explained by the degree of vulnerability to the international environment or by the differences in domestic politics and institutions. However, the influence of the international environment was (in a loose sense) a constant. All countries were affected by the oil shock. Thus, this possible independent variable could not account for the variation. Instead, an alternative variable, the pre-existing domestic political arrangements of a country, influenced how various states responded.

In Katzenstein's perspective, there are two key facets that distinguish economic policy-making across the various countries. First, countries differ in terms of who is part of the ruling coalition—those actors who set policy objectives and decide on the appropriate course of action. Who makes the decisions? Second, one needs to analyze existing institutional arrangements, the policy network in Katzenstein's terms. The policy network consists of the institutional arrangements through which policy can be implemented. More specifically, it directs us to ask whether institutions are intended to foster cooperation and homogeneity in government or whether they are intended to allow for competition and opposition among different branches.

The Ruling Coalition

I argue that the particular nature of the ruling competition derives from four factors. First, the particular historical trajectory of regime development greatly determines who will be part of the policy-setting process. Has the country gradually developed as a vibrant democracy, or does it have an authoritarian past? In general, democratic development entails the curtailing of the absolute power of the monarchy. It also involves the ability of laborers to contract their labor freely, as contrasted with feudal serfdom. Democratic transition should lead to the gradual incorporation of the middle class.[4] If these features are present, then the process of economic

---

4. Moore 1966 provides the classic account of why some states followed a democratic trajectory while others developed as authoritarian states.

development can occur with limited government intervention. Private actors will drive economic development.

Second, a country's overall security environment will affect economic styles. Countries that are highly vulnerable, or for other reasons are often involved in warfare, will have large standing armed forces. This in turn will require government administration to prepare for war, to raise significant revenue, and to draft and equip an army. Citizens' rights might be curtailed in times of crisis. Indeed, history shows that preparation for war often served as justification for high levels of government involvement in the economy. Remember, for example, how governments directed their economies during World War II. Militarized states will thus evince high levels of government intervention in the economy and will tend to be more mercantilist and less democratic.[5]

Third, scholarly ideas and beliefs can influence policy in a very real sense. Adam Smith meant for his theory to educate the politicians in Scotland and England. By contrast, mercantilists such as Gustav Schmoller argued for government intervention in Germany in the late nineteenth century. Similarly, economists, such as John Maynard Keynes in the 1930s or Milton Friedman in the 1970s and 1980s, have greatly influenced government's predisposition to intervene or not to intervene in the economy.[6]

Fourth, as Alexander Gerschenkron has pointed out, the timing of industrial development will critically affect the level of government involvement.[7] Simply put, late development will correlate with more government intervention. This insight is so simple, and yet so powerful, that it deserves more extensive discussion.

Some economists argue that economic development of countries proceeds through a gradual process of sequential stages. For example, Walt Rostow delineates a five-fold process through which states proceed to "take off" as developed countries. On one end of the spectrum stand traditional societies that still engage in simple agricultural production. On the other end stand states that have entered the age of mass consumption and that compete in advanced industrial sectors. All states need to progress through each of the five stages in order to modernize.[8]

By contrast, Gerschenkron notes that late modernizers, that is, states that lagged behind more advanced states, faced different environments than the early modernizers (modernization here is equated with industrialization). While some states might try to develop gradually, others could try to skip stages and attempt to industrialize at an advanced level. The

5. Hintze 1975 notes that Britain and Germany respectively developed as a democracy and as an authoritarian state for exactly these reasons.

6. For a discussion of intellectual trends in economics, see Perlman and McCann 1998.

7. Gerschenkron 1962. For a discussion of how this theory can be used to explain economic policy in Western Europe, as well as East Asia, see Hall 1986 and Amsden 1989.

8. Rostow 1991.

argument can be understood by reflecting on how late industrializers confronted the economic leader of the eighteenth and nineteenth centuries: Britain.

Britain started to industrialize roughly from 1750 on and is generally seen as the first country to do so, propelled by new inventions and the introduction of new devices such as the steam engine, railroads, textile mills, and so on. Since Britain led the way, it faced little competition. Hence, it did not need protectionist barriers to keep rival industrial products out. The converse was true: it preferred a free trading system. Unless other countries put up artificial barriers, their citizens would buy British products, since these were the best, or at least the most affordable, of the day.

Early industrialization also started with modest requirements and proceeded in low cost, low knowledge sectors. Inroads were first made in modernizing textile production. Instead of hand milling and weaving, British producers started to use machinery, reducing labor costs and greatly expanding output. Low cost, low knowledge industries have relatively few efficiencies of scale and few barriers to entry. One did not need a giant plant to be successful in textile weaving and cloth production.

Only later did British manufacturers turn to more sophisticated production of steel, chemicals, and machinery. Investors gradually started to branch out to other, more capital intensive, and higher knowledge sectors. In other words, private actors could take the profits they had made in low-end machine production of textiles and similar sectors and invest in more capital intensive and more complex areas. It is critical to recognize that financing occurred by private entrepreneurs, not by the banks or state.

Finally, the social conditions for industrialization—a reliable and malleable workforce, disciplined into working for fixed times a day, such as a 10- to 12-hour shift—evolved gradually and required little government intervention. The workforce learned side by side with firm owners what modern production entailed. They were not required to transform themselves overnight from peasants into craftsmen.

To conclude, the earlier industrialization occurs, the more likely it is that government will have to play only a relatively small role in development. Government intervention will be modest, and it will tend towards liberal policies in trade.

Later industrializers face a dramatically different environment. In the late nineteenth and early twentieth centuries, countries such as Germany, Japan, and the Soviet Union had to face competitors (particularly Britain and later the United States) that had a clear advantage over them. The early industrializers had established product lines and had developed marketing strategies, brand recognition, and knowledge. Consequently, the late industrializing countries preferred protectionism over free trade to force their own consumers to buy domestic products. Without barriers to entry of foreign imports, the citizens of these still backward states would prefer to buy the better and perhaps cheaper products of the more advanced state.

The same logic holds true for developing countries today. Firms in later developers ask government for help and protection from competition. This is the infant industry argument. Nascent industries in developing countries need protection in order to survive the initial growth stage.

Later developers, if they wish to compete with the more advanced states, also have to compete at the higher end of the spectrum. For example, if a less developed country wants to make money in exports, it must develop a competitive position in sectors such as automobiles, electronics, and aircraft rather than in a low-cost, low-tech sector such as clothing. A country today is less likely to become an economic success story if it tries to become, say, the number one producer of t-shirts. To give one example, in 1950 South Korea was as poor in terms of gross national product per capita as some African states, but by developing a strong position in ship building, electronics, car manufacturing, and other advanced sectors, it has become a competitor to even the most advanced economies of the world.

High end sectors also have high barriers of entry. If one wishes to compete at the high end of aircraft production, billions of dollars are required for the development of new aircraft types.[9] High efficiencies of scale are also needed. In car production, for instance, one needs to be able to engage in large-scale investments in order to be competitive: "For motor vehicles, the minimum efficient scale (MES) is customarily affixed at 250,000 units per year for a single run."[10] China, in its first attempt to become competitive, did not meet these scale requirements and failed, in contrast to South Korea. However, China is currently making another attempt to modernize.

Given the high costs of entry, individual entrepreneurs alone cannot create the large plants necessary to break into these advanced sectors. They need to pool resources. But how can one create the associations, cartels, and banking infrastructure to compete? Government intervention provides the answer. The high costs of entry have led to two government responses. Some governments let banks forge close ties with large conglomerates, as in Germany. In other places, as in South Korea, the state itself led financing through capital controls.[11] The government prohibited entrepreneurs to invest outside of the country while at the same time it limited welfare provisions, which forced individuals to save more to take care of their own needs. These funds in turn could be lent by the government to favored industrial groups that were deemed to be export competitive.

---

9. For that reason government intervention in that sector might even make sense from a liberal perspective. For a discussion, see Brander 1988.

10. Huang 2002, 539.

11. Amsden 1989 describes the South Korean system in great detail. She notes that at one point South Korea had legislation that made capital exports of $1 million punishable by death.

Given the immense social changes necessary to become an advanced industrial state in a short time span, social upheaval is unavoidable. Urbanization, public education, and disruptions of the social fabric profoundly affect previously agricultural societies. Urbanization alone changes the very nature of extended family ties and village communities. Late industrializers also have to develop a strong public education system to educate their workforce.

To conclude, late industrializing countries tend to adopt neo-mercantilist economic policies. They pursue not only protection from external competition but also development of their own national industrial sectors. The government plays a key role in developing the necessary infrastructure and acts as a conduit of the necessary finances needed to break into sectors with high barriers to entry.

The Policy Network

The policy network consists of the institutional arrangements through which policy is carried out. Regardless of who sets policy and whether a country shows a tendency to more government intervention or less, one should examine what kinds of institutions a country possesses. Once decisions are made, institutions will profoundly affect how they are implemented.

Within the policy network, we can distinguish the formal institutions of the state from the institutional arrangements in the private sector. Each of these can in turn be analyzed by the degree to which they are unified or divided. As we move through the various case studies we will see how the United States typifies one end of the spectrum. Its constitutionally devised system of checks and balances leads to a fragmented government machinery. The same is true for the institutions in the private sector. American society looks askance at cooperative institutions among firms and employees. Competition forms the guiding philosophy.

Conversely, many European states and East Asian countries have more unified systems of government. Prime ministerial systems give the executive considerable latitude by unifying the executive and legislature. Similarly, the European corporatist system and the Japanese model give firms and labor various means to coordinate their activities in the private sector. Cooperation between elements of society is valued more highly than in the adversarial style of the United States.

Liberal Capitalism: The United States

The United States stands as the quintessential example of a country where economic liberalism has taken hold. American historical development was so different from that of European and Asian states that it has given rise to the term "American exceptionalism." In the following chapters, these distinctive features of the United States will become clearer as we look at how some other countries organize their economic environments.

The liberal model is not unique to the United States. Britain, particularly under the prime-ministership of Margaret Thatcher (1979–90), adopted many of the same principles. Canada as well has vacillated between more interventionist styles and a liberal, laissez-faire approach. For example, Prime Minister Brian Mulroney (1984–93) tried to scale back government activism and campaigned on a free trade platform, concluding the North American Free Trade Agreement (NAFTA). For these reasons, the model is sometimes referred to as the Anglo-Saxon economic model, but for our purposes, the United States will serve as the clearest exemplar.

The Ruling Coalition

Unlike many other countries, the United States emerged with few impediments to developing as a democracy. While it is true that Britain controlled the 13 states as colonies that had little influence on how London administered them, this in itself did not stifle the future development of the new republic. The English monarchy had already been rebuffed in its ambitions by the Civil War (1640–49) and the Glorious Revolution (1688). There were precedents in English history for arguments that royal power was not absolute. Ultimately, these very principles were used against colonial rule itself. In other words, although subject to monarchical rule, the colonists saw themselves as entitled to no less than the citizens of Britain.

Once the 13 states had shed their colonial status by rebelling against English overrule in 1776, they were ideally positioned to create the first large modern democracy. Having won independence, and without a monarchy, little stood in the way of democratic development. Indeed, the former colonists deliberately tried to forestall any attempt to establish a strong executive that might be akin to a royal dynasty. They were apprehensive of creating a strong government that stood "above" society.

The United States was also exceptional in that it lacked a landed aristocracy and could rely on a reasonably developed middle class. Of course there were wealthy landowners, but they did not constitute a class based on inherited title. In other words, although these landowners constituted a wealthy class, they were not a closed caste based on a privileged position inherited by birth. Moreover, the labor force was free, unfettered by feudal obligations. The southern plantations were an exception based on the systematic repression of Africans who were brought to the Americas as slave laborers. The Civil War settled the issue of free labor decisively. Thus, contrary to developments in Germany, Japan, and other countries, the United States developed as a relatively democratic, non-authoritarian government.

Moreover, North America was blessed with a relatively secure environment. With few bordering states, and those posing little risk, there was no external threat. The United States (and Canada) could get by with only a small standing army.[12] Throughout much of its history, the United States had little to fear from foreign invasion. The wars in which it engaged in the nineteenth century were to a considerable extent due to its own expansionist aims rather than mortal threats to American soil. In addition, individual states distrusted a strong federal government and favored state militias to forestall any encroachment on their territory by other states in the Union.[13] Consequently, as the United States entered the twentieth century, its standing army numbered less than 50,000 men. It was far from a garrison state.

Relatively early industrialization provided a third dynamic propelling the United States to liberalism, as one would expect following Gerschenkron's argument. Even though the United States did not develop as early as Britain did, it managed to benefit from its ties to its former colonial master. The northeast, in particular, became an industrial powerhouse. Fueled by the natural resources of New England and the Appalachian mountain range, it made inroads into textiles and soon thereafter into machine production and heavy industry. Capital became available through private investors and loans from Britain and, to a lesser extent, the Netherlands. Thus, unlike in later industrializers, the key finances required to propel industrial take-off were mobilized by private entrepreneurs with minimal government activism.

Finally, even though the United States had rebelled against colonial overrule, British ideas manifested a profound influence on its subsequent development. Individualism, citizen rights, and distrust of centralized government originated to a considerable extent in the United States itself but were also fueled by European thinkers, particularly those in the French salons who expounded similar ideas in bringing down the French monarchy.

In sum, American economic development did not require a strong state. Private entrepreneurs themselves could muster the means to develop industries and become competitive on the world market. Moreover, its society had experienced a unique historical trajectory that made "top down" economic policies unacceptable.

---

12. Following the War of 1812, in which Britain and the United States clashed over trade restrictions and alleged British support for Indian tribes resisting the American expansion, British and American relations improved gradually, and in 1839 Canada and the United States formalized their border. To the south, the United States threatened and seized territories from Mexico, making that country less of a threat.

13. This fully conforms with Hintze's argument (Hintze 1975).

The Policy Network: Formal Institutions of Checks and Balances

The unique American historical development also had an effect on the nature of its governmental institutions. Apprehensive of reconstituting a strong central government after ousting British rule, the founding fathers envisioned a relatively weak federal government divided between the executive, the legislature, and the courts. Strong agricultural states in the south distrusted the more industrial northeast, and all were on their guard against a strong government that might be seized by rival factions. They thus deliberately devised a system of checks and balances to minimize the powers of the central government while giving individual states all residual rights that were not explicitly allocated to that government.

The fragmentation of the government is evident in several features.[14] The founding fathers opted for a presidential system. Unlike parliamentary systems, in a presidential system the executive does not depend on the support of the legislature to hold office. Indeed, the executive and legislative branches are elected by entirely different electoral systems. While the executive must answer to a national constituency, the Senate and the House of Representatives must cater respectively to individual states and district constituencies.

The legislature itself is divided. Not only are there two chambers but the Senate and House possess important and unique functions. Unlike many parliamentary systems, which usually have two unequal chambers, the American Senate and House are both powerful institutions in their own right. For example, while the Senate has important powers in matters of foreign policy, the House has a key role in the budgetary process. Further fragmenting the legislature, a committee system devolves substantial authority to powerful committees and committee chairs, who might stop a bill from proceeding before it gets to the chamber as a whole. Thus, a committee might be at odds with the larger chamber and nevertheless be able to influence the political agenda.

Moreover, the elections for the executive and the two chambers are staggered, with the president sitting for four years, members of the Senate for six, and House members running for re-election every two years. This further diminishes the likelihood of the same party holding all these elements of office at the same time.

The electoral system has given rise to two dominant parties, the Republican and Democratic. But unlike in the parliamentary system, there is less party discipline. Given that members of the House and Senate rely on local constituencies, they might openly diverge from the party leadership or the president's position. Most campaign funds are raised by the individual candidate, thus giving little leverage to party authorities. In

---

14. For a good discussion of how the American system differs from various parliamentary systems, see Weaver and Rockman 1993.

many parliamentary systems, by contrast, citizens largely vote for the party, so the party leaders can influence the electoral fortunes of individual members.[15]

Completing the triad of federal institutions, the Supreme Court was given significant powers to test legislation. These constitutional tests form yet another potential barrier to any national policy. Given judicial review, courts may strike down legislation that is intended to implement a particular economic policy but fails to meet constitutional provisions. To give one telling example of how judicial activism affects economic policy, consider the Supreme Court's reaction to the New Deal policies of President Roosevelt during the early years of the Great Depression. The Court held that several of these policies were unconstitutional in that the executive and Congress did not have the power to implement some of their key provisions, which violated the freedom of contract. These proposed pieces of legislation dealt with such features of economic policy as price setting and the number of working hours (*Schechter Poultry Corp. v. United States*, 1935) and processing taxes in the agricultural sector (*United States v. Butler*, 1936). Others cases involved aspects of union organization and wage setting. Exasperated, the president argued that "the Court ... has improperly set itself up as a third house of the Congress—a super-legislature, as one of the justices has called it."[16] Threatened by the push for a change in the composition of the Court, and in the face of public demand for the New Deal, the Court relented.

Furthermore, the Washington bureaucracy tends to be more politicized and fragmented than its European or Japanese counterparts. In the latter, the higher rungs of bureaucracy are largely occupied by graduates from a small number of elite schools, thus conferring some social cohesion. These bureaucrats are expected to serve whichever political party or coalition wins an election. In the United States, by contrast, administrators come from a wide variety of social and educational backgrounds. Moreover, when the executive changes political color, many levels of the higher bureaucracy change hands as well.

As if the checks and balances within Washington were not enough, the federal structure grants individual states considerable legal powers of their own. States design key aspects of their legal codes, levy significant tax resources, and can significantly affect any attempt to set national policies through taxation, regulation, incentives, subsidies, and other strategies. Say, for example, that the United States has agreed to lower tariffs on imported cars. Individual states, however, might pass laws stipulating

---

15. For a discussion of party discipline in the two-party, Westminster-type parliamentary system, see Kornberg and Frasure 1971.

16. Roosevelt made these remarks in a famous fireside chat in which he used the new medium, radio, to great advantage. For the text of his address, see http://www.hpol.org/fdr/chat/.

environmental and safety standards, which in practice might be a means of limiting imports. States can also affect policy by having dramatically different environmental or labor standards. California is often cited as one state with stringent standards, while Delaware attracts some industries because it is alleged to have laxer standards.

Policy Network: Society

The American policy network shows considerable heterogeneity among private actors as well. American legislation forbids formal organizations that allow private actors to coordinate their business practices. In other countries peak associations bring together key sectors that share specific interests for periodic consultation. Unlike in East Asian states or Western Europe, such coordination is frowned upon in the United States as government sees this as potential collusion and thus a violation of anti-trust laws.

The United States also lacks a strong finance-industry nexus. Given its early industrial development, capital was traditionally raised by the private sector. Until the early twentieth century, government largely stayed out of regulating banks altogether, leaving it to private entrepreneurs, such as Henry Morgan, to dominate the financial scene. After the Wall Street crash and the bank run of 1929 and the following year, the government took on a more active role, largely to prevent more bank failures. The *Glass-Steagall Act* separated commercial from investment banks and sought to underwrite private deposits through the Federal Deposit Insurance Corporation. (The Act was repealed in 1999.)[17]

Firms largely raise capital by floating stocks and corporate bonds to individuals, who buy these equities through brokerage firms, mutual funds, and pension plans. Contrary to practices in Europe and Japan where far more stocks are owned by banks and related companies, American firms evince far less cross-holding of stock.

Overall there are no formal government institutions where the state brings together government representatives, employers, and labor. At the firm level, the input from labor is relatively weak. Contrast that, for example, with Germany, where workers have formal representation on boards of company directors. In the corporatist model, many organizations intermesh the private and public spheres. In the Netherlands, the Social Economic Council (*Sociaal Economische Raad*) consists of representatives from government, employers, and employee organizations. Its task is to provide advice to the cabinet and Parliament, but it also has a supervisory

---

17. The government intervention in 2008 to shore up the financial sector was similarly driven by concerns about bank failure. The problem was not that government had intervened in financial markets but that the lack of government oversight played a key role in allowing banks and other financial institutions to engage in highly speculative lending.

role over sector specific organizations, which combine employer and employee representatives. It ideally reaches consensus decisions in its advice to government. Such attempts to unify employer and employee interests are virtually unheard of in the more adversarial character of American-style liberalism.

We can conclude with Stephen Krasner that the United States has a weak state.[18] Another astute comparison of the United States with Japan and some European countries is made by John Zysman, who notes that the national government by and large takes a laissez-faire approach towards private business. This stance results from "three structural elements: (1) the apparatus of government, which divides powers ... (2) the court system, which reinforces the fragmentation of policy and the ability of small groups to influence or block government; and (3) the financial system, which stands at arm's length from both government and business."[19] Based on its historical trajectory, American society is wary of government steering or intervention, and hence the state provides a conduit for different interests rather than operating as a strong independent part of the ruling coalition. Furthermore, it lacks a cohesive policy network to carry out policy decisions.

The East Asian Developmental Model: The Rise of Post-War Japan

The Japanese model, as practiced in the decades after World War II, presents almost the diametric opposite of the American system. At the end of the war, the country was utterly devastated. Many of its biggest cities lay in ruins due to firebombing, and two, Hiroshima and Nagasaki, were the target of atomic attacks. Millions had perished, and the industrial basis had been reduced to rubble. Yet within a few short decades, Japan rose to become the second leading capitalist economy, rivaling and displacing American and European firms from their pre-eminence. Its gross domestic product (GDP) in 2007 was almost $4.1 trillion, behind the $13.1 trillion of the United States but well ahead of Germany, whose GDP amounted to $2.7 trillion.[20]

The Japanese success had many causes. Arguably, American support and military bases in Japan allowed the country to concentrate its resources in the private sector rather than spend huge public sums on defense. Symbolically, the public expenditure on defense was for a long time set at no more than 1 per cent of GDP. Others see the Confucian work ethic and disciplined society as possible explanations. It cannot be gainsaid, however, that the government's close cooperation with the private sector has

18. Krasner 1978.
19. Zysman 1983.
20. Figures from OECD Observer, Supplement 1, OECD in Figures 2007 (Paris: OECD, 2007).

been a key feature of the Japanese plan of guided development. This not only was true after World War II but was also a mark of its almost equally remarkable process of modernization from the middle of the nineteenth century on. This has led to a unique way of setting policy objectives and a large amount of cohesion in implementing such decisions.

The Ruling Coalition: The Japanese Path to Authoritarianism

In the sixteenth century, Japan consisted of several warring regions. While the emperor ruled as the symbolic head, in practice political power was dispersed among warlords, the daimyo, and their retinue of armed knights, the samurai. By the end of that century, however, one of the most powerful lords, Tokugawa Ieyasu, managed to defeat his rivals and centralize power. The emperor thereupon appointed him shogun, or supreme general, ushering in the Tokugawa Shogunate, which lasted until 1868.[21]

The political system consisted of military rule and social stratification along a caste system. Politically, the shogun stood at the apex of a hierarchy. Below him were roughly 200 daimyo, who in turn presided over various ranks of knights who numbered in the hundreds of thousands. Socially, the warrior caste formed the pinnacle above peasants and merchants.

To solidify their hold, and to prevent outside influences from upsetting this political and social balance, the Tokugawa shoguns prohibited external contacts, particularly from 1639 on. Although limited contacts were permissible with China and the Dutch Republic (the latter had access to one port near Nagasaki), in effect this marked a period of closure for more than two centuries. But with the Western maritime empires consistently expanding their reach, Japanese isolation could not last forever. Devoid of external contacts and technology, the Japanese inevitably fell further and further behind the developing states of Europe and the Americas. When American Admiral Perry entered Japanese ports in 1853, the Japanese realized they lacked the means to resist demands for American access. The danger of colonization of Japan itself loomed, given that much of Asia had already befallen such a fate. Even China had to grant concessions to the colonial powers.

American intrusion provided an external shock, which led to internal turmoil and political upheaval. In the ensuing decade of civil unrest, Emperor Meiji abandoned his symbolic function and took a more activist position, which transformed the entire political system. The Meiji Restoration (1868) brought the Tokugawa Shogunate to an end as the emperor assumed full powers. A period of forced modernization ensued in which the emperor relied on an implicit alliance of the military and heavy

---

21. A useful description of Japan's political development is Bendix 1978.

industry, the Zaibatsu. Factual power was exercised by an oligarchy of ruling elites and elder statesmen (the genro).

Simultaneous with this "top-down" industrialization (top down as it was instigated by government rather than by society from the bottom up), these elites engaged in an aggressive policy of colonial expansion. Rather than suffering colonization itself, Japan became an imperial power. It successfully fought China in 1895 and acquired Korea (temporarily) and Taiwan. After the startling victory over Russia in 1905, it gained Korea outright in 1910.

This foreign policy benefited both military and heavy industry. From the 1890s on, these groups shared interests on external expansion and internal repression. The increasing role and prestige of the army also provided career opportunities for some of the former military families. At the same time, the army was also used to control democratic elements, peasants, and labor unions, who suffered the consequences of forced modernization. The big corporations benefited not only from the control over the workforce but also from the military expenditures in ship building, steel production, and other materials related to the war effort. In addition, expansion gave the country access to much needed material resources.

Although opponents to this authoritarian system attempted democratization in the 1920s, the military and their allies re-established firm control over the system by the 1930s with further expansionist aims. From then on, war in the Pacific became inevitable.

Japan thus evolved as a militarized authoritarian society from the seventeenth century through the 1930s until the end of World War II. It did not manage to establish a system of checks and balances between aristocracy and monarchy as, for example, Britain managed to do. Instead, the Japanese system, although unique in many respects, resembled European royal absolutism. The middle class and labor were repressed, while the peasantry worked under harsh conditions with no political voice. Although Japan was internally at peace after the Tokugawa unification, it maintained the trappings of a garrison state during this period of isolation. After Perry's appearance, it endured a brief civil war followed by an authoritarian system that relied heavily on military support. After copying the Prussian army and the British Royal Navy, it engaged in a series of major wars and conquests for half a century. In other words, the security environment propelled Japan to adopt an interventionist state system.

Japan's late industrialization similarly led to the need for significant government intervention. During the Tokugawa Shogunate, trade and commerce were forcefully discouraged. In the mid-nineteenth century, Japan was an agricultural society that was challenged by the leading economic powers. In order to catch up after the Meiji restoration, the state actively engaged in capital mobilization by implementing laws that created strategic incentives for a high savings rate by individuals. It also controlled key aspects of the financial sector directly in order to channel investment to favored industries. This strategy continued after World War II and became a critical part of Japanese economic policy (more about this later). It further encouraged collusion among the large firms, repressed labor, and developed a highly advanced public education system.

Some argue that the religious currents of Japan—Buddhism, Confucianism, and Shinto—played a contributing role. The Japanese believe that their emperor is the mythological descendant of a sun goddess and so is an object of worship himself. Regardless of how strongly held that view is today, there can be no doubt that the long lineage of imperial rule by the same family conveys considerable legitimacy. Combined with norms that recommend deferring to seniors and higher authority, these beliefs provided additional support for a strong state.

In short, on all dimensions Japan showed trends exactly opposite to Britain or the United States. Its historical development, security environment, late industrialization, and cultural background provided the space for a statist, interventionist framework. This orientation continued even after World War II, but without the militaristic elements of its past.

The Policy Network: Japanese Governmental Institutions After 1945

American occupation after World War II (1945–52) aimed to change the existing institutional framework. The MacArthur Constitution first engaged in land reform to empower those working in the agricultural sector. Several of the biggest firms were also reorganized.

Interestingly, the United States supported a parliamentary system of government in the reconstruction of Japan. The House of Representatives elects the prime minister (PM), who can also call for new elections if he thinks that his party might gain seats. As in all such systems, the PM requires the continued support of Parliament to maintain office. Legislature and executive thus logically hold the same political position.

Japan's legislature, the Diet, is bicameral but the House of Representatives possesses more important functions and prerogatives than the House of Councilors, the upper chamber. It can also pass certain pieces of legislation without the consent of the House of Councilors. All members of the House of Representatives used to be elected by single non-transferable vote in two to six member districts until the electoral reforms of 1993. Now 300 of the members are elected by single member districts and 180 by party list proportional representation. They hold office for four years if no elections are called.

The House of Councilors consists of 242 members, of which 96 are elected by nation-wide proportional representation. The other 146 come from the prefectures (47), which are multimember districts. Half of them are elected every three years.[22] The legislature divides its work among committees, but they largely function as forums for internal party debates. Moreover, although Japan has provincial governments, these prefectures are not the equivalent of states in a federal structure. They lack real autonomy and must rely on federal financing. This again enhances the ability of the central government to implement its policy objectives.

Although the landscape has been dotted by several contending parties, the Liberal Democratic Party (LDP) won every election from the 1950s until 1993. After being out of power for little over a year following the 1993 electoral reforms, it once again became the main party. Its main contenders have been the Japanese Socialist Party and more recently the Democratic Party of Japan.

The LDP managed to hold on to its dominance of the postwar system partially because its members engaged in a division of labor in multimember districts. Although a "first past the post" system, there was more than one seat at stake in each district, unlike the Westminster system common to Britain and its Dominions. Factional infighting, in which LDP members drew votes away from each other, could have jeopardized the party's dominance. Imagine, for example, three LDP members splitting the vote among themselves in a three member district and each getting fewer votes than the two contenders from rival parties. The LDP would now get to occupy only one seat in the district. To prevent this situation, party members cultivated niche clienteles and thus avoided competing directly with their fellows.[23] Gerrymandering also helped the LDP maintain its hold. The system overweighted LDP strongholds in the agricultural precincts. With protectionist measures for agriculture, the LDP assured itself of their loyalty.[24]

The Japanese system does resemble the American in one respect. Unlike parliamentary systems such as Britain's, where Parliament reigns supreme, it allows for judicial review. The postwar constitution permits the Supreme Court to test the constitutionality of Diet legislation. In practice, however, the Court has been very reluctant to enmesh itself in political disputes. Given that the Cabinet nominates justices, and given that the LDP has dominated the House of Representatives, the Supreme Court has usually followed, rather than challenged, the government's decisions and laws.

Perhaps the best example of Japan's statist disposition and planned economic policy is the lofty position of two bureaucracies—the Ministry of Finance and the Ministry of International Trade and Industry (MITI). Both of these "outrank" the Ministry of Foreign Affairs. Some observers

---

22. For a quick overview of the electoral system, see Kesselman, Krieger, and Joseph 1999, 222. Subsequent changes slightly altered the number of Diet members after 1993.

23. Cowhey 1993.

24. Curtis 1988, ch. 2 discusses the intricacies of how the LDP maintained its dominance for so long.

have noted that Japan does not usually have a foreign policy, only a foreign economic policy. This overstates the situation, certainly in the last decade or two, as Japan has become more activist in many areas such as peace-keeping and diplomatic initiatives, but as Chalmers Johnson points out in a classic work, MITI has been a key facet of Japan's postwar success.[25]

Finally, the bureaucratic elite tends to be recruited from the best insti-tutions, somewhat similar to Britain's Oxford and Cambridge and France's *Grandes Écoles*. The University of Tokyo has been a traditional supplier of high-ranking officials, further leading to homogeneity and consensus.

Peak Associations and Societal Cohesion

The homogeneity in government institutions and the activist role that the state plays is reflected in societal institutions in Japan as well. Government works closely together with private banks and industry. It encourages the formation of peak associations, which are broad organizational groupings that bring many different types of firms together. Aside from peak associa-tions, trade associations also lead to coordination in sectors such as the automobile industry and ship building. However, it would be incorrect to say that firms have always cooperated with one another. Indeed, sometimes firms have used such organizations to disadvantage competitors.[26]

In addition, quite unlike the United States, laws do not prohibit a strong finance and industry nexus (more on this below). Anti-trust legisla-tion remains weak even though the MacArthur Constitution tried to in-troduce such legislation after World War II. However, while there is close cooperation between government and employers, labor has remained on the sidelines. Labor unions are weak, with firms, particularly the larger ones, forestalling unrest by long-term employment and side payments.

The cohesion between government and private enterprise shows up clearly in the financial sector. MITI and the Ministry of Finance deliberate with the private sector to determine in which sectors Japanese firms might develop a competitive advantage. MITI's long-term planning allows firms to gain knowledge of the overall world market prospects. Such planning also signals how the government intends to support firms in seeking open-ings overseas while defending its home market from external incursions. Two Japanese scholars describe the postwar strategy as follows:

> Financial control was implemented through the Bank of Japan and other financial institutions, particularly large banks, with

---

25. Johnson 1982.

26. See, for example, how the large Japanese auto firms used these organizations to deal with the threat of American protectionism by diminishing the role of the smaller car producers. The case study by Simon Reich in the Resources and Case Studies at the end of this section provides a nice discussion of this episode in the Reagan administration.

support from the bureaucracy in the economic field. The banks and the economic bureaucracy functioned as a general staff behind the battlefield in this total war called high economic growth.[27]

In doing this, MITI sometimes clashed with other agencies, which had less faith in its abilities. John Zysman notes that the Bank of Japan saw some of MITI's recommendations as "the most inappropriate for Japan."[28] Nevertheless, MITI often prevailed, particularly if it could get the support of the Ministry of Finance.

Government also has broad policy tools at its disposal that do not target specific firms or sectors but that are critical for the relation of banks and firms. For example, in deciding on the level of social entitlements (social security payments and such), the government can influence the propensity of individuals to save, even when interest rates in a bank are low. For sure, cultural explanations for high savings rates in East Asian countries also carry considerable weight, but with relatively weak entitlement prospects, there are strategic reasons why individuals save for their old age. With individuals not inclined to invest in company stocks and bonds, individuals have few options but to place their money with private banks (the city banks). With high savings rates at relatively low interest, the banks in turn can provide low interest loans to firms that are earmarked by government. Banks floated such low interest rate loans to targeted sectors in steel, chemicals, and automobiles in the 1950s. With the Bank of Japan acting as lender of last resort, the city banks can be assured that the government will prop them up in case of bad loans. At the same time, firms can pursue long-term growth strategies because they can acquire capital at a low interest rate and do not have to contend with fickle stockholders who want immediate profits, which is the case when firms depend on private equity.

The neo-mercantilist model is premised on a close relation between industry and banks with considerable state involvement: "The stock market is not a means of raising new funds for industry from the household sector. Nor does the bond market provide an alternative to bank loans as the basic source of company finance."[29] MITI planners identify preferred sectors and long-term strategies that allow such sectors and firms to be export competitive. The Ministry of Finance in turn settles on an optimal financial mix of macro-economic policies to make adequate funds available to these firms. Schematically this is captured in Figure 8.1.

27. Eisuke and Yukio 1988, 47. The book by Okimoto and Rohlen in which this essay is contained also has other essays that support the argument.
28. As quoted in Zysman 1983, 240.
29. Zysman 1983, 245.

Figure 8.1 | **The Industry, Government, and Finance Nexus in Japan**

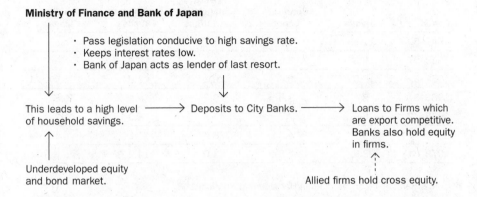

We can conclude, therefore, that historically the Japanese state has always played an activist role. After World War II it has continued to do so, but it has shed the militaristic component of its mercantilist past decisively. Particularly in the decades up to the late 1980s, the Japanese government actively pursued a policy of fostering development in industrial sectors that it deemed vital for the country's welfare as a whole. Government allowed close cooperation between industries (cartels) and the banking sector to target particular opportunities. Moreover, cohesion among the different branches of government and societal institutions gave it the institutional framework to carry out such policy.

Government regulated interest rates and acted as the insurer of last resort. While it allowed for domestic competition among Japanese firms, it protected its companies from external competition through tariffs and subsidies. Acquiring funds at low cost, firms were able to pursue a long-range game. Finance did not depend on individual investors who had limited time horizons. Looking at how this system evolved between the 1950s and the 1980s and comparing it with the United States, two observers concluded:

> We lean toward a very simple explanation for the differences in the structure of interest group representation in the United States and Japan: the network of associations in Japan arose under a mercantilist, nationalist state; by contrast, the network of associations in the United States developed under a state that seldom resorted to direct intervention.[30]

While this system has propelled Japan to become the world's second largest economy, it has also revealed disadvantages. Homogeneity and

---

30. Lynn and McKeown 1988, 174.

Table 8.1 | **External Sources of Industrial Funds 1947–81**

Period	Stocks	Corporate bonds	Private financial institutions	Government funds	Foreign loans
1947–52	11.5%	3.2%	71.7%	13.6%	n.a.
1953–57	16.3	3.6	70.9	9.3	n.a.
1958–62	16.6	5.6	70.1	7.8	1.9%
1963–67	8.4	3.6	79.8	8.1	0.8
1968–72	6.5	2.7	82.8	8.0	1.2
1973–77	5.9	4.3	78.5	11.1	n.a.
1978–81	8.3	4.6	73.0	14.2	n.a.

Source: Bank of Japan, as cited in Hamada and Horiuchi 1987.

cohesion allowed for capture by special interests, even corruption. These problems surfaced in the late 1980s when it became clear that many of the bank loans were not performing. Rather than acknowledge the problem, the Japanese government refused to deal with it and instead propped up the banks. Corruption scandals had always been an issue, but new revelations in the 1980s and 1990s revealed how close ties between government and industries led to suboptimal performance in such industries as construction.

Finally, as we will discuss shortly, we must ask to what extent these neo-mercantilist strategies can be maintained in the face of integration into the global economy. Overt protectionism violates the terms of the General Agreement on Tariffs and Trade (now the World Trade Organization). Ever since the American trade balance turned negative in the 1970s, Japan's very high, positive trade balance has created a source of contention, leading to American demands that Japan repeal activist government policies designed to favor its domestic firms. With the American negative trade balance for 2008 over $800 billion, and Japan's positive trade balance over $60 billion, these sources of contention will continue to exist.[31]

The Corporatist Model: The German Economic Miracle

The German Historical Tradition:
From Statist Intervention to Social Compact

Although separated by thousands of miles, and composed of distinct cultures and peoples, the German historical trajectory in many ways resembles that of Japan. As we saw in our earlier discussion of the prelude

31. The British journal *The Economist* provides weekly information on trade and current account balances; see the Resources list at the end of Part II for its website address.

to World War I, Prussia developed as a militarized authoritarian society in the seventeenth century. Instead of creating checks and balances between aristocracy and monarchy, as emerged in Britain, Prussia forged a political system based on royal absolutism. The king could rule without parliamentary oversight. In exchange for the support from the Junkers, he granted the aristocracy extensive autonomy over their landed estates and the peasantry (the Second Serfdom), and made them tax exempt.[32]

By the middle of the nineteenth century, industrialization had progressed in many European countries, with Britain comfortably in the lead. Although Prussia and the other German states lagged in their development, a new class emerged that did not have a stake in landed production but had commercial interests. The political system, however, was still dominated by the Prussian king and the Junkers. Germany remained a group of several dozen disjointed territories, each of which was autonomous in many matters of policy.

Economically, the emerging industrial groups and middle class wanted protection from British exports, since Britain, as the leader of the Industrial Revolution, produced machines and manufactured goods at a better price and quality than anybody else. At the same time agricultural interests, particularly the landlords in Prussia, wanted protection of agricultural commodities. The prices of these commodities, especially grains, suffered from an emerging new economic power house across the Atlantic: the United States.

This set the stage for another political bargain, which forestalled democratic development and led Germany to develop a mercantilist economic policy. The commoners, of course, favored more democracy, whereas the king and the Junkers opposed it. However, all groups favored a united Germany, as they understood that it would be better able to compete both militarily and economically with its rivals. Moreover, with dozens of distinct political units, unification would also remove the many barriers to trade across their boundaries.

Under the leadership of the Prussian king and his chancellor, Otto von Bismarck, Prussia engaged in several wars. Defeating Denmark, Austria, and then France, Bismarck unified Germany under the Prussian king who then became the emperor of the reconstituted empire. The emperor offered protectionism to big industrial interests (in common parlance, the Iron Group) and to agricultural interests (denoted as the Rye interests after the predominant grain produced in the Prussian lands). This Iron and Rye Coalition excluded labor from meaningful cooperation, and the Socialist Party was outlawed. Bismarck tried to deflect social unrest and labor opposition by introducing the beginnings of a social insurance scheme, a precursor of elements of the later welfare state.

---

32. Craig 1955, 4. His book remains the classic source for the Prussian army's role in Germany's historical development.

Two common objectives thus united mercantile interests with aristocracy and agricultural groups: unification and protectionism. Political unification under a Prussian king thus went hand in hand with mercantilist protection. However, demands for more democracy were rebuffed, and the military and the officer corps continued to play an important role in subsequent German politics.

Despite a brief democratic interlude after World War I during the Weimar Republic (1918–33), this pattern reappeared with a vengeance during the Nazi regime. The Weimar Republic introduced a multi-party system, but the fragmentation of the political spectrum led to weak governments. Once again a coalition emerged between military interests and heavy industry, and once again these forces were anti-democratic in nature. Hitler used the support of these two groups to usurp power and install the Nazi regime. Only utter defeat in World War II brought a dramatic reversal of Germany's anti-democratic past.

From this historical overview, it should be clear that Germany's mercantilist tendencies can be explained not only by its slow democratic development but also by its late industrialization as well as its security environment. Both the insights of Otto Hintze and Gerschenkron's late industrialization thesis provide key insights into the German trajectory. From the seventeenth century on, Prussia emerged as one of the premier military powers in Europe, and Germany continued as such when it unified. Its militaristic inclinations stifled democratic tendencies—bearing out Hintze's perspectives. Moreover, its industrial development only started in earnest in the latter half of the nineteenth century, well behind Britain, requiring the intervention of a strong state—as Gerschenkron has noted.

It should come as no surprise that theoretical doctrines that justified a strong state held considerable sway. The government was keen to appoint professors, such as Gustav Schmoller, who advocated mercantilist policies and a strong Germany, to important educational posts. Germany thus lacked a tradition that championed individual rights and liberal trade.

To sum up, its historical trajectory, late industrialization, militaristic past, and ideology propelled Germany to develop mercantilist economic policies. State formation, protectionism, and government intervention historically went hand in hand.

After the war, the configuration of forces changed dramatically. Many of the lands that had belonged to prominent aristocratic families were taken over by the socialist governments in East Germany and Poland. Parts of Prussia, Silesia, and Pomerania went to an expanded Poland, while the Soviet Union occupied the territory around Konigsberg. In the occupied areas, in what would become West Germany in 1949, the allied forces initially set out to dismantle the large industrial complexes that had made Germany a military and economic power. Its armed forces were greatly reduced in strength, and a democratic system put in place of the previous authoritarian regime.

However, given the history of state activism, it should come as no surprise that the German government retained an important role in setting policy objectives. Unlike the pre-war "top down" style, it developed a far more inclusive form of setting economic policy. Influenced by liberal-capitalist trends, the government opted for an open economy with few protectionist measures. Instead of protectionism and government support, it sought to enhance the ability of the private sector to compete in exports. Labor also became part of this grand coalition in favor of export-led growth. However, labor did not shape foreign economic policy but was given a co-decision-making role at the corporate level through various pieces of legislation that gave voice to the unions. The postwar German ruling coalition thus became a social compact between the government, employer organizations, and organized labor.

The German Policy Network[33]

The policy network that the allies put in place after the end of World War II reflects elements of the democratic systems of the occupying forces. First, the allies created a viable parliamentary system. The prime minister (the chancellor) requires the approval of the legislature, which can topple the government and call new elections. The legislature has tended to be dominated by two parties: the Socialist Democratic Party (SDP) and the Christian Democrats (the CDU/CSU alliance). Several smaller parties—the Greens, Free Democrats (the FDP), and Democratic Socialists (old communists)—round out the political spectrum. A five per cent threshold requirement keeps even smaller parties from parliamentary representation, thus limiting fragmentation. Given that the PM requires legislative support, executive and legislature usually have similar preferences.[34]

The legislature, somewhat atypical compared to most parliamentary systems, has a bicameral structure consisting of the Bundestag and Bundesrat, which both have significant powers. The Bundesrat is composed of representatives of the individual states—the Länder—but their function is not to carry out state directives but rather to make sure the states can implement the decisions of the Bundestag. The PM can call elections and thus enhance parliamentary support, if she believes an election will strengthen the position of the parties in the governing coalition.

---

33. Given our focus on capitalist systems, and given that East Germany was reunited with the West in 1990, after the collapse of the communist regimes, we focus only on West German development.

34. For an overview of the German political system, see Kesselman, Krieger, and Joseph 1999.

The parties exercise strong party discipline. The votes for the Bundestag are cast in a complicated system, in which some of the members are elected by local constituencies and others by a national party list. Given that party elites decide on the placement of candidates on the party lists, the party leadership exercises considerable power over the rank and file.

The unity of German institutions is further enhanced by a highly qualified, but not politicized bureaucracy. While the highest placed administrators might rotate when the government shifts, lower rungs are permanent civil servants expected to serve whichever party or coalition holds office. The bureaucracy implements rather than sets policy goals.

In other respects, the system also shows heterogeneity. First, it possesses a federal system in which considerable authority is delegated to the individual states. This is partially a reflection of Germany's historical past and partially by design of the allied forces who helped redesign Germany's constitution after the war. Powers that are not explicitly enumerated in the constitution and delegated to the federal government are supposed to reside at the state level (the subsidiarity principle). Second, and reflecting American interests, although it is a parliamentary system the German legislature is subject to judicial review. Unlike the British parliament, which reigns supreme, the German Supreme Court (the *Bundesverfassungsgericht*) can strike down legislation that it deems unconstitutional.

Social Cohesion and Co-Decision-Making

While the institutions of government show some traits that indicate a unified system and some that indicate more diversity, the institutions among social actors are clearly cohesive. Business interests are well organized in peak associations. For example, the Federation of German Industry (BDI) brings together the key sectors of German manufacturing and production. Moreover, service sector organizations and labor unions are strong, well organized, and formally represented by law on the boards of directors of some major companies. In addition, bureaucracies and private interest groups work closely together: "The policy network is a close cooperative relationship linking the ministerial bureaucracy to interest groups in industry, trade, and banking."[35]

Although the German government and private sectors work closely together, the system differs from the Japanese case in that labor is part of the social bargain. The generous welfare system compensates employees who suffer from adjustment costs: if a person loses her job, the government and employers fund retraining and welfare payments. This has made adjustment to global competitive pressures easier to accept.[36]

---

35. Kreile 1978, 194.
36. Esser and Fach 1989 provide a good example of how this works in particular sectors.

Finally, there are close connections between the financial sector and industry. There is considerable cross-holding and credit-based financing. In the mid-1970s one could conclude that "banks hold more than 25 percent of voting capital in 28 of the 100 largest enterprises."[37] But contrary to Japan, which is also a stakeholder system, the state does not directly allocate credit nor does it coordinate activities in the private sector, as MITI and the Ministry of Finance do. Coordination in Germany is done by the private banks. Firms in both systems derive their funding from loans by banks and other firms rather than from individual stockholders. As is the case with Japanese firms, this has given German corporations the ability to have a long-run perspective in contrast to the shorter time horizons that individual stockholders often have in the American system.[38]

The German arrangements can be described as social corporatism. There are formal institutional arrangements that facilitate cooperative decision-making between government, employers, and labor. This diminishes the differences between private actors and the public sector, advancing an organic view of co-decision-making. It is consensus oriented rather than conflictual.

To sum up, firms need to be responsive to the international market and compete on price and quality. In order to do so, the government allows for collusion and cooperation between industries and banks. Labor is given a voice in corporate decision-making and takes part in discussions when external competition makes it necessary to phase out certain sectors. Thus, phase-outs become politically feasible thanks to unemployment benefits, re-education programs, and early retirement schemes.

The Germans have developed a different variant of capitalism than either the United States or Japan by blending liberal capitalism with social welfare provisions: "The harsh prescriptions of liberalism are softened in Germany when the social disruptions caused by industrial change are judged to represent social and political costs that are simply unacceptable."[39]

Conclusion

It is important to restate that the descriptions of the various logics of capitalism are ideal types that characterize essential features of the postwar capitalist economies. The United States, Japan, and Germany were chosen as examples of these ideal types that in many ways come (or perhaps came) close to meeting the characteristics of liberal capitalism, neo-mercantilism, and corporatism. Yet even these three countries do not always exemplify the ideal types in all aspects. The American government is not altogether averse to protectionism, particularly if key domestic constituencies are at

---

37. As cited by Kreile 1978, 211.
38. Zysman 1983, 265.
39. Zysman 1983, 252.

Figure 8.2 | **Overview of the Ruling Coalitions and Policy Networks in Three Countries**

	United States	**Germany**	**Japan**
Ruling Coalition	Liberal	Mercantilist till WW II. But after 1945 liberal in trade, co-decision-making with private sector.	Neo-mercantilist. Guided economy, protectionist
Policy Network			
(a) State	Fragmented	Unified with a degree of federalism	Unified
(b) Society	Fragmented	Unified	Unified
Policy Style	Little coordination	Coordination by private banks and corporatist compact	Government-led economic policy

More liberal $\longleftarrow$ $\longrightarrow$ More interventionist

stake. Similarly, Japan has incorporated many aspects of liberal capitalism, particularly during the last two decades. Nevertheless, it is fair to say that for most of the decades after 1945, these countries evinced distinctive styles of development.

This account inevitably provides a somewhat stylized portrait. That is, it has paid particular attention to those aspects that resemble the ideal types rather than confuse the reader with pointing out subtle deviations. Moreover, important changes have occurred in each of these economies, particularly during the last decade and a half. However, in order to examine whether different national strategies are still possible in this era of globalization, we first have to clarify their points of origin. We can then map the developments in each country over time—a single case diachronic comparison. We can, furthermore, compare whether the distinctive forms of capitalism at an earlier period differ from the modes of economic organization in these three countries in the contemporary period, thus comparing them synchronically and diachronically. Before we can tackle the question of whether convergence among these types has occurred, we need to turn first to the role played by international economic organizations, most notably the World Trade Organization (WTO).

NINE

The International Economic Order and the Question of Convergence

International Regimes and Hegemonic Stability Theory

Regimes as Collective Goods

As we discussed in Chapter 6, collective action problems are in essence multi-person Prisoner's Dilemma games.[1] With public goods each individual benefits from mutual cooperation, but at the same time each individual's first preference is to defect while hoping others will provide for the good in question. Provision of the good may occur if there is one actor who might benefit disproportionately from the good or who is willing to bear the costs for some other reason. The smaller the group, the more likely is provision of that good, because transaction and enforcement costs will be lower.

The logic of public goods theory can be used to understand the global economic order, given that the rules governing this order can be understood as a collective good. More specifically, the rules that regulate international trade and finance constitute a regime, which is a blend of formal rules and procedures but which also has less explicit underlying norms and principles "around which actor expectations converge in a given issue-area."[2] Principles and norms specify the goals of interaction—what is the regime for? What do we see as its ultimate objective? The rules and procedures specify the means to obtain such goals and are thus narrower in scope.

A regime can be considered as a collective good in that all actors benefit from having such a set of rules. Following liberal trade theory, specialization and unrestricted trade would make each actor better off. Each state will specialize in those areas in which it has a comparative advantage and trade for other goods. In the pursuit of the state's own interests, such specialization and trade will maximize the total amount of goods available.

1. Hardin 1982.
2. Krasner 1983, 1.

Nevertheless, states also have an incentive to violate the rules if they can get away with it. Neo-mercantilists attempt to protect their domestic market. The rules of the liberal trading order allow them to export their products to other countries and shield their own constituencies. Moreover, such states might be more inclined to be more concerned with relative gains than liberal perspectives would suggest. Even states that usually adhere to liberal tenets might sometimes defect from the regime if political elites believe there are domestic political gains in doing so. The government of President Ronald Reagan (1981–89) opted for restraints on Japanese imports of automobiles.[3] More recently, George W. Bush's presidency violated WTO rules in steel and agriculture, which were both key sectors from which he hoped to gain popular support.

Regardless of whether states are liberal or mercantilist, both types seek to roll the costs of enforcement and rule creation onto others. Creating and enforcing such rules imposes economic and political costs. The leading economy must perform various functions and risk trade wars when it seeks to penalize violators of these rules. Should the larger economies fail to provide such leadership, then the collective good will be in jeopardy.

Hegemonic Stability Theory

Charles Kindleberger has provided a persuasive argument that a collective goods perspective can explain both the collapse of the international trading system in the 1930s and the emergence of the international order created after 1945. He argues that since liberal trade can be understood as a collective good, the creation and maintenance of such a regime requires a dominant actor willing to provide that good. The system requires one state that is economically more powerful than the others and is willing to lead; in other words, it requires a hegemonic state:

> The international economic and monetary system needs leadership, a country which is prepared ... under some system of rules that it has internalized, to set standards of conduct for other countries; and to seek to get others to follow them, to take on an undue share of the burdens of the system ...[4]

The hegemon benefits disproportionately from such a regime, given that it is the leading economy and will likely be able to export its goods and services abroad. However, in creating a liberal trading system, other states will benefit as well. The hegemon creates a liberal trading system and maintains and enforces the rules of liberal trade; in so doing it maintains the stability of that system.

---

3. See Reich 1989, Pew Case Study 119, in the Resources list at the end of Part II.
4. Kindleberger 1973, 28.

Kindleberger argues that economic leadership entails fulfilling several functions. First, the hegemon needs to establish and defend a fixed exchange rate or, at the very least, control currency fluctuations, because any participating state might be inclined to devalue its currency. Devaluation would raise the price of foreign products while, conversely, making one's own products cheaper for foreign consumers. If all states engage in such behavior, we might witness a downward spiral of competitive devaluation. Each state will retaliate against another state's devaluation. This is exactly what happened in the 1930s when Britain went off the gold standard, and countries competitively devalued their currencies: "Each successive devaluation imposed substantial costs on other countries and eventually triggered offsetting devaluations."[5] With currency exchange rates in constant flux, it is much more difficult to conduct business across national boundaries. Imagine a business owner who is constantly faced by dramatic currency fluctuations. At a minimum such instability will raise transaction and information costs.

Secondly, the leader must keep its own market open to create an incentive for the other states and to be consistent in its demands for openness. Aside from creating an incentive, this also is a means to penalize defectors. Given that the hegemon has a large market, it will be attractive for any country to export its goods there. The threat of being excluded from that market can act as a strong deterrent to defection from the international rules.

Third, the leading actor must provide for open markets so that other actors can sell their goods in the hegemon's market. In order to prevent "beggar thy neighbor" policies, the hegemon must keep its tariffs low and provide positive incentives for others to do likewise. This is particularly the case during economic downturns, so that governments will not pursue short-run gains at the expense of overall stability. At the same time, the hegemon should retaliate and punish those who pursue protectionist strategies. In short, in order to lead, the hegemon should have a large and accessible domestic market and the ability to retaliate or otherwise inflict a penalty on transgressors. The long-term benefit to the hegemon, as the leading producer, is the ability to sell its goods abroad.

Finally, the hegemon must engage in countercyclical lending. Capital should flow from the leading economy to the other states, even if the hegemon goes through a momentary downturn. A domestic recession in the hegemon should correlate with foreign lending and investment. Imagine a situation where the economy of the hegemon is not doing well in a given year. Investors will now take their money elsewhere and invest in places where they think they will get a better return. This will lead to growth of the recipient economies. In order to get the products they need, these emerging economies will now start to buy more goods from the hegemon,

5. Oye 1986, 178.

which, being the dominant economy of the day, still provides the most sophisticated technologies and products of its time. Thus, the hegemon will be pulled out of its own economic slump. More intuitively, one might argue that the dominant economy must make capital available for the system to work. If other states lack capital, trade will be reduced.

Kindleberger's main interest was to explain the Great Depression. Why had the international economic system collapsed so dramatically in the 1930s? His answer was simple: the system had lacked a hegemonic leader.

British Hegemonic Leadership

Britain in the nineteenth century fulfilled all the roles that went with hegemonic leadership. It tried to support stable exchange rates through the gold standard. It also by and large maintained an open market. And London was the financial center of the world, from which capital flowed to emerging markets such as in Latin America and the United States.

For most of the nineteenth century Britain was the undisputed economic leader. But by the turn of that century it was challenged and surpassed by Germany and the United States. Even so, after the German defeat in World War I, Britain tried to re-establish its position as the key player in international trade by trying to create a stable exchange rate system, and it did so by a fixed exchange rate based on the gold standard. This system required Central Banks to agree to officially commit themselves to a set conversion of gold into currency and vice versa.[6] Each country also had to agree to the unrestricted export of gold to allow for gold shipments to address trade imbalances. The ratio of gold to money would remain fixed.

On the one hand, this created advantages for the hegemon. As said, fixed exchange rates facilitate liberal trade. But it also conveyed other benefits. By establishing the pound as the main currency for exchange, Britain in effect operated as banker to the world. Like any private bank, it could make money from lending funds or by providing financial services to its clients.

On the other hand, the hegemon also incurred costs. It had to enforce fixed exchange rates, and it had to be willing to make short-run sacrifices. For complicated reasons that we need not discuss here, this system was unstable. The pound was set too high from the outset, particularly *vis-à-vis* the French franc. French products were thus relatively cheap while British goods were not. In a perfect system, the gold standard should have led to downward pressure on prices and wages in Britain, which would make British products cheaper. But this was politically unacceptable. People

---

6. For a collection of essays on how the gold standard worked across history, see Eichengreen 1985.

refused to accept lower wages. The problem was well understood by the governing elites of Britain. Commenting on deflation, the Macmillan inquiry committee of 1931 worried that if such adjustment were made impossible "by social causes from transmitting its full effect to money-wages and other costs, it may be that the whole machine will crack before the reaction back to equilibrium has been brought about."[7] These social causes—that is, public resistance to lower wages—derailed the standard. The necessary adjustment did not take place, and the gold standard could not be maintained. Consequently, Britain went off gold, and states started to engage in competitive devaluations.

Britain similarly became less inclined to maintain an open market at home. It was no longer the leading producer in the world in many manufacturing sectors. Both the United States and Germany had supplanted it in key areas such as chemicals, steel production, and automobiles. Given that consumers in other countries were no longer inclined to choose British products over others, its share of world trade declined markedly. Its lead in world manufacturing had similarly diminished. In 1880 it accounted for 23 per cent of world manufacturing, by 1913 its share measured slightly less than 14 per cent, and by 1928 its share had dropped to around 10 per cent.[8] Consequently, Britain had less interest in pursuing leadership and lowering its tariffs. Conversely, because its share of the world market had declined, its ability to retaliate or offer incentives for others to lower their tariffs had diminished. In other words, if Britain threatened to close its markets in retaliation to other countries pursuing protectionism, these other countries could turn elsewhere. The British economy lacked the leverage it once exercised.

Finally, the British financial sector also changed its orientation. At that time there were few formal government institutions, or international organizations, to perform countercyclical lending. International financial flows were largely determined by private capital. As the overall British position weakened, its financial reserves and the capital outflows to other countries also declined. It could operate as the world's banker no longer. Instead, capital turned inward to investments in their own colonies rather than looking for emerging markets elsewhere.

In sum, Britain no longer had the capability to lead internationally. It turned inward. Its capital increasingly flowed to areas that were still part of the British Empire—the colonies and the largely self-governing Dominions. Its trade also gyrated to those parts of the world. But if Britain no longer could lead, why did the new economic giant, the United States, not step in to take over this role?

7. As cited in Eichengreen 1985, 194.
8. Figures from Paul Bairoch as cited in Kennedy 1985, 12.

The United States Passes the Buck

It is not fully clear whether the United States really had the capability to help stabilize exchange rates. Kindleberger argues that it had sufficient gold reserves, but others note how dollar reserves sank from $7.4 billion in 1929 to $2.4 billion in 1932.[9] If one can debate the American ability to lead, its lack of will to do so was clear. The American government preferred to support prices, particularly of agricultural goods given the importance of that sector for the overall economy. Moreover, farmers were an important political constituency that Washington dared not anger.

This primacy of internal politics over internationalism was even more pronounced in trade policy. While the American domestic market was very large, its share of world trade was relatively small. By keeping its market open, it could have provided incentives for other states to do likewise. But, given that international trade made up only a small portion of overall national product, the American incentive to pursue open markets was relatively low. Hence, American corporations fell back on the domestic market rather than actively pursue international openness.

Moreover, President Herbert Hoover had made promises during his electoral campaign that he would support higher prices for agricultural goods. These had fallen worldwide in the slump of the 1920s. On his election, therefore, Hoover pushed for tariffs and Congress responded likewise. The government passed the Smoot-Hawley tariffs in 1930. Originally intended for farm protection, they ultimately covered many goods, raising tariffs overall by 40 per cent. This not only made export to the United States difficult, but complicated other countries' ability to pay back loans from World War I.

The United States also failed to engage in countercyclical lending. Although American financial capabilities increased, its private capital tended to stay at home during economic downturns. Why this was so is due to various factors. American investors had little experience in international lending. They were at the beginning of the learning curve. Moreover, the United States provided many new opportunities for entrepreneurial investment internally, such as in the sparsely populated west. If older, more established industries showed low returns on investment, capital could easily find new opportunities. The United States, unlike Britain, was not a mature economy but still showed many new venues for entrepreneurship. Why would capital seek returns elsewhere?

To conclude, Britain was no longer able to lead and had less and less incentive to do so. The United States could have taken on the mantle of leadership, but it failed to do so for domestic political reasons. Kindleberger describes it in vivid terms that capture the logic of the multi-person Prisoner's Dilemma:

---

9. Heaton 1948, 703.

The world economic system was unstable unless some country stabilized it, as Britain had done in the nineteenth century and up to 1913. In 1929, the British couldn't and the United States wouldn't. When every country turned to protect its national private interest, the world public interest went down the drain, and with it the private interests of all.[10]

The world thus lacked hegemonic leadership. Countries defected from the fixed exchange rate, and a cycle of competitive devaluations set in. In retaliation to the Smoot-Hawley tariffs, other countries erected barriers of their own. In 1931 France put 1,100 goods on a quota list, raising some tariffs, such as that on wheat, by 200 per cent. Germany put a 300 per cent duty on rye (given the traditionally strong influence of the landed aristocracy, the Junkers), and Britain raised duties by 10 per cent across the board.[11]

American Leadership After 1945

The consequences of a lack of leadership were disastrous. Not only did world trade plummet and unemployment skyrocket, but the dire economic conditions set the stage for extremist politicians, contributing to the outbreak of a world war. While war still raged, the government of the United States realized it could no longer forsake its leadership role, and together with Britain it devised a new international economic order.

Through agreements made at Bretton Woods, New Hampshire, in 1944, the United States established that exchange rates would fall within 1 per cent of the fixed rate. In 1947 it reintroduced the (modified) gold exchange standard and set the formal exchange at $35 for one ounce of gold. The United States also took the lead in setting up international institutions to make capital available to the other countries. Public institutions such as the World Bank and the International Monetary Fund (IMF) were created to supply capital and balance periodic trade deficits. In addition, the Marshall Plan started to funnel money to the destroyed West European countries, so that their economies could be rebuilt. American private capital also had matured. It started to flow in increasing quantities to the devastated states of Europe. American direct investments created overseas plants making cars, chemicals, and other products.[12]

American leadership was most pronounced in creating a liberal trading system with explicit rules of behavior. The United States, through the General Agreement on Tariffs and Trade (GATT, 1947), set about creating a liberal trading system across all the leading capitalist countries. GATT

---

10. Kindleberger 1973, 291.
11. Heaton 1948, 698.
12. Gilpin 1975.

established several key principles of international trade. First, states were not allowed to discriminate. Any agreement signed bilaterally had to be extended to all participants. The "Most Favored Nation" clause required that if one country established very favorable trade conditions for another country (the most favored country), then those conditions had to be extended to all. Second, all contracting parties committed themselves to the reduction of trade barriers. Third, unconditional reciprocity required that any concessions granted should be reciprocated without caveats by the recipient. Fourth, transparency forbade hidden barriers to trade meant to circumvent the spirit of the agreement.

The GATT agreement was periodically renegotiated and updated through various rounds that gave it greater specificity. During the 1950s, several ad-hoc smaller rounds advanced liberalization. The Dillon Round of 1960–62 aimed at a more comprehensive and far-reaching breakthrough, but its item by item approach met with little success. By contrast, the Kennedy Round (1962–67) was highly successful. It resulted in a 35 per cent across the board reduction on approximately 60,000 items.[13] However, it did not address non-tariff barriers, nor did it tackle voluntary export restraints (VERS) and orderly marketing arrangements in which states "voluntarily" agreed to limit trade but which in fact masked coercive tactics of the restricting state.

The Tokyo Round (1973–79) explicitly aimed to categorize and deal with non-tariff barriers, such as, for example, health codes, environmental standards, or safety regulations. In principle such codes and standards were not violations of GATT if they were indeed intended to maintain safety or protect the environment. However, given that overt tariffs were forbidden by GATT, states started to use such codes to covertly protect domestic producers.

The Tokyo Round achieved some success in that it reduced overall tariffs by about 27 per cent, but it did not resolve other items. Non-tariff barriers were inherently difficult to categorize. What constituted a legitimate health regulation, and what was a form of veiled protectionism? For example, the European Union (EU) in 2003 passed regulations dealing with the trade in genetically modified foods.[14] The United States subsequently argued that in passing these regulations, Europe had unfairly restricted imports of American genetically modified foods. Is the EU indeed concerned about health effects—the United States argues there are none—or is it trying to keep cheaper and perhaps higher quality American agricultural products from competing with European farmers?

GATT's Article 19 also continued to create problems. This article, the so-called safeguard clause, permitted states to violate GATT rules if serious injury to domestic industry could result from liberal trade. However, the

13. Gilpin 1987 provides a good overview of these various rounds.
14. EU regulations 1829/2003 and 1830/2003.

safeguard clause could be broadly interpreted by any state that thought foreign products were more competitive. Such a broad interpretation undermined the very spirit of GATT.

Furthermore, at the initial signing of the agreement, the United States had insisted that agriculture not be included. The agricultural lobby was powerful, and the executive feared a political backlash. When the United States later wanted to bring certain agricultural provisions into GATT, other states objected for similar reasons. In addition, decolonization had added many new nations to the international system. These less developed countries (the LDCs) faced highly developed economies, and as one would expect given the late development thesis, they argued that their economies required state intervention and the use of protectionism to foster domestic industries. GATT, so they argued, favored the already developed states.

The Uruguay Round (1986–94) tried to address these problems. By now the number of participating states had grown to more than 100. Agriculture continued to have strong domestic constituencies, even in advanced states such as France and Japan. Moreover, the world economy had changed dramatically since the 1940s. GATT had focused on trade of material goods, but trade in services had become a critical component by the mid-1980s. Services accounted for one-quarter of world trade and accounted for 60 per cent of world GNP.

The ensuing discussions were complicated and controversial. At several junctures the Round seemed to collapse. Non-tariff barriers were inherently difficult to categorize, and agricultural interests almost drove the European Community[15] and the United States to a series of trade conflicts in 1986 and 1992. Nevertheless, it was clear that more liberalization would benefit the main actors. By some estimates at that time, the United States would gain $70 billion, the EC $60 billion, and Japan $50 billion from opening the markets further. In total, efficiency gains would amount to $250 billion. Later estimates doubled that amount.

After eight years of protracted negotiations, the Uruguay Round was successfully concluded: the GATT 1947 text was expanded and incorporated as GATT 1994. It remained an agreement and was not renamed so it did not require ratification by the American Senate. It established a new organization, the World Trade Organization (WTO), and located it in Geneva. It also institutionalized a new and much more vigorous dispute settlement mechanism. The process now became mandatory, and the accused party could no longer stop the procedure by refusing to acquiesce

---

15. The European Economic Community, a coalition of six Western European governments, was formed in 1957 to facilitate a single market in trade. In 1967 it fused with the European Coal and Steel Community (ECSC) and the European Atomic Energy Community (Euratom) to become the European Community. In 1993, it was renamed the European Union (EU) and widened its interests to include foreign affairs, immigration, and justice issues. The EU now has 27 members.

to panel composition. It also established a strict timetable, particularly for cases categorized as "urgent matters." Prior to the new procedure, dispute settlement could take so long that states were reluctant to bring cases to GATT since by the time a finding was reached, the case would have become irrelevant.

Shortly thereafter two additional agreements were signed: GATS, the General Agreement on Trade in Services, and TRIPS, Trade Related Aspects of Intellectual Property Rights. This was critical as the leading actors, particularly the United States, were concerned about piracy of intellectual property such as copying of pharmaceuticals, music, movies, and software.

Subsequent progress, however, has been slow. The Doha Round, which commenced in 2001, was intended to pay particular attention to the plight of the developing countries. It particularly made reference to

> ... the long-term objective referred to in the Agreement to establish a fair and market-oriented trading system through a programme of fundamental reform encompassing strengthened rules and specific commitments on support and protection in order to correct and prevent restrictions and distortions in world agricultural markets.[16]

However, the Round soon ran into trouble when the developed countries balked at further liberalization of their agricultural sectors. By the fall of 2008 WTO Director Pascal Lamy had to concede that finalization of the Doha Round would at best occur in 2009.[17]

The WTO has increasingly come under pressure for not responding to the continued plight of the LDCs, and it has been criticized for sacrificing environmental concerns for gains in trade.[18] (I discuss the environmental critique in Part III.) Even proponents of the WTO have conceded that the distribution of gains achieved by liberation have flowed disproportionately to the developed countries.

Still the Era of Hegemonic Leadership?

It remains a matter of debate whether the current problems surrounding the WTO can be explained by hegemonic stability arguments. One might note that the United States has long been a declining hegemon in relative terms. Already by 1972 it had to retreat from fixed exchange rates and move

16. WTO ministerial declaration of 2001; http://www.wto.org/english/thewto_e/minist_e/min01_e/mindecl_e.htm#agriculture.

17. Stephen Castle and Mark Landler, "After 7 Years, Talks on Trade Collapse," *New York Times*, 30 July 2008.

18. For a scholarly critique, see Kaplinsky 2001. Oxfam 2002 provides critical insights by a prominent non-governmental organization.

towards mutually negotiated exchange ratios (the Smithsonian Agreement). Its declining relative share of World GNP and its large trade imbalances cast doubt on its ability to function as the leader in the system.

Moreover, domestic calculations have led American leaders to opt for trade barriers rather than liberal trade. Republican presidents have been little better than Democratic ones, although the latter tend to cater more to labor unions and segments of the population that are wary of liberal trade agreements. As we mentioned earlier, Republican President Ronald Reagan brokered "voluntary" export restrictions with the Japanese. More recently, the administration of George W. Bush engaged in interventionist and protectionist strategies that contravened WTO rules. In May 2002, he came out in favor of a bill "which would increase farm spending by some 70 per cent and envisions spending more than $100 billion over six years."[19] In an another attempt to garner support in key electoral states, he implemented retaliatory tariffs for the benefit of the steel industry, which raised prices on imported steel by 30 per cent. The WTO ruled in favor of the EU, which had challenged the policy, and permitted it to impose sanctions on imports from the United States. Fully cognizant that domestic electoral politics were driving the American decision, "the Europeans pulled out an electoral map and proudly announced they would single out products made in the states Mr. Bush most needs to win a second term."[20] Making matters even worse, the WTO ruled against the United States on tax breaks that gave American corporations' offshore operations competitive advantages. The WTO also authorized the EU, Canada, Mexico, Japan, India, South Korea, and Brazil to retaliate against American duties imposed on their goods, which were allegedly being dumped on the American market.[21] These episodes raise serious doubts about the American hegemonic leadership. Hence, one might argue that the difficulties surrounding the latest rounds must be attributed to a declining capability and a declining will to lead the international system.

Conversely, one might submit that the difficulties might be due to the increasing complexity and intractability of the issues in question. Non-tariff barriers are inherently more difficult to deal with than overt tariffs. Trade in services is also less transparent than trade in goods, making deregulation of such trade more complicated. Add to that the increasing number of WTO members with vastly different levels of development. Thus, whereas the early GATT rounds involved several dozen relatively developed

19. David Stout, "House Overwhelmingly Passes Bill Raising Farm Subsidies," *New York Times*, 2 May 2002.

20. David Sanger, "Backing Down on Steel Tariffs, U.S. Strengthens Trade Group," *New York Times*, 5 December 2003. See also Elizabeth Backer, "U.S. Tariffs on Steel Are Illegal, World Trade Organization Says," *New York Times*, 11 November 2003.

21. Alan Cowell, "Europeans Plan to Press for Tariffs Against U.S," *New York Times*, 6 December 2003; Paul Meller, "W.T.O. Authorizes Trade Sanctions Against the United States," *New York Times*, 27 November 2004.

economies, the later rounds faced greater numbers, making the provision of a regime (a collective good) more subject to free riding.

Rather than speak of hegemonic leadership by one actor, it would be more accurate to describe the WTO system as currently driven by a cohort of the largest economies. The Quad—consisting of the United States, the EU, Japan, and Canada—has been the key entity propelling the Uruguay Round, as well as the TRIPS and GATS agreements. Increasingly also, the larger emerging economies have started to play an ever increasing role.

These reflections do not necessarily invalidate a collective goods perspective of international regimes. However, it does draw attention to the often neglected aspect in collective goods theory that such goods can also be provided by small groups acting together rather than by a single dominant actor. Consequently, scholars such as David Lake and Duncan Snidal have challenged hegemonic stability theory on theoretical as well as empirical grounds.[22] Even if the American ability and will to lead have at times been lacking, the international regime might well survive through the cooperation of the world's leading economies.

Globalization and Convergence

Arguments for Convergence

In the half-century since the formation of this new liberal trading system, epitomized by the WTO, interactions in trade and finance have increased to an unprecedented scale. States and private actors have come to depend more and more on international trade. Consequently, trade has become an ever larger percentage of GNP. In the 1940s, international trade made up less than 10 per cent of American GDP.[23] By 2000, it accounted for 26 per cent.

Given this increased international pressure, we might expect the various types of economic decision-making to converge. The three different styles that we identified—liberal, corporatist, and neo-mercantilist forms of government policy (identified with the United States, Germany, and Japan respectively)—should start to look the same.

There are various reasons why we might expect convergence. First, the GATT and now the WTO with its related agreements have made overt protectionism illegal. Even more subtle government intervention through such methods as non-tariff barriers, tax breaks, and government contracts have come under scrutiny. Simply put, neo-mercantilism and traditional

---

22. Lake 1984; Snidal 1985.

23. GDP (gross domestic product) measures the total cost of goods and services produced within a country. GNP (gross national product) measures the total cost of goods and services produced in a country, plus income earned by its citizens abroad, minus income earned by foreigners in the country.

corporatist intervention might no longer be possible. We may thus expect public and private sector interaction to look increasingly similar across countries. Organizations such as NAFTA and the EU have had an even greater impact. The EU in particular has created a hierarchical structure with relatively autonomous European-wide organizations that have issued directives and regulations that greatly diminish national autonomy. However, given that our interest is in cross-regional comparison of the three most different types of systems, our main interest here goes to the impact of the WTO.[24]

Second, Darwinian selection might eliminate government and corporate policies that are inefficient. In a strong version of this view, countries or corporations that engage in inefficient practices will be weeded out. Whether governments and companies learn is largely irrelevant in this perspective. Blind evolution and selection will weed out those practices that are not competitive, and the trend will be towards similarity of units that are competitive.[25] A less strong version of Darwinian arguments couples selection and learning. Both private and public actors try to mimic the most successful type of economic arrangement in order to compete more effectively. They realize that if they do not learn, or do not learn the right lessons, these countries' corporations will fail to be competitive on the international market. Actors thus engage in mimicry and copy best practices. For example, during the heyday of Japanese success when the American economy languished in the early 1980s, both American decision-makers and companies started to study Japanese government policy and corporate behavior. Earlier in the century, American corporate structure and organization had broken new ground, and European companies tried to emulate them.[26]

Finally, at the micro-level we might expect more convergence in corporate organization because alliances and mergers are creating truly transnational companies. Corporations are not just copying the competition; they are integrating across borders and blurring the very distinction of national companies.[27]

Is there evidence for such convergence? We should analyze this question at two levels. At the micro-level, we can examine whether companies are starting to look alike in terms of corporate structure and organization. At the macro-level, we need to see whether government policies have started to resemble each other. In the Japanese case, we might thus look

24. For a discussion of how NAFTA and the EU differ and how the EU in particular has created a far more hierarchical regional organization than NAFTA, see Cooley and Spruyt 2009.

25. Thompson 2001. Of particular relevance to political economy are the essays in this collection by Spruyt and by Kim and Hart.

26. Chandler 1990.

27. Bartlett and Ghoshal 1998 thus argue that we have entered the era of the transnational firm in which firms must engage in continuous worldwide learning.

for less activism and less protectionism. In Germany, we might see if the elements of consensus decision-making are unraveling. And in the United States, we might look for signs that government is perhaps becoming more active in management.

Signs of Change but Continued Divergence

There has indeed been some convergence at both the micro and macro levels. However, the empirical evidence so far suggests that historical trajectories and institutional arrangements continue to show distinct patterns. Thus, while the differences have become less stark, we continue to observe considerable differences in national economic styles.

Louis Pauly and Simon Reich examined in some detail whether the global integration of markets affected the corporate behavior and organization of multinational companies.[28] They explicitly engaged in a comparison of the United States, Japan, and Germany, observing that all three had different national economic styles (as we discussed above). Since all three were heavily exposed to the global international economic environment, one would expect that the external variable—the competitive pressure caused by globalization—would have a similar effect. (International exposure could be treated as a constant and could not be adduced to explain variation in national economic styles, leaving internal variables as the key explanation—a comparison using method of difference.) Focusing particularly on corporate governance and financing, research and development, and investment and intra-firm trade, Pauly and Reich found that divergent national economic styles and ideologies continued to affect corporate behavior and corporate structure in all these aspects. Historical past, ideology, and institutional arrangements continued to propel these companies to continue on their previously established trajectories. Corporate behavior remained path dependent.

Another researcher, Richard Whitley, came to a similar conclusion when he examined corporate behavior. His research started from the assumption that business systems had become more internationalized. Besides expanding into foreign markets with their exports, companies also increasingly invested more funds in subsidiaries overseas. Indeed, in some cases mergers and alliances had basically created transnational business systems.[29] Whitley hypothesized that international competition and managerial coordination would lead to convergence. To examine his expectation, Whitley engaged in a cross-country comparison of business systems and examined the ownership relations within companies, alliances across companies and sectors, and employee-management relations.

---

28. Pauly and Reich 1997.
29. Whitley 1998.

He concluded that, despite higher levels of internationalization, business systems continued to show nationally specific variation.

In short, until very recently, national economic styles and differences in corporate objectives and corporate structure have persisted in the face of globalization. However, things might have started to change in the last few years. Both Germany and Japan have started to change their financial systems. As we have seen, their respective governments' intervention and the close business-finance nexus formed critical components of the overall relations of government to the private sector. In both countries, we see evidence that private equity is starting to play a greater role. Companies in these countries have started to raise money from private stockholders rather than rely on the government or bank relations. Japan has for the first time started to let banks that carried many bad loans fail.

And yet, while there might be a trend to similar policies and arrangements, differences still remain. German corporate governance has undergone changes, but companies have not passively reacted. Instead, they have selectively engaged the increasing pressures of globalization. National patterns are still very recognizable. Looking at corporate governance, Alexander Börsch compared the Anglo-Saxon model, which he calls a shareholder system, to the continental European and Japanese model, which he terms a stakeholder system. While certain aspects of governance have changed, many other aspects continue to conform with previous trajectories. Thus, "the outcome is not convergence or imitation of the shareholder value model in all or even most of its aspects, but partial and selective adaptation without a fundamental change in the structures and strategies of German corporate governance."[30]

Moreover, despite pressures brought about by globalization, corporate finance, a key feature of the German co-determination system, has remained markedly different from the American model. Although things have changed in degree, one observer could legitimately claim that "big European companies ... still rely for the large bulk of their funding on artificially cheap loans from their relationship banks."[31] Thus, while there has been a gradual shift towards equities financing, "external financing remains long term in nature; approximately two-thirds of all external funds of German enterprises have maturities of more than one year."[32]

The same conclusion can be reached for Japan despite the pressures that the economic downturn of the late 1980s and 1990s put on the traditional Japanese neo-mercantilist approach. This downturn correlated with a crisis in the financial sector. The problem in bank loans arose from unfounded expectations in the real estate markets (seemingly foreshadowing similar problems in the American market in 2008). Subsequently, some

---

30. Börsch 2007, 10.
31. Edward Lucy, "Half Full or Half Empty." *Financial Times*, 20 December 1999.
32. Börsch 2007, 59.

regulatory reforms were put into place. The United States also put pressure on Japan to engage in even more fundamental economic reforms.[33] Nevertheless, even after such reforms, a recent analysis of Japanese industrial organization saw relatively little change. The analysis is worth quoting at length:

> Our results provide little evidence that economic and regulatory changes in the early 1990s influenced the Japanese intercorporate network, and in particular keiretsu organization. In spite of significant changes in the Japanese economy during the early 1990s and the globalization of markets, the keiretsu system appears to have remained intact. Perhaps the most striking finding is that, despite arguments for reduced dependence on bank financing, we observe little evidence of such change.[34]

Steven Vogel, too, observes that there have been significant changes in the Japanese industry-finance nexus following the economic downturn of the late 1980s and 1990s. The varieties of capitalism thesis is still relevant, but its applicability depends on the size and type of firms and banks. Larger corporations have become more selective in the types of financing they acquire and have distanced themselves somewhat from their main relationship banks. In this sense, some Japanese companies have started to look more like their Anglo-Saxon counterparts.

Smaller companies, however, have maintained, or even strengthened, their main bank ties. Indeed, Vogel notes "the stubborn resilience of main bank relations rather than their demise."[35] Assessing the overall changes of institutions at the micro (company) level and the macro (government) level, he notes that while some Japanese politicians and corporate elites wanted their system to move closer to the liberal-capitalist type, changes only occurred selectively.

> Yet a funny thing happened on Japan's way to the U.S. model: it never got there. As government officials and industry leaders scrutinized their options they selected reforms to modify or reinforce existing institutions rather than to abandon them.[36]

To conclude then, we are no doubt witnessing an era of profound global pressures on national systems. Nevertheless, despite these pressures

---

33. Edmund Andrews, "U.S. Says Japan Must Make Bolder Economic Changes," *New York Times*, 29 September 2002.

34. McGuire and Dow 2003. (A keiretsu is an alliance of interrelated firms centering around a parent bank or banks.)

35. Vogel 2006, 129.

36. Vogel 2006, 3.

for convergence, history still casts a long shadow. Practices that are decades and even centuries old continue to influence institutional arrangements and the expectations that citizens have of markets and of their government. Indeed, although cross-holdings in Japan declined for more than a decade, they started to go back up after 2004. Whether the financial crisis that hit the world in 2008 will change the industry-finance nexus remains to be seen. Even though stock market losses have directly affected Japanese banks' balance sheets, corporate leaders have already argued that the cross-holding of industry and bank shares will continue in the future.[37]

For this reason, this chapter has focused on clarifying the roots of the current national economic systems. Before we can understand the changes in these systems, and debate whether or not the current global economic order is inducing convergence among these diverse types, we first need to understand the bases from which they originated.

---

37. "Criss-Crossed Capitalism," *The Economist* 389: 8605 (8 November 2008): 80.

RESOURCES

Useful Websites and Resources

Check to see if your library provides access to some of these sources. Many are also directly available online, at no charge.

Centre for Economic Policy Research
http://www.cepr.org/default_static.htm
This research center disseminates reports and policy briefs on economic and other matters.

The Economist
By subscription. http://www.economist.com/research/
Weekly magazine presents non-technical world and economic news and also provides useful country research reports.

International Monetary Fund
http://www.imf.org/external/
The IMF monitors economic and financial developments, and lends to countries with balance of payments difficulties. Website provides information on the organization, data, membership, and statistics.

Organization for Economic Cooperation and Development
http://www.oecd.org/home/
The OECD is one of the world's largest publishers in the fields of economics and public policy. Its publications disseminate the organization's intellectual output both on paper and online. It is a useful source for statistical information.

World Trade Organization
http://www.wto.org/
This is the organization that emerged out of the Uruguay Round of the GATT negotiations in 1994. The site provides information on the organization, membership, treaty texts, and statistics.

Case Studies

Odell, John, and Margit Tchakerian. 1988. *European Community Enlargement and the United States.* Pew Case 130. Washington, DC: GUISD Pew Case Study Center.

Reich, Simon. 1989. *The Reagan Administration, the Auto Producers, and the 1981 Agreement with Japan.* Pew Case 119. Washington, DC: GUISD Pew Case Study Center.

Ryan, Michael, and Teresita Ramos-Soler. 1996. *Beer Brawls: GATT "Settles" the Market access Dispute Between U.S. and Canadian Brewers.* Pew Case 721. Washington, DC: GUISD Pew Case Study Center.

PART III
GLOBAL CHALLENGES: ENERGY AND THE ENVIRONMENT

TEN

Tools of the Trade: Common Pool Resources and Imperfect Markets

The Logic of Collective Action and Common Pool Resources

As discussed in Part II, collective goods have two characteristics. They are non-rival and non-exclusive. Non-rivalry entails that the quantity of the good in question does not diminish with individual consumption. My intake of oxygen does not in any meaningful way diminish the amount of oxygen available to you. Non-exclusiveness means that one cannot prevent others from enjoying that good. You can enjoy clean air as much as I do.

Consequently, the provision of a good that has such characteristics runs the risk of free riding. From an individualist perspective, and calculating as a rational economic actor, people will prefer to enjoy the benefits of a service, but, given that they cannot be excluded from that service even if they do not contribute, they will opt to free ride. Simply put, it is rational to enjoy the benefits of a service (as they flow directly to me) while rolling the costs of service provision over onto other actors. The collective result is that the service will be underprovided or not provided at all.

The logic of collective action can provide a powerful explanation for the depletion of common pool resources. Moreover, it can also clarify some of the dynamics in global energy markets.

Common pool resources are goods that are not individually owned and accessible to all. They are not governed by private property rights, and so others cannot be excluded from access to and use of them. Moreover, individual actions only marginally deplete the total amount of the resource available. An individual can directly reap the full benefit of that resource, while the costs of him using that resource (the marginal depletion of the total quantity) can be rolled over to all other individuals. Benefits are precise, costs are diffuse.

Thus, as with free riding, individuals will behave opportunistically and try to maximize private gains without focusing on the total costs, which are borne by the group as a whole. The producer calculates only the cost to himself and prices the product he offers accordingly. The externalities—the actual social costs that are not factored into the individual producer's cost-benefit calculation—are borne by the whole group. Such individual calculations, however, when aggregated, can have disastrous collective effects.

Environmental degradation often occurs due to such a logic, what biologists have termed "The Tragedy of the Commons," based on the over-grazing of common pastures in England. In late medieval England, villages had certain lots of lands that were not directly subject to feudal lords. The village as a whole, and thus each village inhabitant, had the right to graze their sheep on these common pastures. However, no individual had an incentive to limit the number of sheep on these common pastures. The benefits of doing so accrued directly to the individual—more sheep meant more wool and money. The costs, however—overgrazing and destruction of the pastures—were borne by the community as a whole. The result was an overall decline in the use value of such arable lands.

Whether this presents a historically accurate account of the end of common pastures in England is less important than the fundamental in-sight that commonly owned resources, or resources that are not owned by anyone (*res nullius*), will be subject to such depredation.[1] Rational, indi-vidualist calculations will collectively have a disastrous outcome—exactly the contrary of Adam Smith's "invisible hand" in economics.

Several solutions are possible to the problem. First, one can privatize the good in question. If, for example, the common pastures were divided among the various villagers as private property, then each villager would have an incentive to judiciously manage the property under his care. The costs of overexploitation would now fall directly on the farmer. If he overgrazed one year, then the following year he would have to bear the consequences himself. Benefits and costs in other words would be aligned. However, as economists have shown, assigning private property rights to common pool resources is no panacea.[2] If private actors have a high dis-count rate, that is, if they highly value current profits and care less about future gains, then the common resource might still be overexploited.

Privatization has been applied in practice. For example, the problem of overexploitation of littoral seas—waters close to shore—has been par-tially addressed by allowing states to extend their jurisdiction. Originally states could lay claim to an area three miles off their coast. This was gradually expanded in common practice. The 1982 UN Law of the Sea Convention (UNCLOS III) agreement extended this territorial zone to 12 miles and also gave states the right to an Exclusive Economic Zone 200

---

1. The tragedy of the commons was well recognized before contemporary economists turned to the study of these problems. In the early nineteenth century, William Lloyd noted the problem of cattle overgrazing common lands and gave a theoretical account of why it had happened (Lloyd 1977).

2. Clark 1977.

miles offshore. Given that many fish stocks populate this part of the ocean, this essentially privatized their exploitation.[3]

Second, one could establish a governing body that allocated and governed the use of such resources. This collective body would still treat the resource as a collectively owned good, but it would decide how much use each individual could make of that resource. Thus, in our example, the village elders might determine the maximum number of sheep that a given pasture might hold without the danger of overgrazing and then allocate each villager a certain quota of sheep. This collective governance, of course, has problems of its own. Who will take the lead in organizing the collectivity? Who will take on the burdens of monitoring and potentially penalizing transgressors? In other words, collective governance itself requires actors to overcome the problem of free riding. Consequently, as with economic regimes, some argue that a dominant actor (a hegemon) or group of actors needs to take the lead. The equivalent of hegemonic stability theory in the economic realm is hegemonic leadership in the creation of environmental regimes. And, indeed, at times the United States and the EU have acted in such leadership capacity, as with the Montreal Protocol on chlorofluorocarbons (CFCs).

The Coase Theorem: Bargaining Solutions for Externalities

Ronald Coase formulated the case for privatization and gained a Nobel prize for his insights.[4] Cases involving environmental degradation often involve actions by one party A, impinging on another party B, without A having to take the negative effects on B into account. For example, if a steel factory in Ohio produces acid rain, and if that pollution downstream reduces the environmental milieu in Quebec, killing fish and trees, then the cost of producing steel by the factory in Ohio should take the cost of the environmental degradation into account. But in reality that does not happen. The steel producer simply calculates the resources and labor he requires to produce the steel while the market pays that producer in accordance with competitive prices. The cost of environmental degradation is not taken into account. It is a negative externality—external because it does not figure into the price of the product.

Prior to Coase's insights it was commonly thought that such situations required governmental intervention. In order to make the polluter pay, government should establish rules and enforce them. Coase, however, introduced a new solution. According to his theorem, if property rights were clearly assigned—and it did not matter to whom those rights were

---

3. For a detailed discussion of the various law of the sea conferences and the various issues associated with reaching agreement, see Holick 1981.
4. Coase 1960.

assigned—then the two parties should be able to arrive at an efficient bargaining solution.

For simplicity's sake, let us take the example above and suppose we are dealing with two parties. Assume that among the victims of environmental degradation is the owner of a lodge near the Saguenay River in Quebec. Acid rain from steel mills in Ohio has diminished tourism, and she has suffered a loss in revenue. In order to prevent this pollution, the steel producer in Ohio could diminish its overall output, at some cost to itself. If the lodge owner is assigned the right to be free from the noxious acid rain fallout—that is, if the Ohio producer is held liable—then it would be beneficial for the steel producer to negotiate compensation with the lodge owner. The lodge owner will calculate how much pollution she is willing to put up with in exchange for reimbursement from the steel corporation, while the producer will calculate the marginal benefits of production against the marginal costs of remunerating the lodge owner. Conversely, if the steel producer were given the right to produce steel and not be held liable, then it would pay for the lodge owner to negotiate with the steel producer to reduce emissions. Coase argues that either solution will result in the same equilibrium outcome.

In order for the Coase theorem to hold, two key conditions must be met. First, transaction costs must be low. That is, it should be relatively easy to sign an agreement to which both parties will comply. Second, property rights must be well defined although we do not need to be concerned to whom we should allocate these property rights. The allocation of course matters to the individuals; that is, the lodge owner would prefer that the steel producer be held liable and incur no costs. However, if one takes total costs into account on both sides—Coase calls this a reciprocal situation—property rights can be assigned to either, and they will then negotiate to the same equilibrium.

If such is the case, then bilateral agreements between countries can resolve such environmental disputes without the necessity of having an international organization (or hegemonic actor) dictating policy. In reality, though, transaction costs are rarely zero. Moreover, game theory suggests that with more than two players, an equilibrium solution is far more difficult to achieve. Finally, international affairs do not have an overarching legal framework with a government assigning property rights to one of the actors.

Consequently, the Coase theorem requires international institutions in order to work. Keohane, analyzing international regimes in finance, trade, and oil, suggests that international institutions serve to reduce transaction costs and clarify legal frameworks.[5] Therefore, privatization of commons and bilateral bargaining might not be a solution for common pool resources.

---

5. Keohane 1984, 85–92.

Bargaining Leverage due to Price Inelasticity and Transaction Specific Assets

Besides shedding light on collective action problems, scholarship in economics and business has provided other useful analytic tools. Two concepts in particular—price elasticity and the nature of transaction specific assets—are relevant to understanding energy as well as environmental politics. Both concepts provide an understanding of who has the bargaining advantage in international negotiations on natural resources.

Price Elasticity

Price elasticity refers to whether or not the demand for a good is price sensitive. If the demand for a product or resource diminishes if the price for that product increases, then the good in question is deemed price elastic. As the price goes up, the supply increases—since producers now get paid more for that product—but, conversely, demand decreases—as consumers are not willing or able to pay the higher price. If a good is price inelastic, it means that the demand for a good does not react or barely declines as the price goes up. Suppliers of course will be willing to produce more at the higher price, and consumers will pay the higher cost.

Most goods are price elastic. If a particular good becomes more expensive, consumers will not purchase the good and will do without it, or they will look for alternatives. Since most goods and many natural resources have substitutes, consumers will switch to those alternatives if a good is priced too high. In a few cases, as in the energy sector, some goods—oil in particular—have very few substitutes. Consequently, consumers will pay high prices to keep getting oil from oil-producing countries. If producers can band together to control supply and push up prices, and the product is price inelastic, then consumers will be faced with limited supplies and critical, non-substitutable, higher priced resources.

A group of producers working together to set prices, a cartel, can exercise considerable leverage over consumers. Since consumers have no alternatives to the good in question, they must pay the prices demanded by the producers. Such producers might not merely have economic objectives but also make political demands, as the Organization of the Petroleum Exporting Countries (OPEC) has done in the past.

Transaction Specificity

Transaction specific assets are assets that are deployed for a particular purpose and use and that cannot easily be redeployed to some other function or area. In this sense the asset is deemed specific for the purposes of that transaction only. Such invested assets do not have a readily available alternative location. A clear example is an investment to extricate a particular mineral or an investment that needs to be at that specific setting. Such investments are also called site-specific investments. When a Canadian oil producer invests in machinery specifically built to exploit tar sands in Alberta, there is no alternative for those purchased machines. Similarly, if a copper producer, say Anaconda, invests in the infrastructure to mine copper in Chile, then that copper mine is a transaction specific asset.

The key point is that such transaction specific assets make the investor subject to hold-up by the partner. This insight is derived from Oliver Williamson's study of corporate organization.[6] Williamson concluded that when transaction specific assets are in play, then companies tend to diminish uncertainty and potential hold-up by integrating the two separate firms into one. This explains, for example, the high level of vertical integration in the American automobile sector. When General Motors (GM) feared that one of its suppliers, Fisher Auto Body, would take advantage of GM because their relationship involved many transaction specific assets, GM decided it would be best to buy up and integrate with the supplier. The solution to the problem was to create a hierarchical organization.

Williamson's insights into the potential for hold-up among companies and the relevant solution to that problem has its analytic parallel among states. If, say, the Chilean government wants to change the bargain it has struck with Anaconda after that firm has built the copper mine, then Anaconda has little alternative but to comply. Site specific investments, such as mines, oil refineries, and plantations, are vulnerable to expropriation and seizure.[7] In order to prevent hold-up, companies have lobbied their home governments to protect them from possible seizure of their assets. Political scientists have noted a correlation between the nature of investments abroad and the emergence of formal empire.[8]

Many investments in energy extraction are transaction specific. In the past, these investments went hand in hand with imperialist politics. For example, the Dutch government reacted to the demands from extractive industries by extending their hold of Indonesia, thus safeguarding investments in oil (Shell), tin extraction (Billiton), and plantations. Similarly, Britain pursued control over Iran to vouchsafe access to oil, a key necessity for its Royal Navy. Today, many international relations are influenced by the role of transaction specific energy transfers and investments. Russia can hold its neighboring states hostage by controlling deliveries of oil and gas. China eyes Central Asian supplies with a geostrategic perspective.

The following two cases hardly constitute the universe of global issues that confront humankind. However, both deal with key issues; the global warming case in particular illustrates the problems facing environmental

---

6. Williamson 1975.
7. For a fine example of how the seizure of American mines in Chile worked out, see Moran 1974.
8. Frieden 1994; Lipson 1985.

collective goods. Thus, they demonstrate how one might use these "tools of the trade" to understand such issues as regulation of ocean resources, water rights, and public health.[9]

---

9. On the oceans and concerns regarding the depletion of fish stocks, see Hannesson 2004. For collections of essays on a variety of global public goods issues, see Dolsak and Ostrom 2003, and Kaul et al. 2003.

ELEVEN

The Politics of Energy

It is imperative that petroleum resources be freed from monopoly control of the few ... The world petroleum cartel is an authoritarian, dominating power over a great vital world industry.[1]

The Industrial Revolution and Transformation of Human Society

For millions of years our forebears were limited in their mobility and level of development by their inability to master energy other than that provided by the human body. *Australopithecus* and other ancestors more closely resembled our simian cousins than modern humans. Neanderthals, and the later *Homo sapiens* (the "intelligent man"), who appeared around 200,000 years ago in Africa, gradually developed the intelligence to manipulate their environment far more than their predecessors. Paleontological evidence indicates they used fire and fabricated tools.

Homo sapiens mastered the use of mammals probably around 12–15,000 years ago with the first domestication of dogs and horses. Until then, they had to rely on their own speed and strength to transport themselves and their goods. It would take thousands more years before *Homo sapiens* developed instruments that could use inanimate energy, particularly wind energy. Even so, until the early Renaissance, the most developed areas of their day—Western Europe, the Chinese Empire, the Ottoman Empire, and the great American civilizations—would still be recognizable to individuals who had lived a thousand years earlier. Society still relied on the horse for transport and the burning of wood, dung, and coal for warmth. Sailing ships and oar were still the means to cross the seas.

Consequently, the Industrial Revolution that commenced around the middle of the eighteenth century signaled a quantum leap in how individuals interacted with nature and how they used natural resources to provide energy. The demand for energy leapt exponentially, social and political

---

1. The American Attorney General was not fulminating at OPEC but at the stranglehold of the "seven sisters," the major oil companies, whose cartel preceded that of OPEC. As quoted in Sampson 1975, 149.

organization went through a dramatic transformation, and the human footprint from then on altered the very landscape.[2]

Coal became the key source of energy use. It was critical to fire up the furnaces that could turn ores into metals for use in myriad mechanical devices. It was also critical for propelling the dynamos that produced electric energy and the railroads. And, prior to the advent of electric lighting, gas produced from coal was used for lighting. For these reasons, industrialization took off in areas where coal was abundant. In Britain this meant development in its western areas that previously had been at the periphery of the country. Industrial cities such as Manchester sprung up virtually overnight. In the United States, the northeast and later the areas of the Great Lakes provided such critical resources.

By the late nineteenth century, a new source of fuel became ever more important: oil. Until then it had largely been of use only in lighting; although various kinds of oil could be used for this purpose, whale oil, rather than carbon fuels extracted from the ground, was preferred. However, the invention of the combustion engine created a much larger demand for oil within just a few decades. While the automobile did not become widespread until the early twentieth century, the benefits of using oil for propulsion were soon clear to the military. With the change from sail to steam-driven ships, the great navies of the nineteenth century had to secure reliable access to ports to re-coal their ships. Indeed, the Royal Navy created an extended array of overseas bases exactly for this purpose. Already by World War I, however, the British admiralty preferred to switch to oil rather than rely on large quantities of coal to propel its ships. For that reason, Winston Churchill advocated British expansion into Persia (most of the other Middle East reserves were still unknown) and financially supported the Anglo-Persian Oil Company in exchange for a guaranteed oil supply. So, from the very beginning, the exploration of oil was linked to large private firms and national security interests.

Another major energy source also emerged in conjunction with security concerns: nuclear energy. The first use of nuclear energy was of course the atomic bombs at the end of World War II. The United States, fearing German development of atomic weapons, engaged in a tremendous effort to develop the bomb first. As much as one-seventh of its national electricity production was diverted to produce the two nuclear fission weapons that were used against Japan. After World War II, many nations envisioned multiple peaceful uses for nuclear energy. For one, such energy could be used to generate electricity. And again the military had keen interests in using new sources of energy. Nuclear power allowed ships and submarines to stay at sea for extended periods of time, and thus nuclear propelled ships

---

2. See Crone 1989 for a compelling narrative of how industrialization changed society.

and submarines soon appeared. Mercantile ships also explored nuclear propulsion. Even nuclear powered planes were contemplated.

Bureaucratic interests propelled such developments as well. Agencies and private companies that had been involved in the production of the atomic bombs feared that the end of the war would lead to declining budgets and potentially threaten their role or existence. Consequently, they became aggressively involved in seeking alternative, peaceful uses for nuclear energy.

Advantages and Disadvantages of Various Types of Energy

Coal, nuclear energy, and oil all come with benefits and costs. Electricity is less problematic in and of itself, but it still requires coal, nuclear energy, and oil and gas in order to be generated.

Coal retains a key role in the energy supply of such advanced industrial countries as the United States and is still important for generating electricity. In developing countries such as China, its role is even more pronounced. It is cheap and widely spread geographically. Despite these advantages its use is highly problematic. In mid-nineteenth-century Britain, as in coal-burning countries today, smog—the combination of smoke created by coal-burning furnaces and household heating and fog—created major health problems. Coal produces far more carbon when burned than oil or gas. It is, consequently, a major contributor to global warming (more on this later). Bringing coal to the surface is also not without danger. Thousands of miners have perished in China's attempts to meet the energy needs of its rapid industrialization.

Because of these health and environmental concerns, governments and citizens have tried to scale back the use of coal, but environmental and health concerns have clashed with the desire for economic growth. Given China's current pace of economic development and its reliance on coal, it recently bypassed the United States as the primary producer of greenhouse gases. The surge in oil and gas prices in 2007 and 2008, moreover, led even the developed economies to increase their use of coal. Consequently, 2007 saw a record consumption of coal in the United States, with most being used for the generation of electricity.[3]

At one time, nuclear energy promised to be the energy resource of the future. Indeed, some countries, such as France, made nuclear energy a key component of their overall energy policy. Because of the energy crisis of the 1970s, the French government undertook a systematic plan to build dozens of standardized nuclear reactors. In the United States, by contrast, private utility companies created a much more limited nuclear response.

However, the danger associated with handling radioactive materials was apparent at the very beginning. Serious accidents have also eroded

---

3. A useful website for the study of energy resources is http://www.eia.doe.gov/.

confidence about its safety. In the United States, the accident at Three Mile Island in Pennsylvania in 1980 almost precipitated the emergency evacuation of hundreds of thousands of residents. Luckily, a meltdown of the reactor core was averted. The Chernobyl accident in the Soviet Union in 1986 was far more serious. The reactor did melt down, and more than 50 people died as a result of the explosion and radiation. The surrounding area had to be evacuated, and the site remains entombed in concrete to this day.

Nuclear energy has another serious drawback in that it creates radioactive waste. This byproduct retains dangerous levels of radioactivity for thousands of years. While in the short run such waste can be buried deep underground or encased in concrete and dropped in the ocean, its very longevity raises health and environmental concerns.

In addition, the distinction between the development of nuclear know-how for peaceful purposes and military objectives is not always easy to draw. Clearly, many countries that have built nuclear reactors for peaceful purposes—and there are dozens of them—could also develop nuclear weapons if they chose, but they have largely refrained from doing so. However, this is not the case for some countries that have recently developed or are about to develop nuclear capabilities. Pakistan gained nuclear capability from the Netherlands as far back as the 1970s with the avowed aim to use such knowledge for energy purposes. By the 1990s, however, it became clear that Pakistan was using this information to develop its own nuclear arsenal. Similarly, North Korea claimed its nuclear program was intended to develop an independent source of energy supply. Its 2006 test of a nuclear device gave lie to that claim. Iran now argues that its nuclear program is meant to develop an alternative source of energy supply. The United States and its European allies, however, remain skeptical.

Oil as a Special Category

Coal and nuclear energy thus both raise complicated questions involving environmental concerns, economic development, and security issues. But hydrocarbons—oil and natural gas—raise such questions even more starkly. Oil and, to a lesser extent, natural gas are so important to all economies of the world, and are so linked to national security, that they merit extensive discussion.

Oil became the lynchpin of modern economies with the invention of the combustion engine and its use in automobiles and all types of machinery. This exploding demand gave rise to some of the biggest capitalist firms of all time. By the end of the nineteenth century, much of the Middle East was still part of the Turkish Empire, and oil exploration had not occurred there. The key production areas were the United States and parts of Africa and Asia, especially Indonesia. American, British, and Dutch corporations controlled these deposits and became corporate giants. In the United States, Standard Oil dominated the scene. Even after its break-up, due to anti-trust regulations in 1911, its spin-offs went on to become some of the biggest oil companies in the world, eventually becoming Exxon and Mobil. The British Anglo-Persian Oil Company became one of the first to start exploring the Middle East through its discoveries of oil in Iran (the firm was later renamed Anglo-Iranian and went on to become the contemporary British Petroleum). Shell Oil (now Royal Dutch Shell) built its fortunes on explorations in Indonesia.

All in all, by the 1920s, seven huge firms—dubbed the Seven Sisters—controlled the oil sector. Working together and cooperating in secret, they tried to restrict the access of other companies to the oil fields and control the price of oil on the world market. In one (in)famous episode, Henry Deterding, the Chairman of Shell, contacted by encoded communications representatives of the various oil companies, supposedly for a grouse hunt in Scotland but in reality in an attempt to control the world's oil.[4] Indeed, so strong was their position that they even tried to exclude other firms from beginning exploration of Saudi Arabia. The Red Line Agreement (1928) prohibited the signatories from independently exploring the areas that were previously part of the Ottoman Empire. It was eventually overthrown and brought the vast Arabian peninsula to the fore as the world's primary supply region.

Decolonization and nationalist sentiments in the less developed countries started to change the landscape. In Iran, covert action by the CIA in the 1950s averted attempts to nationalize the oil industry. However, this success of the former imperial powers and the United States was just temporary. Newly independent governments increasingly asserted their sovereign rights over their natural resources. They pooled their political power in the Organization of the Petroleum Exporting Countries (OPEC), which was created at the Baghdad Conference in September 1960 by Iran, Iraq, Kuwait, Saudi Arabia, and Venezuela. Later joined by nine others, OPEC currently consists of 13 members.

Centered in the oil-producing states of the Middle East, OPEC particularly flexed its muscles during the 1970s. Economic gain and political motives propelled it to restrict output and dramatically raise prices. Politically, the Middle East states were motivated to use their leverage in oil to oppose Israel and its allies. Economically, they aimed to reap dramatically higher rents. Subsequently, the price of a barrel of oil went from roughly $2 a barrel in the early 1970s to $40 by the end of the decade. OPEC also restricted deliveries to allies of Israel—the United States, Portugal, and the Netherlands—in the wake of the Yom Kippur War of October 1973.

---

4. Sampson 1975, 86. He provides a fine cloak-and-dagger account of the oil industry.

Oil is not only critical to the energy supply of virtually every country, but it is also a product with few substitutes. Demand for oil is thus inelastic and is marginally affected by the price in the short to medium run. OPEC could thus raise prices with impunity. Oil's inelasticity coupled with the fact that the largest oil deposits are in the volatile Middle East makes it a source of contestation.

Many of the largest oil-producing states are also hardly democratic. There is considerable evidence that countries that have abundant natural resources that generate large revenue usually end up with undemocratic forms of government.[5] This argument—the rentier state thesis—suggests that oil and gas revenues in particular allow leaders to avoid demands for democratic input since they can raise revenue without having to tax the population, severing the age-old connection between representation and taxation that was mentioned in earlier parts of the book.

The production and use of oil and gas is thus fraught with economic and political quandaries. Their use also poses a serious environmental risk. Even though oil and particularly gas burn cleaner than coal, the use of hydrocarbons in energy supply greatly contributes to the greenhouse effect. When burned, they emit carbon dioxide, CO_2, which is thought to be a key factor in global warming.

All these problems are compounded by an ever-increasing demand for oil and gas. It is fair to state that economic development and the strength of the overall world economy hinge around the stability and pricing of oil: "Oil price movements not only link directly to shifts in consumption in the industrialized regions ... but also correlate with changes in GDP growth— the entire pace of world economic activity."[6] The demand in the developed countries has been less explosive in past decades due to greater efficiency in energy use. By some calculations, per capita energy consumption in North America was lower in 1992 than in 1973, and the growth rate in consumption for the industrial world (not counting the socialist economies) had declined dramatically.[7] However, the rapid development of large populations in China and India will significantly raise global demand.

The use of oil and gas, therefore, presents a collective action problem. On the one hand, continued use at this level threatens humankind with potentially catastrophic environmental degradation. On the other, oil and gas are still a critical source of energy and vital for national economies. Thus, individual states have been more concerned with assuring sufficient supply and access for themselves and their private corporations rather than coordinating on any international regulation of production. The International Energy Agency (IEA) serves largely as a clearinghouse for information but does not address issues such as energy security or access.

5. Some of the key arguments are evaluated by Cooley 2001.
6. Goldstein et al. 1997, 260.
7. Lin 1984, 789f.

OPEC and Production Cartels

Although OPEC was formed in 1960, it came into its own in the 1970s when the cartel managed to raise the price for a barrel of oil twenty-fold. The geographically concentrated nature of oil resources and the limited number of producers make such a cartel possible. According to estimates, the total proved oil reserves amount to 1.3 trillion barrels of oil. Of this total, Saudi Arabia has the most, followed by Canada, Iran, Iraq, Kuwait, the United Arab Emirates, Venezuela, Russia, and the United States, which has only 22 billion barrels left. Libya, Nigeria, and Angola all have more oil than the United States.[8] Despite the early claims that Central Asia would become a new Middle East, countries such as Kazakhstan (9 billion) and Azerbaijan (7 billion) have far less oil than the big Middle East producers.

This means that the top 10 oil-producing states have more than 80 per cent of the world's oil reserves. Of the total, OPEC accounts for two-thirds of reserves. Moreover, the high estimates of Canada's reserves are based on the ability to recover non-conventional sources of oil, mostly from tar sands.[9] If one were to exclude non-conventional sources, then OPEC would occupy an even more commanding position.

Given that oil is an inelastic good and given the small number of oil producers, the oil-producing countries can command substantial rents.[10] As long as they can jointly regulate the amount of oil that is produced and brought to market, they can drive up the price. That is, by regulating supply through specifying how much each OPEC member can produce each year, OPEC can reduce the total amount of oil available to consumers. With a limited supply, the laws of supply and demand dictate that demand for a scarce product will push up the price. During periodic OPEC conferences, the members agree to certain production quotas, which are lower than the production capacity. Moreover, given that most of the OPEC members are in the Arab Middle East, these states share certain political goals, particularly their antagonism to Israel. As we saw above, collusion in oil production has in the past also served to punish Israel and its Western allies.

---

8. Saudi Arabia has 264 billion barrels, Canada 179 billion, Iran 138 billion, Iraq 115 billion, Kuwait and the United Arab Emirates each have about 100 billion, Venezuela has 79 billion, Russia 60 billion. Figures are proved reserves by January 2006. See CIA, *The World Factbook*, https://www.cia.gov/library/publications/the-world-factbook/rankorder/2178rank. html.

9. For a discussion of alternatives to oil, see Deffeyes 2006. He also discusses oil production from tar sands and the difficulties associated with that production. (Tar sands are mixtures of sand and water and a dense form of petroleum called bitumen.)

10. Economic rent is the difference between what a factor of production is paid and how much it would need to be paid to remain at its current use. So if, say, oil production would continue if producers were paid $5 a barrel, but the market price ends up being $40, then the rent comes to $35.

Nevertheless, as with all cartels, OPEC faces a collective action problem. If all members agree to follow through on production quotas, all stand to gain from the higher price of oil. However, from an individual perspective, if a state produces more oil than agreed, it will gain more revenue. If the other states stick with their agreed quotas, then the price will remain high since overall supply will remain constricted, and the defecting state will benefit from the high price while selling more oil than it was allocated by the cartel. A state might also defect by simultaneously undercutting the market price of oil. For example, if OPEC manages to put the market price of a barrel of oil at $40 (as it succeeded in doing in the late 1970s), a defecting country might undercut the price by bringing oil to the market at $39. This would still be well above production costs. Needless to say, consumers would flock to that producer. If the defecting producer is willing to produce as much as it can, it can reap huge windfall profits.

However, if all individual producers engage in such self-interested behavior and free ride, then the collective effect will be a breakdown of the overall production and price agreement. This is what happened in the 1980s and 1990s. Economically, states attempted to profit individually by violating OPEC agreements. Politically, the Middle East fell in disarray, most notably because of the Iraq-Iran war and the Iraqi invasion of Kuwait in 1991.

As with all collective action problems, free riding can be minimized by the actions of a hegemonic actor. In OPEC's case, this role has been played by Saudi Arabia. The Saudi government, controlling by far the largest oil reserves, can threaten to flood the market to penalize transgressors of OPEC agreements. In other words, if a member threatens to produce more than a given quota or below the agreed price, then Saudi Arabia can ramp up production to such an extent that the market price will drop substantially. In such an instance, the defector would be worse off than if it had adhered to the original agreement.[11]

The Saudi government was quite successful in maintaining OPEC cohesion through its hegemonic leadership in the 1970s. But after the early 1980s, this became ever more difficult. As said, the Middle East, which already was unstable due to tensions surrounding the Arab-Israeli conflict, erupted in several wars. The participants in those wars now had added incentives to maximize their oil revenues beyond the standard economic incentives—their military expenditures after all needed to be covered. (Iraq at its peak had the fifth largest military in the world by some estimates.)

---

11. Producers of other resources envisioned reaping the benefits of cartels in a similar manner. During the 1970s, cartels were formed to control tin, bauxite, and even coffee. However, these products proved to have substitutes. As prices rose, consumers switched to alternatives. Thus, unlike oil, prices in these commodities were elastic. See Arad *et al.* 1979, ch. 2.

The global context had changed as well. Although the consumption of oil is inelastic in the short run, the dramatic oil shocks of the 1970s spurred oil-consuming nations to adopt energy policies that aimed at reducing oil dependency. As we saw in Part II of this book, economic policies reflect the long-run historical and institutional development of the state. Governments tend to vary in their responses to economic crises, choosing neo-mercantilist policies, private sector and state cooperation, or primarily private sector based strategies.[12] The oil shocks precipitated in some states (such as France) the direct intervention by the state in energy production. The French government nationalized energy firms, negotiated energy contracts, and engaged in a state-led nuclear energy program. Other states opted for competitive adjustment. The Japanese and German governments favored guidance mechanisms to help private enterprise cope with the energy problems. Although not quite as interventionist as its European and Japanese counterparts, the Canadian government too intervened in energy policy.[13] The National Energy program aimed at reducing the stake of foreign multinational corporations (MNCs), greater Canadian ownership of the oil industry, and more revenue for the federal government. (It met with limited success as MNCs, together with local businesses and provincial governments, particularly Alberta, resisted the push from Ottawa.) The United States opted for reliance on price mechanisms, believing that higher prices would lead to greater production and a search for new sources of energy, while at the same time consumption would drop.

All these strategies reflected what was domestically possible in the various advanced capitalist countries. Combined, they led to diminishing demand for oil and thus less leverage for OPEC and Saudi Arabia.

As we also noted in Part II, the global economy has dramatically changed the nature of traditional economic relations. Globalization of trade and financial relations profoundly affected how some of the Middle East oil producers saw the world in the late twentieth century. Flush with capital from the price explosion between 1973 and 1980, they put their funds in Western banks and firms. These "petrodollars" were then used by the developed countries not only as liquidity to buy more oil but also to lend funds to non-oil producing states in Latin America. Some of these countries were subsequently unable to pay back these loans, which led to the Latin American debt crisis in the 1980s.

The interconnectedness of financial relations has also given the Middle East producers a stake in the welfare of companies and countries other than their own. If, for example, a sizeable number of shares of Mercedes Benz are owned by Arab investors, then those investors have an interest in maintaining a significant demand for Mercedes Benz products. If higher oil prices push developed states into a recession, the company,

---

12. Ikenberry 1986.
13. Jenkins 1986.

and its Arab investors, will fare poorly. Simply put, it is not clear that Saudi Arabia and some of the other Arab states are that keen on having OPEC dictate prices to such a level that worldwide recession will result.

Moreover, while Saudi Arabia controls by far the largest proved oil reserves, it is only marginally the largest oil producer. In 2006, it produced about 10.7 million barrels of oil per day, while Russia produced about 9.7 million and the United States 8.3 (followed by Iran with 4 million, and China, Canada, and Mexico with 3–4 million barrels).[14] Russia in its attempt to modernize its economy has shown little inclination to scale back its production. Half of its foreign trade comes from oil and gas exports. So while Saudi Arabia no doubt is a very important player, it controls less than one-sixth of total oil production.

Finally, the high price of oil in the 1970s made it economically attractive to explore new areas for oil production. The Alaska North Slope, the North Sea, and Canada were further explored and developed. Non-conventional sources of oil such as shale oil also became profitable. Consequently, prices remained stable for more than two decades after the oil shock, with momentary swings based on political instability. By 1997 the real price of a barrel of oil had fallen to $10. Does this decline of OPEC cohesion combined with the search for new sources of oil and alternative energy supplies mean that energy has become less of a hot political issue? Such optimism unfortunately is misplaced.

The Future of Oil

The politics surrounding fossil fuels, particularly oil, underscores a key argument throughout this book. We have witnessed the emergence of a truly global economy with highly interdependent actors. Not only have states become sensitive to one another's actions, they have become mutually vulnerable. That is, not only are the actions of one state felt by other states, but those actions can have adverse effects on the other states' welfare and economy.[15]

Oil makes states interdependent and mutually vulnerable for several reasons. First, as noted above, oil has become the key source of energy production, and economic development is inextricably linked with oil prices. The oil shock of the 1970s was a hard blow to the developed economies, but the less developed states that did not produce their own oil suffered even worse consequences. Given this worldwide dependence on oil, the producing states will be inclined to continue using their oil reserves for political leverage. Even militarily and economically powerful states might not be able to resist this pressure, as power resources in one domain do

---

14. See CIA, *World Factbook* 2006 (see note 8 above).

15. The distinction between vulnerability and sensitivity is well articulated by Keohane and Nye 1977.

not necessarily translate into another. Thus, even though the United States, Japan, and Germany were the undisputed economic leaders in the 1970s, they could do little to pressure OPEC to lower oil prices.

Second, this leverage is enhanced by the inelasticity of oil and the geographic concentration of reserves. Consumers might balk at higher prices and the political demands of the producing states, but they will be inclined to give in to those demands as they see little alternative. During the Yom Kippur War of 1973, the threat of an Arab oil boycott propelled many European states to refuse landing rights to American military transport planes that were destined for Israel. There is little reason to believe that the political leverage provided by oil has diminished since then.

Third, investments in the oil sector are inevitably transaction specific. States and firms that invest in the exploration of oil and gas fields, and pipelines to transport oil and gas, are potentially subject to nationalization and renegotiation by the host country. Conversely, many of the producing states will be wary of having their sovereign resources exploited by the developed consumer states—as no doubt was the case during the colonial era.

For these reasons then, the politics of oil involves far more than the usual issues surrounding the trade of commodities. It blurs the distinction of low politics (traditionally economic issues) and high politics (security issues). Our discussion of OPEC and the oil shock of the 1970s demonstrates this succinctly, but the same logic has played out in more recent developments.

Even if OPEC cannot collude or does not wish to collude as effectively as in the 1970s, the high demand for oil has raised both the price of oil as well as the stakes for securing access. China is concerned that its double-digit economic growth will be stymied by either insufficient access to oil or high oil prices. Consequently, it has sought closer ties with the Sudanese government despite the abysmal human rights record of the latter. Similarly, it sees access to Central Asian oil as a geostrategic issue, not an economic one. Given its own authoritarian system, combined with its economic needs, China has far fewer reservations about doing business with authoritarian states in the region than do some of its Western counterparts.

In the former Soviet Union the politics of oil is similarly fraught with tension. Many of the newly independent states continue to depend on Russia for their oil and natural gas. Most of the pipelines that bring these energy sources to these states also run through Russian territory. The resurgence of Russia, bolstered partially by the rise in oil prices after 2005 and partially by renewed nationalist sentiment under Prime Minister, previously President, Putin, has led Moscow to use the transaction specific nature of these assets to its advantage. It has raised prices to some states such as Georgia and the Ukraine and threatened to cut off deliveries altogether. Economic motives coincided with political ones as Russia sought to pressure them to alter some of their internal policies.[16] It has, furthermore, tried to influence the layout of Kazakhstan's oil and gas lines.[17]

Moscow has also increasingly intervened directly in the oil and gas sector. It expropriated some private firms that seemed to be acting contrary to Putin's political objectives. It broke up the Yukos concern, allegedly for tax reasons but probably also because its CEO had criticized the president.[18] The state is now directly involved in production of oil and gas. Gazprom, the largest producer of natural gas in the world, is a privately traded company, but the shares owned by the state give Moscow a controlling interest.

Western MNCs have experienced the heavy hand of Moscow in various ways. BP and Shell Oil have both invested heavily in developing new areas in Siberia and Central Asia, but Russia changed the agreement that Shell had reached regarding its Sakhalin investments. BP has run afoul of the Russian government as well, with the latter claiming that some BP technical experts lacked work permits and that BP contributed to environmental degradation. In response, BP pulled its technical experts out of Russia.[19]

Conclusion

Oil politics is fraught with potential danger and intertwines with economic, security, and environmental issues. Prior to World War II, the developed capitalist countries could largely rely on supplies from other developed countries, most notably the United States. But even though the United States proved a reliable supplier, the pursuit of energy supplies dovetailed with the pursuit of empire, and Britain and the Netherlands eagerly sought to produce oil in Persia and Indonesia.

After 1945, the picture changed dramatically. American production in 1938 was approximately 3.5 million barrels per day, and it accounted for 62 per cent of the world's total.[20] By 1972, in absolute terms, it had tripled production, but as a share of the world's total it had dropped to no more than 21 per cent. The Middle East, by contrast, accounted for no

---

16. Andrew Kramer, "Russia Cuts Off Gas to Ukraine in Cost Dispute," *New York Times*, 2 January 2006; C.J. Chivers, "Georgia, Short of Gas, Is Hit With a Blackout," *New York Times*, 27 January 2006.

17. For details and analysis of Russia's attempts to control Kazakhstan's oil and pipelines, see Marten 2007.

18. See the Kohl and Rendall case study in the Resources and Case Studies section at the end of Part III.

19. Andrew Kramer, "Russia Increases Pressure on BP," *International Herald Tribune*, 25 March 2008.

20. Vernon 1976, 33.

more than 6 per cent of the world's total in 1938 but had risen to 41 per cent by 1972.[21]

Producers also managed to overcome collective action problems, demanded higher prices, and pushed for economic and political concessions. OPEC, through the leadership of Saudi Arabia, managed to do so with particular success in the 1970s and, to a lesser extent, more recently after 2005, with the price of a barrel of oil reaching $140 by the middle of 2008 (although it dropped below $40 by the end of the year). Individual states, such as Russia, have also used their oil and gas supplies to engage in hard bargaining, bordering on outright coercion of their neighboring states. Developing countries such as China and India fear that their growth spurts will be stymied by dwindling world reserves and higher prices.

For these reasons some have argued that an international energy regime is required to stabilize the price of oil and guarantee secure access. Some scholars argue that there is in fact a loose multilateral regime composed of various elements such as the IEA, OPEC, and various bilateral and multilateral agreements, some of which are aimed at environmental objectives.[22] However, while some elements of this regime, such as OPEC, are relatively solid (as we noted above), other parts are only marginally effective. Particularly the cooperation between importing states in times of oil crises has been sparse.

Multilateral cooperation faces traditional collective action problems. While importing states might benefit from hanging together to vouchsafe secure supplies, in practice in the past, each state has pursued its own objectives. At best, the IEA works as a loose insurance scheme, but in reality it has often had only a marginal effect.

With dwindling supplies of their own, many highly industrialized countries have become ever more dependent on Mideast oil. The turmoil in that region, and the revival of radical Islamist movements, hardly guarantees a stable supply for the future. In addition, some scholars provide considerable evidence in favor of Hubbert's Peak—the prediction that oil production would peak around 2000. While there is discussion surrounding the exact date, the argument that oil, as a non-renewable resource, will become ever more difficult to find—and exploit—at the same rate as before seems quite compelling.[23] Moreover, industrial development of the BRIC countries—Brazil, India, China, and a resurgent Russia—has raised global demand. Combine the inelasticity of oil with uncertain supply and rising demand, and the result is that the future of global energy politics will likely be volatile for decades to come.

---

21. British Petroleum, and Statistical Review of the World Oil Industry, as cited in Vernon 1976, 33.

22. See Victor and Cullenward 2006.

23. For an accessible discussion of the arguments for and against Hubbert's claims, see Deffeyes 2006.

TWELVE

Global Warming
and Ozone Depletion

*There is ample reason to believe that the problems of our time
will not be solved in the routine course of events. For one
thing, the numerous crises of the present exist simultaneously
and with a strongly woven interrelationship between them.*[1]

The Planet's Atmosphere at Risk

The growth of the world's population and the Industrial Revolution have
placed increasing burdens on the globe's ecology. As more and more nations industrialize, and as human use of energy sources and raw materials
continues to increase, the human "footprint" grows commensurably.

No one can open a newspaper or other news medium without being confronted by a multitude of environmental issues. The oceans, once
thought vast areas with boundless resources, are being depleted of fish.
Some estimates indicate that fish stocks will suffer complete collapse in
50 years if nothing is done. Whereas littoral seas were already suffering
environmental degradation, now the environment of the deep ocean itself
is threatened. Prized fish, such as bluefin tuna, which roam the Atlantic
but spawn largely in the Gulf of Mexico and the Mediterranean, are particularly vulnerable.[2]

On land, the availability of fresh water is of growing concern as
more and more ground water supplies are being tapped. Increasing population and agricultural demands require ever more fresh water. More than

---

1. The call for dramatic action to address population growth, environmental
degradation, and the intense use of non-renewable resources came from the Second Report
to the Club of Rome in 1974. See Mesarovic and Pestel 1974, 10.

2. Cornelia Dean, "Study Predicts Disastrous Loss of Fish," *International Herald
Tribune*, 4–5 November 2006; Andrew Revkin, "Tracking the Imperiled Bluefin From
Ocean to Sushi Platter," *New York Times*, 3 May 2005. For a study of various problems
regarding the oceans, see Woodward 2007, which also contains a useful set of references to
other work.

a billion people worldwide lack clean drinking water, and global warming is expected to reduce the supply.[3]

There are other concerns with biodiversity now that species are becoming extinct at an alarming rate. Deforestation, particularly of the once vast rainforests, plays a large role in this extinction and also has serious consequences for soil erosion and even local climates. E.O. Wilson has been one of the most prominent voices on this issue.[4]

Global warming has most recently captured the headlines as a scientific consensus has emerged.[5] One of the key organizations that has been created to assess the consequences of climate change is the Intergovernmental Panel on Climate Change (IPCC).[6] The IPCC issued a report, with 250 authors and almost 500 peer reviewers, that carbon emissions would almost double by 2030, if nothing at all were done.[7]

Recent years have been among the warmest since measurements have been taken. While global warming predicts an overall rise of average temperature, the regional effects are varied. Some areas are expected to experience higher than average summer temperatures, while others might experience more hurricanes, and yet others higher than average snowfall. In 2006, the top-ten list of human disasters did not include merely devastating earthquakes or hurricanes, but also the thousands of people who perished in Western Europe during the heat wave of that summer. The pictures of rapidly receding glaciers have become commonplace. And former American Vice-President Al Gore was rewarded the Nobel Prize for bringing the issue to a broader audience.[8]

Needless to say, we cannot cover a large number of such global environmental issues in this short book. However, as in previous chapters, we will discuss a particular case to see if we can begin to develop the methodological and theoretical tools through which we can think about environmental issues in general. The case we will focus on in this chapter is that of global warming.

More specifically, we will focus on the emergence of a comprehensive ban on chlorofluorocarbons (CFCs) through the Montreal Protocol and the relative failure of the Kyoto Protocol, which sought to control greenhouse

---

3. Jennifer Barone, "Better Water," *Discover*, May 2008: 31–32.

4. For work by the E.O. Wilson foundation, see http://www.eowilson.org/index.php.

5. The critics of the global warming thesis have become a small minority as overwhelming evidence has started to mount. James Kanter and Andrew Revkin, "World Scientists Near Consensus on Warming," *New York Times*, 30 January 2007; Elisabeth Rosenthal and Andrew Revkin, "Science Panel Calls Global Warming 'Unequivocal,'" *New York Times*, 3 February 2007.

6. See http://www.ipcc.ch/.

7. McKibben 2007. This review essay debunks the argument that the evidence on global warming is mixed.

8. Gore 1993. The documentary film, *An Inconvenient Truth*, released in 2005, reached millions of viewers.

gas emissions. The study of global energy issues in the last chapter dealt with rising global demand for commodities that are privately owned, as individual states have legitimate title to the resources in their subsoil. The quality of the earth's atmosphere, by contrast, presents the proto-typical collective good. All benefit from maintaining that quality, but the dangers of free riding are obvious. We conclude with some reflections about the effects of the liberal trade regime, fostered by the WTO (which we discussed in Part II), and the environment.

The Montreal Protocol, 1987

The Emergence of the Issue

In 1974 two scientists, Frank Sherwood Rowland and Mario Molina, first hypothesized that CFCs could be detrimental to the ozone in the stratosphere. Because the ozone layer forms a critical barrier and protects humans from harmful solar rays, their thesis was soon investigated by such other scientific organizations as the UN Environment Program (UNEP), as well as American institutions such as the Bureau of Oceans and International Environmental and Scientific Affairs (OES), the Environmental Protection Agency (EPA), the National Oceanic and Atmospheric Administration (NOAA), and the National Aeronautics and Space Administration (NASA).[9] Scientists in many other countries similarly started to investigate the issue.

Research increasingly indicated that Rowland and Molina were correct. Since CFCs have a long life, immediate action was called for. Even if production did not increase but remained static, the long-term effects were still very serious. Calculations showed that millions of people might be affected by skin cancer should nothing be done. The discovery of a hole in the ozone layer above Antarctica in 1985 added to the sense of urgency.

If transaction costs were low and property rights clearly assigned, then perhaps environmental issues, such as this one, might be left to bilateral bargaining. However, many instances of environmental degradation, including CFC emissions, do not have such characteristics. There were so many producers of CFCs that transaction costs were hardly negligible. Moreover, as suggested earlier, the Coase theorem might hold in bilateral negotiations, but large numbers of actors prevent a stable bargaining solution from emerging. CFCs posed a classic collective action problem. Costs for reducing CFCs would fall to the individual reducing emissions, while benefits would be spread over many states.

CFCs thus raised the risk of a tragedy of the commons. Recall that pure public goods have two traits. They are non-exclusive in that others cannot be excluded from enjoying them. And they are non-rival in that

---

9. Morrisette 1989 provides a good overview of the technical aspects and some of the process through which the protocol came into existence.

one person's consumption does not diminish their availability to another person. Tragedy of the commons cases are imperfect public goods. They are non-exclusive in that none can be excluded from enjoying that good. However, they are rival in that consumption by one actor diminishes the availability to others. If a country engages in accelerated industrialization while producing CFCs that harm the atmosphere, that state will enjoy the benefits from industrialization while the costs will be rolled over onto others. Put another way, the benefits of continuing production along the same lines would accrue directly to the transgressor, but the total amount of ozone in the atmosphere would be thereby diminished. Consequently, managing CFCs required a different solution than simple bilateral negotiations. Multilateral agreements and international leadership were required.

Despite the importance of the issue, countries were reluctant to move decisively to regulation. Producing CFCs provided direct benefits to the producers and diffuse costs to other countries. Thus, opposition to reducing and/or freezing CFCs came from various quarters. In the United States a business group, the Alliance for Responsible CFC Policy, argued, not totally without justification, that the scientific evidence was incomplete. It favored further investigation. Departments in the American government were similarly concerned about how a drastic curtailing of CFCs would hurt business or military interests. CFCs had multiple industrial uses as refrigerants, fire retardants, and solvents in the semi-conductor industry. So the Departments of Interior, Commerce, and Defense all opposed an international accord.

Other countries, particularly Britain and France, similarly feared the adverse effects of such an agreement. Although many European countries favored more drastic action, the European Community adopted the British-French position that would freeze production but not consumption, as the United States preferred.

How then did these countries come to agree on the comprehensive Montreal Protocol? One perspective, advanced particularly by Peter Haas, argues for the critical role played by an epistemic community, a group of experts working nationally and transnationally to influence the public and elites. The epistemic community in this case consisted of a "knowledge based network of specialists, who shared beliefs in cause-and-effect relations, validity tests, and underlying principled values and pursued common policy goals."[10] These chemists, physicists, and other scientists who studied the ozone problem defined the issue area of ozone depletion, putting CFCs on the policy agenda and delimiting the subsequent options for decision-makers.

No doubt the role of experts mattered a great deal, but other factors played a critical role as well. First, the American executive managed to overcome some of the domestic opposition. Although various departments

10. Haas 1992, 187.

had conflicting views, the costs of adjustment were considered manageable. President Reagan, although hardly a proponent of environmental regulation in general, was willing to entertain an international agreement and override objections from some of the agencies.

Second, CFC production had few commercial producers. The global production market was dominated by 16 large firms. This reduced the collective action problem. Among these large firms, DuPont dwarfed its competitors and accounted for almost one-quarter of total world production. Once DuPont became convinced of the negative effects of CFCs and was willing to search for alternatives, other companies had to follow the market leader. Among the producers, DuPont thus acted as a hegemonic leader.

In the international arena, the United States played a similar role. Once it had decided to take the lead in regulating CFCs, the probability of an agreement became much more likely. In addition, many of the European Community countries had favored aggressive action from the outset, as had Canada and the Scandinavian countries. When Germany joined this group, also partially driven by domestic political concerns having to do with various environmental problems, the opposition by Britain and France diminished.

The developed states also built in side payments and special clauses for the less developed countries. Thus, a combination of domestic changes in the hegemon and cooperation between the United States and like-minded allies led to the creation of a regime on CFCs. The Montreal Protocol was achieved even though scientific evidence was not fully conclusive. Thirty-one countries immediately ratified the agreement.

Subsequent evidence that emerged shortly after the initial protocol validated the earlier research. Other countries, such as Brazil, then joined although they initially had been lukewarm about the CFC problem. And yet others, such as Britain, became strong proponents of drastic reduction, even though they had been earlier opponents.

Domestic Institutions and External Policy

The contrast between the United States and Britain raises an interesting point. In the United States new scientific evidence emerged much faster in the political arena than in Britain. Conversely, once the evidence had percolated to the top of the political spectrum in Britain—that is, once the Thatcher cabinet had come around—it quickly implemented far-reaching policies.

No doubt divergent interests played an important role in explaining the different positions these two countries took in the early negotiations. Arguably their institutional arrangements were also relevant. This observation squares with the policy network argument developed in Part II. The

United States has a fragmented policy network, consisting of numerous competing institutions with diverse competencies. In such a political system, new ideas can more readily emerge. One need not convince an entire monolithic structure but can try to convince members of one of the houses of Congress, or a committee or subcommittee at the federal level, or one of the more influential states such as California. Conversely, by that same logic, a fragmented system, with its multiple checks and balances, makes subsequent implementation slow, once a policy has been adopted.[11]

By contrast, the unified policy network in Britain means that new ideas do not easily find their way to the top. So, in the CFC case it was difficult for new scientific evidence to influence policy. However, once those ideas took root, they could be swiftly implemented from the top down, given the unity between executive and legislature, the lack of judicial oversight, and the unified governmental structure.

Results of the Montreal Protocol

The Montreal Protocol has been regarded as extremely successful. It called for the elimination of CFCs by January 1996. It also designated halon gases for elimination by 1994. Hydrochlorofluorocarbons (HCFCs) were another issue of concern; their consumption was to be frozen by 1996, production by 2004, and full elimination by 2030. Overall compliance has been high.

NASA observed in 2001 that the expansion of the hole in the ozone layer had halted. However, it seems to have increased again. Nevertheless, the reduction of CFCs has vastly reduced its rapid deterioration. By mid-2008, 193 countries had signed the protocol—the initial Vienna Convention and the Montreal Protocol.[12] Various amendments to the protocol were similarly signed by a large majority of the member states of the UN.[13]

The Kyoto Protocol

The Montreal Protocol aimed at reducing substances that contributed to ozone depletion. Gases that contributed to ozone depletion are also considered greenhouse gases, so reducing CFCs, the primary target of the Montreal Protocol, has had an added beneficial effect in tackling global warming.

---

11. Hall 1989 makes this argument for the spread of Keynesianism. The United States showed how Keynes's ideas quickly emerged but were implemented slowly. In Britain, by contrast, the initial uptake was slow, but once the government came around, it swiftly implemented Keynesian policies.

12. The Vienna Convention of 1985 created the general obligation to protect the ozone layer and called for further research. The Montreal Protocol established specific objectives to reduce production and consumption of CFCs.

13. See http://ozone.unep.org/.

However, in the 1980s and 1990s, it became increasingly evident that other gases—such as carbon dioxide, methane, and nitrous oxide—were contributing to global warming at an alarming rate. Scientists concluded that the average global temperature had risen by about three-quarters of a degree since the late 1800s. If left unchecked, it is expected to rise by another 2–4 degrees Celsius within this century. The world currently emits 7 billion tons of carbon a year, and the concentration of CO_2 has almost doubled since the beginning of the Industrial Revolution. If we continue to increase our emissions at the current pace, the world will produce 14 billion tons of carbon per year. At that point CO_2 will have doubled in the atmosphere, and severe climate change will be inevitable.[14] Furthermore, other gases such as HCFCs and hydrofluorocarbons (HFCs), which were covered less stringently by the Montreal Protocol, are now recognized as potent greenhouse gases as well.

Global warming will be felt in every sphere of life. At a minimum, the adjustment costs will be extremely high, and in some areas it will be catastrophic. It will occur in every region of the globe, although its effects will be distributed unevenly. Hurricanes might become more frequent and extreme in the mid-Atlantic. Temperatures in the upper northern and lower southern hemispheres are expected to undergo more significant increases than around the equator. Across the globe, precipitation, wind patterns, and average temperatures will all undergo changes. Plant and animal species will suffer significantly as well, with some possibly becoming extinct. The diminishing polar ice cap has already put the polar bear population under stress, and coral reefs in the tropics are diminishing. The rising temperature, by thinning the polar ice caps and reducing glaciers, will raise the average sea level, threatening low-lying countries such as Bangladesh and the Netherlands.

Given the cataclysmic nature of global warming, urgent multilateral action is required. Every country contributes to the problem. Burning fossil fuels produces carbon dioxide. Agriculture and other land uses generate methane and nitrous oxide. Consequently, left unchecked, each country will continue to produce greenhouse gases, while hoping that other countries will bear the cost of adjustment and reduction. In other words, as with ozone reduction, global warming presents a classic collective action problem.

To address this problem, countries convened under the auspices of the UN Framework Convention on Climate Change, which was adopted in Rio de Janeiro in 1992. Negotiations began in 1995 for an amendment to the convention in the form of a protocol,[15] and a final agreement was

---

14. Socolow and Pacala 2006 provide a variety of recommendations to reduce this level of emissions. Each of these recommendations in itself will be insufficient, but each provides a piece of a solution (a wedge as they call them) that jointly can address the problem.

15. See http://unfccc.int/2860.php.

reached in Kyoto in 1997. It was unanimously adopted and was to enter into force by 2005.

The Kyoto Protocol set mandatory targets on the emission of greenhouse gases. Some states were to reduce their emissions while others would be allowed to increase them, but only to a set level. Reduction targets ranged around 8 per cent for many of the European countries and 7 per cent for the United States. Russia would remain about the same, while countries such as Australia and Iceland would be allowed to increase their emissions by 10 per cent. Countries undergoing transitions to market economies, such as Russia, were given some leeway. The EU subsequently made internal arrangements to redistribute the target burden. More advanced states in the EU, such as Denmark and Germany, set much higher reduction targets than 8 per cent (Germany aimed for 25 per cent), while less prosperous members, such as Greece and Portugal, were allowed to increase their emissions by as much as 25–27 per cent. This still allowed the EU as a whole to meet the Kyoto standards.

Kyoto offers participants various means to meet these targets. To offset increases in emissions in some areas, states could compensate by creating "sinks." For example, extension of forested areas could compensate for falling behind in the reduction in CO_2 emissions. The protocol even allowed for the trading of emissions standards. If a country fell short of its target, it could either create more sinks domestically or trade with another country that had not filled its allowed quota. The advanced economies could pay less advanced economies funds to create sinks in the latter countries. This Clean Development Mechanism (CDM) allowed the industrialized states to meet their targets by contributing to the reduction of greenhouse gases in developing countries. By this system, developing countries also stood to gain from their participation. Otherwise they could legitimately argue that they were not the primary producers of greenhouse gases and that the target rates would threaten their economic development. The cap-and-trade scheme was thought to be a mutually advantageous means of giving these countries a stake in making Kyoto work.

The protocol, however, ran into trouble before entering into force. Although approving it, the Clinton administration in the United States never submitted the agreement to the Senate for ratification since the president believed that it would fail to pass. Despite a near consensus in the scientific community, the succeeding Bush administration continued to argue that more research was required and did not ratify the agreement. A *New York Times* editorial launched a scathing critique of the administration's position:

> Washington was intent on making sure that the conferees required no more of the United States than what it is already doing ... which amounts to virtually nothing. At least the Americans'

shameful foot-dragging did not bring the entire process to a complete halt, and for this the other industrialized countries, chiefly Britain and Canada, deserve considerable praise.[16]

Even Australia, which was allowed to increase its emissions, initially withdrew its support but ratified finally in 2007. Major greenhouse emitters among the developing states, such as Brazil, India, and particularly China, have signed the treaty but are not bound by target rates.

Explaining the Emergence of the Kyoto Protocol

Kyoto thus aims at privatizing what is a global commons issue. Indeed, the cap-and-trade scheme to some extent follows a Coasian logic in that it expects the participants to arrive at an efficient outcome through privatization and the ability to trade emissions quotas.[17]

As of 2008, more than 180 countries had ratified the protocol. The United States, however, continues to hold out. With one of the key leading economies standing aside, one may well wonder how the protocol came into being in the first place. If hegemonic leadership, both by private firms (such as DuPont) and by the United States, was a key factor in bringing about the Montreal agreement, then how did Kyoto emerge?

First, although the Clinton administration did not put the protocol forward for ratification by the Senate, the administration, partially spurred on by Vice-President Al Gore, supported the Kyoto negotiations. It was only due to congressional reluctance and Clinton's embroilment in some personal scandals that the executive altered its focus.[18]

This shows once again that hegemonic stability theory requires a careful analysis of domestic politics. Although the United States was clearly one of the leading economies and even though the executive favored the agreement, the fragmented nature of institutions prevented a coherent national policy. By 1995 the Clinton administration had lost control of both the House and the Senate (and never regained either chamber). As the Republican Party traditionally was more oriented towards business concerns, Congress responded skeptically to any proposal that would limit greenhouse emissions and impose burdens on American firms. With Republican President George W. Bush in control of both House and Senate, support for Kyoto dwindled even further.

Leadership on the Kyoto Protocol thus fell to the developed states acting in tandem. Just as scholars have noted that hegemonic leadership

---

16. Editorial, "America's Shame in Montreal," *New York Times*, 13 December 2005.

17. Hannesson 2004 provides an interesting discussion of how property rights might be assigned in fisheries, another common pool resource issue.

18. For a good account of the lack of American leadership and the influence of domestic politics, see Falkner 2005.

is neither necessary nor sufficient to achieve international cooperation in economic affairs, the same holds true in this case. Although the United States was initially a partner in creating the protocol, the effort to reduce greenhouse emissions has been carried by a small group of the other leading economies, which took on the leadership role: "Whereas in the 1970s and 1980s, the United States frequently branded European countries as environmental laggards, it is the European Union (EU) that now claims the mantle of international leadership in sustainable development."[19]

Evaluating Kyoto

The Kyoto Protocol has been criticized from various perspectives, particularly the CDM mechanism that created the cap-and-trade scheme, which allows a country to offset its emissions.[20] So, for example, the release of a ton of greenhouse gas can be offset by avoiding the release of the greenhouse gas elsewhere or by reducing greenhouse gas emissions in some other country. Such offsets can come from promoting energy efficiency, or the use of renewable energy, or by sponsoring sinks, such as increasing forested areas.

Some environmental groups argue against the scheme as it allows the developed countries to sidestep real reductions in emissions by simply purchasing offsets in the developing world. Rather than tackle constituents and their sport utility vehicles, it is cheaper and politically easier to purchase offsets. Environmental groups and economists have also criticized the current set-up.[21] By some calculations, the CDM system is not at all cost effective. For example, China, which is not bound by targets itself and can thus pick up offsets, is eager to take on CDM projects but then taxes them at a high rate.

Moreover, the idea that carbon sinks offset emissions favors large countries over small. Thus, developed small countries, such as the Netherlands or Denmark, that have few forested or non-developed land areas are deemed to have few sinks. Despite aggressive policies aimed at reducing emissions, these countries are evaluated more stringently than the United States even though the latter might have done less to reduce emissions. That is, the United States can claim to meet standards by simply maintaining large undeveloped areas rather than engaging in painful adjustment and reduction.

The system also creates perverse incentives. Producers of HFCs stand to gain from producing this potent greenhouse gas (it is created as a side product in refrigerants) and then capturing it in order to reap financial benefits from developed countries that pay for this offset. Thus, rather

19. Falkner 2005, 585.
20. For a critical evaluation of Kyoto centering on its lack of enforcement, see Barrett 2003, ch. 15.
21. See Wara and Victor 2008.

than reduce the actual product in the first place, the CDM system might lead some calculating producers to keep producing HFCs. Developing countries thus avoid the costs of actually reducing the HFCs in their production processes and then receive payments from the developed countries to capture these gases.

Finally, it is difficult to determine the effect of CDM offsets. Some sustainable projects would have resulted regardless of the offset mechanism. For example, if a developing country opts for generating electricity through a renewable source, such as hydroelectric power, should this be construed as an offset or would they have chosen that method anyway?

Even if the CDM system can be improved, the fact that the United States has still refused to sign and that some of the rapidly developing countries (Brazil, India, and China) are not bound by the protocol, one may wonder whether Kyoto will achieve its objective. The two largest contributors to greenhouse emissions—the United States and China—are not bound by targets.

Indeed, some have argued that while the United States has not acted as a hegemonic leader, it has exercised a hegemonic veto. With its dominant position, it can manage to derail international agreements even though such accords are supported by a large number of states.[22] There are signs that even the conservative camp in the United States is coming around to accepting the near consensus on global warming. Which direction future governments might take is still open to question.

Does the Liberal Trade Regime Threaten the Environment?

In Part II of this book we discussed how the membership of GATT and now the WTO has dramatically expanded. Worldwide trade barriers have fallen. Significant economic gains have been achieved through liberalization, although there is debate to what extent some of the less developed countries have benefited equally with the more developed countries. Environmentalists, however, raise serious concerns regarding the benefits of the current WTO arrangements.[23]

Although the "Washington consensus" suggests that liberalization of trade has occurred because governments have adopted a laissez-faire policy, this has in fact not been the case. States have been essential actors in creating the conditions for international trade. Governments have created infrastructural conditions and have often subsidized exports through key policies by targeting favored industries. In the process environmental costs have been externalized. The negative externalities associated with higher production and more commerce are not reflected in market prices. So, for example, although liberalization of trade has led to dynamic growth in

22. Falkner 2005, 591.
23. This segment relies particularly on Conca 2000.

countries such as China and Brazil, the true costs of such expansion—the degradation of the environment and destruction of the rain forest—are not reflected in the real market prices of their products.

Moreover, the dispute resolution system arguably weakens existing environmental standards. For example, the WTO panels ruled against American standards aimed at protecting dolphins and sea turtles. In the "Tuna-Dolphin case" the American *Marine Mammal Protection Act* regulated how yellowfin tuna may be caught and how dolphins (which end up as side catch) ought to be protected.[24] The American government argued that Mexico could not demonstrate that its fishing fleet met these standards and that therefore tuna from Mexico (and from intermediary countries) could not be imported into the United States. The GATT panel (as this case took place before the 1994 change in procedure that accompanied the creation of the WTO) held against the United States. The legislative act was interpreted as opening the door to protectionist practices. In the end Mexico and the United States settled the issue through bilateral negotiations.

In the "Shrimp-Turtle case," India, Pakistan, Malaysia, and Thailand brought suit against the United States (WTO Dispute cases 58, 61).[25] The *American Endangered Species Act* of 1973 aimed to protect several species of sea turtles. American shrimp trawlers were required to use "turtle excluder devices," which allowed accidentally caught turtles to escape. Countries that did not use such devices were prohibited from exporting shrimp into the United States. In the 1998 ruling, the Appellate Body of the WTO acknowledged that countries may legitimately protect endangered species and engage in environmental protection. However, it argued that the United States had discriminated among WTO member states as it offered financial and technical assistance to some countries to adjust their fishing methods, but not to all. Consequently, it held in favor of the plaintiffs.

It is also argued that the WTO leads to a "race to the bottom." Liberalization means that producers will move to locations with the least restrictions. In American regulatory discussions, a similar claim has been made. Companies would tend to move to states with laxer environmental standards (Delaware) and avoid states with tough environmental codes (California). In practice this has not been obvious as companies make decisions regarding their location based on many factors. Similarly, with regard to the WTO, some suggest that greater liberalization will actually lead to higher corporate standards.

Some environmentalists note a general tension between WTO rules and other international agreements. For example, international agreements on endangered species or hard woods aim exactly to limit trade in certain areas, whereas the WTO is all about unrestricted trade.

24. See http://www.wto.org/english/tratop_e/envir_e/edis04_e.htm.
25. See http://www.wto.org/english/tratop_e/envir_e/edis08_e.htm.

Finally, WTO rules at times clash with existing local norms and codes. In many instances, informal social systems have found ways to limit environmental degradation. Smaller communities have social norms and other means of protecting local commons. The internationalization of such local commons renders such regulative devices useless.

Conclusion

The environment shows how interconnected the global community has truly become. For millennia the imprint of human activity was relatively small. We were subject to climate and environmental changes rather than being the catalysts of such changes. Today we run the risk of profoundly affecting virtually every aspect of the human biosphere.

In this sense, global warming poses not only environmental but also economic and security challenges. Environmental degradation has been directly linked to violent conflict.[26] Consequently, some experts have argued that we should broaden our conceptualization of security beyond the traditional meaning that refers to the clash of arms. The study of "human security" sees security threats as encompassing a broad array of dangers that are posed to human well-being. Others submit that ecological problems are quite distinct from traditional security studies and should be studied as distinct problem areas.[27]

Whichever perspective one adopts, it is clear that only multilateral governance can offer some redress of the severe ecological problems facing humanity. This is not to say that this is the only means of tackling these issues. Contrary to the earlier regime literature, which sought solutions at the inter-state level alone, many actors at the sub-state, non-governmental level can play a critical role as well.[28] But whatever the contributions of international and national non-governmental organizations, multilateral accords among the governing elites of the international community must be a key element if there is to be any significant progress. Only time can tell whether the world's largest economy (the United States)[29] and the large

---

26. Homer-Dixon 1994. Conversely, Conca 2001 suggests that environmental challenges might lead actors to search for solutions. This low-level functional cooperation in turn might lead actors to cooperate in other areas as well, thus reducing tensions.

27. See the discussions by Paris 2001 and Deudney 1990.

28. Conca 2006 argues this particularly with regard to local environmental issues, but it seems that his point speaks as well to the broader generative grammar behind inter-state accords.

29. By fall 2008, the United States had failed to sign key international agreements such as the Kyoto Protocol and the Law of the Sea Convention (UNCLOS III), even though the latter was endorsed by the Bush administration. To date more than 150 countries have signed the UNCLOS agreement. Canada signed the Kyoto Protocol in 1998 and ratified it in 2002. Canada ratified UNCLOS III in 2003.

and rapidly expanding economies (China, India, and Brazil) will be willing to wear the mantle of co-hegemonic leadership in these efforts.

RESOURCES

Useful Websites: Energy

The Energy Information Agency (United States)
http://www.eia.doe.gov/
Provides information on individual countries as well as current and historical data.

The Organization of Petroleum Exporting Countries
http://www.opec.org/home/
OPEC's official website.

Stanford University Program on Energy and Sustainable Development
http://pesd.stanford.edu/
PESD is a multi-year, interdisciplinary program that draws on the fields of political science, law, and economics. Covers issues such as energy and development, national oil companies, and climate change.

Case Studies: Energy

Kohl, Wilfred, and Carroll Rendall. 1991. *OPEC and the World Oil Market: The March 1983 London Agreement*. Pew Case 123. Washington, DC: GUISD Pew Case Study Center.
Rotnem, Thomas. 2005. *Political Economy in Putin's Russia: The YUKOS Affair and the Demise of an "Oligarch."* Pew Case 280. Washington, DC: GUISD Pew Case Study Center.

Useful Websites: Environment

Climate Change Policies and Measures Database
http://www.iea.org/textbase/pm/index_clim.html

This database tracks measures taken to reduce greenhouse gas emissions by members of the International Energy Agency (IEA). It also records information on the policies of non-IEA member states such as Brazil, China, India, the EU, etc. Updated regularly.

EarthTrends
http://earthtrends.wri.org/index.php

The World Resources Institute offers a remarkable collection of data and databases covering ten environmental topic areas in five formats: a searchable database with time series data for over 600 variables; charts and vital statistics on topics from over 220 countries; maps providing visual representations of environmental information; feature stories; and data tables that are global snapshots of each topic area, synthesized by country and region-level information. See, especially, "Research Topics/ Site Map" to start your search.

Environment Canada
http://www.ec.gc.ca/

Provides useful information on international and national environmental issues.

Greenpeace
http://www.greenpeace.org/

Greenpeace forms a worldwide non-governmental organization with daughter organizations in virtually every country. It provides reports and critical assessments, as well as appeals to organize society to prevent environmental degradation.

The Intergovernmental Panel on Climate Change
http://www.ipcc.ch/index.htm

The IPCC is a scientific intergovernmental body set up by the World Meteorological Organization (WMD) and by the UN Environment Programme (UNEP) to assess on a comprehensive, objective, open, and transparent basis the latest scientific, technical, and socio-economic literature produced worldwide relevant to the understanding of the risk of human-induced climate change. Provides online accessible materials and has a useful list of links to other organizations.

The International Institute for Sustainable Development
http://www.iisd.ca/
Contains information from various perspectives. Also provides a list with useful links to other sites. The website tracks information on issue areas such as sustainable development; biodiversity and wildlife; climate and atmosphere; and water, wetlands, oceans, and coasts.

The Ozone Secretariat at the United Nations Environment Programme
http://ozone.unep.org/
This Secretariat provides information on the Vienna Convention for the Protection of the Ozone Layer and for the Montreal Protocol.

Case Studies: Environment

Goodman, Allan. 1992. "The Negotiations Leading to the 1987 Montreal Protocol on Substances that Deplete the Ozone Layer." Pew Case 447. Washington, DC: GUISD Pew Case Study Center.
Pitzl, Jerry, and Emily Stewart. 2000. "The U.S. Position on the Kyoto Protocol: Senate Ratification or Not?" Pew Case 240. Washington, DC: GUISD Pew Case Study Center.

BIBLIOGRAPHY

Ahrari, Mohammed. 1986. *OPEC: The Failing Giant*. Lexington, KT: University of Kentucky Press.

Allison, Graham. 1971. *Essence of Decision: Explaining the Cuban Missile Crisis*. Boston, MA: Little, Brown and Company.

Almond, Gabriel, and Stephen Genco. 1977. "Clouds, Clocks, and the Study of Politics." *World Politics* 29(4): 489–522.

Amsden, Alice. 1989. *Asia's Next Giant: South Korea and Late Industrialization*. New York: Oxford University Press.

Arad, Ruth, *et al*. 1979. *Sharing Global Resources*. New York: McGraw Hill.

Ashley, Richard. 1986. "The Poverty of Neorealism." In Robert Keohane, ed., *Neorealism and Its Critics*. New York: Columbia University Press.

Aslund, Anders. 1995. *How Russia Became a Market Economy*. Washington, DC: The Brookings Institution.

Auerswald, David. 2006. "Deterring Non-State WMD Attacks." *Political Science Quarterly* 121(4): 543–68.

Axelrod, Robert. 1984. *The Evolution of Cooperation*. New York: Basic Books.

Baldwin, David, ed. 1993. *Neorealism and Neoliberalism*. New York: Columbia University Press.

Barrett, Scott. 2003. *Environment and Statecraft*. New York: Oxford University Press.

Bartlett, Christopher, and Sumantra Ghoshal. 1998. *Managing Across Borders*. Boston, MA: Harvard Business School Press.

Bendix, Reinhard. 1978. *Kings or People*. Berkeley, CA: University of California Press.

Berghahn, V.R. 1973. *Germany and the Approach of War in 1914*. New York: St. Martin's Press.

Blyth, Mark, and Hendrik Spruyt. 2003. "Our Past as Prologue." *Review of International Political Economy* 10(4): 607–20.

Börsch, Alexander. 2007. *Global Pressure, National System*. Ithaca, NY: Cornell University Press.

Brander, James. 1988. "Rationales for Strategic Trade and Industrial Policy." In Paul Krugman, ed., *Strategic Trade Policy and the New International Economics*. Cambridge, MA: MIT Press.

Breslauer, George, and Philip Tetlock, eds. 1991. *Learning in U.S. and Soviet Foreign Policy*. Boulder, CO: Westview Press.

Brooks, Risa. 2008. *Shaping Strategy*. Princeton, NJ: Princeton University Press.

Bryant, Ralph. 1987. *International Financial Intermediation*. Washington, DC: The Brookings Institution.

Bunce, Valerie. 1985. "The Empire Strikes Back: the Transformation of the Eastern Bloc From a Soviet Asset to a Soviet Liability." *International Organization* 39(1): 1–46.

Byman, Daniel, and Kenneth Pollack. 2001. "Let Us Now Praise Great Men: Bringing the Statesman Back In." *International Security* 25(4): 107–46.

Chagnon, Napoleon. 1968. *The Fierce People*. New York: Holt, Rinehart and Winston.

Chandler, Alfred. 1990. *Scale and Scope: The Dynamics of Industrial Capitalism*. Cambridge, MA: Harvard University Press.

Clark, Colin. 1977 [1833]. "The Economics of Overexploitation." In Garrett Hardin and John Baden, eds., *Managing the Commons*. San Francisco, CA: W.H. Freeman.

Coase, Ronald. 1960. "The Problem of Social Cost." *The Journal of Law and Economics* 3: 1–44.

Cohen, Stephen. 1977. *Modern Capitalist Planning: The French Model*. Berkeley, CA: University of California Press.

Colton, Timothy. 1990. "Perspectives on Civil-Military Relations in the Soviet Union." In Timothy Colton and Thane Gustafson, eds., *Soldiers and the Soviet State*. Princeton, NJ: Princeton University Press.

Conca, Ken. 2000. "The WTO and the Undermining of Global Environmental Governance." *Review of International Political Economy* 7(3): 484–94.

——. 2001. "Environmental Cooperation and International Peace." In Paul Diehl and Nils Gleditsch, eds., *Environmental Conflict*. Boulder, CO: Westview Press.

——. 2006. *Governing Water*. Cambridge, MA: MIT Press.

Cooley, Alexander. 2001. "Booms and Busts: Theorizing Institutional Formation and Change in Oil States." *Review of International Political Economy* 8(1): 163–80.

Cooley, Alexander, and Hendrik Spruyt. 2009. *Contracting States: Sovereign Transfers in International Relations*. Princeton, NJ: Princeton University Press.

Cowhey, Peter. 1993. "Elect Locally—Order Globally: Domestic Politics and Multilateral Cooperation." In John Ruggie, ed., *Multilateralism Matters*. New York: Columbia University Press.

Craig, Gordon. 1955. *The Politics of the Prussian Army 1640–1945*. London: Oxford University Press.

Craig, Gordon, and Alexander George. 1983. *Force and Statecraft*. New York: Oxford University Press.

Crone, Patricia. 1989. *Pre-Industrial Societies*. Oxford: Basil Blackwell.

Curtis, Gerald. 1988. *The Japanese Way of Politics*. New York: Columbia University Press.

Deffeyes, Kenneth. 2006. *Beyond Oil*. New York: Hill and Wang.

Desch, Michael. 1993. "Why the Soviet Military Supported Gorbachev But Why the Russian Military Might Only Support Yeltsin for a Price." *Journal of Strategic Studies* 16(4): 455–89.

Deudney, Daniel. 1990. "The Case Against Linking Environmental Degradation and National Security." *Millennium* 19(3): 461–76.

Dolsak, Nives, and Elinor Ostrom, eds. 2003. *The Commons in the New Millennium*. Cambridge, MA: MIT Press.

Durkheim, Emile. 1933. *The Division of Labor in Society*. New York: Free Press.

Eckstein, Harry. 1975. "Case Study and Theory in Political Science." In Fred Greenstein and Nelson Polsby, eds., *Handbook of Political Science*. Vol. 7. Reading, MA: Addison-Wesley.

Eichengreen, Barry, ed. 1985. *The Gold Standard in Theory and History*. New York: Methuen.

Eisuke, Sakakibara, and Noguchi Yukio. 1988. "Organization for Economic Reconstruction." In Daniel Okimoto and Thomas Rohlen, eds., *Inside the Japanese System*. Stanford, CA: Stanford University Press.

Elbe, Stefan. 2002. "HIV/AIDS and the Changing Landscape of War in Africa." *International Security* 27(2): 159–77.

Elman, Colin. 1996. "Horses for Courses: Why not Neorealist Theories of Foreign Policy." *Security Studies* 6(1): 7–51.

Elman, Miriam Fendius. 1997. *Paths to Peace: Is Democracy the Answer?* Cambridge, MA: MIT Press.

Elster, Jon. 1989. *Nuts and Bolts.* New York: Cambridge University Press.

Esser, Josef, and Wolfgang Fach. 1989. "Crisis Management. Made in Germany." In Peter Katzenstein, ed., *Industry and Politics in West Germany.* Ithaca, NY: Cornell University Press.

Evans, Peter. 1979. *Dependent Development.* Princeton, NJ: Princeton University Press.

Falkenrath, Richard. 2001. "Problems of Preparedness: U.S. Readiness for a Domestic Terrorist Attack." *International Security* 25(4): 147–86.

Falkner, Robert. 2005. "American Hegemony and the Global Environment." *International Studies Review* 7(4): 585–99.

Feaver, Peter. 1999. "Civil-Military Relations." *The Annual Review of Political Science* 2: 211–41.

Flibbert, Andrew. 2006. "The Road to Baghdad: Ideas and Intellectuals in Explanations of the Iraq War." *Security Studies* 15(2): 310–52.

Freedman, Lawrence, and Efraim Karsh. 1991. "How Kuwait Was Won: Strategy in the Gulf War." *International Security* 16(2): 5–41.

Freud, Sigmund. 1961 [1930]. *Civilization and Its Discontents.* New York: W.W. Norton.

Frieden, Jeffry. 1994. "International Investment and Colonial Control." *International Organization* 48(4): 559–94.

Gaddis, John. 1993. "The Long Peace: Elements of Stability in the Postwar International System." In Sean Lynn-Jones and Steven Miller, eds., *The Cold War and After.* Cambridge, MA: MIT Press.

Gash, Norman. 1968. *The Age of Peel.* London: Edward Arnold.

Gellner, Ernest. 1983. *Nations and Nationalism.* Ithaca, NY: Cornell University Press.

George, Alexander. 1979. "Case Studies and Theory Development: The Method of Structured, Focused Comparison." In Paul Lauren, ed., *Diplomacy: New Approaches in History, Theory, and Policy.* New York: The Free Press.

George, Alexander, and Andrew Bennett. 2004. *Case Studies and Theory Development.* Cambridge, MA: MIT Press.

George, Alexander, and Richard Smoke. 1974. *Deterrence in American Foreign Policy.* New York: Columbia University Press.

Gerschenkron, Alexander. 1962. *Economic Backwardness in Historical Perspective.* Cambridge, MA: Harvard University Press.

Gerth. H., and C. Wright Mills. 1946. *From Max Weber.* New York: Oxford University Press.

Gilpin, Robert. 1975. *U.S. Power and the Multinational Corporation.* New York: Basic Books.

———. 1981. *War and Change in World Politics.* Cambridge: Cambridge University Press.

———. 1987. *The Political Economy of International Relations.* Princeton, NJ: Princeton University Press.

Goldstein, Joshua, Xiaoming Huang, and Burcu Akan. 1997. "Energy in the World Economy, 1950–1982." *International Studies Quarterly* 41(2): 241–66.

Gore, Al. 1993. *Earth in the Balance.* New York: Penguin.

Gray, Colin. 2007. "The Implications of Preemptive and Preventive War Doctrines: A Reconsideration." Washington, DC: U.S Army War College, Strategic Studies Institute.

Guillemin, Jeanne. 2005. *Biological Weapons.* New York: Columbia University Press.

Gulick, Edward Vose. 1955. *Europe's Classical Balance of Power.* New York: W.W. Norton.

Haas, Peter, 1992. "Banning CFCs." *International Organization* 46(1): 187–224.

Hall, Peter. 1986. *Governing the Economy: The Politics of State Intervention in Britain and France.* New York: Oxford University Press.

———. 1989. *The Political Power of Economic Ideas*. Princeton, NJ: Princeton University Press.

Hamada, Koichi, and Akiyoshi Horiuchi. 1987. "The Political Economy of the Financial Market." In Kozo Yamamura and Yasukichi Yasuba, eds., *The Political Economy of Japan*. Vol. 1. Stanford, CA: Stanford University Press.

Hannesson, Rögnvaldur. 2004. *The Privatization of the Oceans*. Cambridge, MA: MIT Press.

Hardin, Russell. 1982. *Collective Action*. Baltimore, MD: Johns Hopkins University Press.

Harvard Nuclear Study Group. 1983. *Living With Nuclear Weapons*. Toronto: Bantam Books.

Heaton, Herbert. 1948. *Economic History of Europe*. New York: Harper and Row.

Herz, John. 1976. *The Nation-State and the Crisis of World Politics*. New York: David McKay.

Hintze, Otto. 1975. *The Historical Essays of Otto Hintze*. Felix Gilbert, ed. New York: Oxford University Press.

Holick, Ann. 1981. *U.S. Foreign Policy and the Law of the Sea*. Princeton, NJ: Princeton University Press.

Homer-Dixon, Thomas. 1994. "Environmental Scarcities and Violent Conflict." *International Security* 19(1): 5–40.

Huang, Yasheng. 2002. "Between Two Coordination Failures: Automotive Industrial Policy in China with a Comparison to Korea." *Review of International Political Economy* 9(3): 538–73.

Ikenberry, G. John. 1986. "The Irony of State Strength: Comparative Responses to the Oil Shocks in the 1970s." *International Organization* 40(1): 105–38.

Jenkins, Barbara. 1986. "Reexamining the 'Obsolescing Bargain': A Case Study of Canada's National Energy Program." *International Organization* 40(1): 139–66.

Jentleson, Bruce, Ariel Levite, and Larry Berman. 1993. "Protracted Foreign Military Intervention: A Structured Focused Comparative Analysis." In Dan Caldwell and Timothy McKeown, eds., *Diplomacy, Force, and Leadership*. Boulder, CO: Westview Press.

Jervis, Robert. 1976. *Perception and Misperception in International Politics*. Princeton, NJ: Princeton University Press.

———. 1989. *The Meaning of the Nuclear Revolution*. Ithaca, NY: Cornell University Press.

———. 2003a. "The Confrontation between Iraq and the U.S.: Implications for the Theory and Practice of Deterrence." *European Journal of International Relations* 9(2): 315–37.

———. 2003b. "Understanding the Bush Doctrine." *Political Science Quarterly* 118(3): 365–88.

Johnson, Chalmers. 1982. *MITI and the Japanese Miracle*. Stanford, CA: Stanford University Press.

Joll, James. 1992. *The Origins of the First World War*. New York: Longman.

Jones, Eric. 1987. *The European Miracle*. Cambridge: Cambridge University Press.

Kaplan, Fred. 1983. *The Wizards of Armageddon*. New York: Simon and Schuster.

Kaplinsky, Raphael. 2001. "Is Globalization All It is Cracked up to Be?" *Review of International Political Economy* 8(1): 45–65.

Katzenstein, Peter, ed. 1978. *Between Power and Plenty*. Madison, WI: University of Wisconsin Press.

Kaul, Inge, *et al.*, eds. 2003. *Providing Global Public Goods*. New York: Oxford University Press.

Keegan, John. 1978. *The Face of Battle*. London: Penguin Books.

Kennan, George (X). 1946/1947. "The Sources of Soviet Conduct." *Foreign Affairs* 25(4): 566–82.

———. 1984. *The Fateful Alliance*. New York: Pantheon Books.

Kennedy, Paul. 1985. "The First World War and the International Power System." In Steven Miller, ed., *Military Strategy and the Origins of the First World War*. Princeton, NJ: Princeton University Press.

Kennedy, Robert. 1969. *Thirteen Days*. New York: W.W. Norton.

Keohane, Robert. 1984. *After Hegemony*. Princeton, NJ: Princeton University Press.

——, ed. 1986. *Neorealism and Its Critics*. New York: Columbia University Press.

Keohane, Robert, and Joseph Nye. 1977. *Power and Interdependence: World Politics in Transition*. Boston, MA: Little Brown and Co.

——. 1987. "Power and Interdependence Revisited." *International Organization* 41(4): 725–53.

Kesselman, Mark, Joël Krieger, and William Joseph. 1999. *Introduction to Comparative Politics*. New York: Houghton Mifflin.

Kester, W. Carl. 1996. "American and Japanese Corporate Governance: Convergence to Best Practice?" In Suzanne Berger and Ronald Dore, eds., *National Diversity and Global Capitalism*. Ithaca, NY: Cornell University Press.

Kindleberger, Charles. 1973. *The World in Depression, 1929–1939*. Berkeley, CA: University of California Press.

King, Gary, Robert Keohane, and Sidney Verba. 1994. *Designing Social Inquiry*. Princeton, NJ: Princeton University Press.

Kinzer, Stephen. 2007. *Overthrow: America's Century of Regime Change From Hawaii to Iraq*. New York: Henry Holt.

Kissinger, Henry. 2000 [1957]. *The World Restored: Metternich, Castlereagh, and the Problems of Peace, 1812–22*. New York: Weidenfeld and Nicolson.

Kornberg, Allan, and Robert Frasure. 1971. "Policy Differences in British Parliamentary Parties." *American Political Science Review* 65(3): 694–703.

Krasner, Stephen. 1978. "United States Commercial and Monetary Policy." In Peter Katzenstein, ed., *Between Power and Plenty*. Madison, WI: University of Wisconsin Press.

——, ed. 1983. *International Regimes*. Ithaca, NY: Cornell University Press.

Krauss, Ellis. 1992. "Political Economy: Policymaking and Industrial Policy in Japan." *PS: Political Science and Politics* 25(1): 44–57.

Kreile, Michael. 1978. "West Germany: The Dynamics of Expansion." In Peter Katzenstein, ed., *Between Power and Plenty*. Madison, WI: University of Wisconsin Press.

Kula, Witold. 1986. *Measures and Men*. Princeton, NJ: Princeton University Press.

Lake, David. 1984. "Beneath the Commerce of Nations: A Theory of International Economic Structures." *International Studies Quarterly* 28(2): 143–70.

Layne, Christopher. 1993. "The Unipolar Illusion: Why New Great Powers Will Rise." In Sean Lynn-Jones and Steven Miller, eds., *The Cold War and After*. Cambridge, MA: MIT Press.

Lenin, V.I. 1939 [1916]. *Imperialism: The Highest Stage of Capitalism*. New York: International Publishers.

Levy, Walter. 1982. *Oil Strategy and Politics*. Melvin Conant, ed. Boulder, CO: Westview Press.

Lieberson, Stanley. 1992. Small N's and Big Conclusions: An Examination of the Reasoning in Comparative Studies Based on a Small Number of Cases. In Charles Ragin and Howard Becker, eds., *What is a Case? Exploring the Foundations of Social Inquiry*. Cambridge: Cambridge University Press.

Lijphart, Arend. 1971. Comparative Politics and the Comparative Method. *American Political Science Review* 65(3): 682–93.

Lin, Ching-yuan. 1984. "The Global Pattern of Energy Consumption Before and After the 1974 Oil Crisis." *Economic Development and Cultural Change* 32(4): 781–802.

Linden, Carl. 1990. *Khrushchev and the Soviet Leadership*. Baltimore, MD: Johns Hopkins University Press.

Lipson, Charles. 1985. *Standing Guard*. Berkeley, CA: University of California Press.

Little, David. 1991. *Varieties of Social Explanation*. Boulder, CO: Westview Press.

Lloyd, William. 1977 [1833]. "On the Checks to Population." In Garrett Hardin and John Baden, eds., *Managing the Commons*. San Francisco, CA: W.H. Freeman.

Lorenz, Konrad. 1966. *On Aggression*. New York: Harcourt, Brace, Jovanovich.

Lynn, Leonard, and Timothy McKeown. 1988. *Organizing Business: Trade Associations in America and Japan*. Washington, DC: American Enterprise Institute.

Lynn-Jones, Sean, and Steven Miller, eds. 1993. *The Cold War and After*. Cambridge, MA: MIT Press.

Mann, Michael. 1986. *The Sources of Social Power*. Cambridge: Cambridge University Press.

Marfleet, Greg, and Colleen Miller. 2005. "Failure after 1441: Bush and Chirac in the UN Security Council." *Foreign Policy Analysis* 1(3): 333–60.

Marten, Kimberly. 2007. Russian Efforts to Control Kazakhstan's Oil: The Kumkol Case." *Post-Soviet Affairs* 23(1): 18–37.

Martin, Lisa. 2000. *Democratic Commitments*. Princeton, NJ: Princeton University Press.

Mattli, Walter. 1999. *The Logic of Regional Integration*. New York: Cambridge University Press.

Mayers, Teena. 1986. *Understanding Nuclear Weapons and Arms Control*. Washington, DC: Pergamon-Brassey's.

Mazarr, Michael. 2007. "The Iraq War and Agenda Setting." *Foreign Policy Analysis* 3(1): 1–23.

McGuire, J., and S. Dow. 2003. "The Persistence and Implications of Japanese Keiretsu Organization." *Journal of International Business* 34(4): 374–88.

McKibben, Bill. 2007. "Can Anyone Stop It?" *New York Review of Books* 54(16): 38–40.

McNeill, William. 1982. *The Pursuit of Power*. Chicago, IL: University of Chicago Press.

Mearsheimer, John. 1990. "Back to the Future." *International Security* 15(1): 5–56.

Mesarovic, Mihaljo, and Eduard Pestel. 1974. *Mankind at the Turning Point: The Second Report to the Club of Rome*. New York: New American Library.

Miller, Steven, ed. 1985. *Military Strategy and the Origins of the First World War*. Princeton, NJ: Princeton University Press.

Milner, Helen. 1987. "Resisting the Protectionist Temptation: Industry and the Making of Trade Policy in France and the United States during the 1970s." *International Organization* 41(4): 639–66.

Moore, Barrington. 1966. *Social Origins of Dictatorship and Democracy*. Boston, MA: Beacon Press.

Moran, Theodore H. 1974. *Multinational Corporations and the Politics of Dependence: Copper in Chile*. Princeton, NJ: Princeton University Press.

Morgenthau, Hans. 1966. *Politics Among Nations*. 4th ed. New York: Knopf.

Morrisette, Peter. 1989. "The Evolution of Policy Responses to Stratosphereic Ozone Depletion." *Natural Resources Journal* 29: 793–820.

Munton, Don, and David Welch. 2007. *The Cuban Missile Crisis*. New York: Oxford University Press.

Nye, Joseph. 1987. "Nuclear Learning and U.S.-Soviet Security Regimes." *International Organization* 41(3): 371–402.

Olson, Mancur. 1965. *The Logic of Collective Action*. Cambridge, MA: Harvard University Press.

Oxfam. 2002. *Rigged Rules and Double Standards*. Boston, MA: Oxfam International.

Oye, Kenneth, ed. 1986. *Cooperation Under Anarchy*. Princeton, NJ: Princeton University Press.

Paris, Roland. 2001. "Human Security: Paradigm Shift or Hot Air." *International Security* 26(2): 87–102.

Park, Kyung-Ae. 2004. "North Korea in 2003." *Asian Survey* 44(1): 139–46.

Parker, Geoffrey. 1979. "Warfare." In Peter Burke, ed., *New Cambridge Modern History*. Vol.13. Cambridge: Cambridge University Press.

——. 1988. *The Military Revolution*. New York: Cambridge University Press.

——. 1995. *The Cambridge Illustrated History of Warfare*. New York: Cambridge University Press.

Pauly, Louis, and Simon Reich. 1997. "National Structures and Multinational Corporate Behavior." *International Organization* 51(1): 1–30.

Pempel, T.J. 1978. "Japanese Foreign Economic Policy." In Peter Katzenstein, ed., *Between Power and Plenty*. Madison, WI: University of Wisconsin Press.

Perlman, Mark, and Charles McCann. 1998. *The Pillars of Economic Understanding*. Ann Arbor, MI: The University of Michigan Press.

Posen, Barry. 1993. "Nationalism, the Mass Army, and Military Power." *International Security* 18(2): 80–124.

Ricardo, David. 1973 [1817]. *The Principles of Political Economy and Taxation*. London: Dent.

Ricks, Thomas. 2007. *Fiasco*. New York: Verso.

Rose, Gideon. 1998. "Neoclassical Realism and Theories of Foreign Policy." *World Politics* 51(1): 144–72.

Rosenberg, Hans. 1943/1944. "The Rise of the Junkers in Brandenburg-Prussia, 1410–1653." *American Historical Review* Part I, 49(1):1–22; Part II, 49(2): 228–42.

——. 1966. *Bureaucracy, Aristocracy, and Autocracy: The Prussian Experience 1660–1815*. Boston, MA: Beacon Press.

Rostow, W.W. 1991. *The Stages of Economic Growth*. New York: Cambridge University Press.

Russett, Bruce. 1985 "The Mysterious Case of Vanishing Hegemony: or Is Mark Twain Really Dead?" *International Organization* 39(2): 207–31.

Russett, Bruce, and Bruce Blair, eds. 1979. *Progress in Arms Control?* Readings from *Scientific American*. San Francisco, CA: W.H. Freeman.

Ryan, Alan, ed. 1973. *The Philosophy of Social Explanation*. Oxford: Oxford University Press.

Sagan, Scott. 1993. *The Limits of Safety*. Princeton, NJ: Princeton University Press.

——. 1996/1997. "Why Do States Build Nuclear Weapons." *International Security* 21(3): 54–86.

Sampson, Anthony. 1975. *The Seven Sisters*. New York: The Viking Press.

Scammel, G.V. 1981. *The World Encompassed: The First European Maritime Empires c.800–1650*. Berkeley, CA: University of California Press.

Schumpeter, Joseph. 1961. "Imperialism as a Social Atavism." In Harrison Wright, ed. *The New Imperialism*. Lexington, MA: D.C. Heath and Company.

Slater, Philip. 1976. *The Pursuit of Loneliness*. Boston, MA: Beacon Press.

Snidal, Duncan. 1985. "The Limits of Hegemonic Stability Theory." *International Organization* 39(4): 579–614.

Snow, Donald. 1991. *National Security*. New York: St. Martin's.

Snyder, Jack. 1984. *Ideology of the Offensive: Military Decision Making and the Disasters of 1914*. Ithaca, NY: Cornell University Press.

Socolow, Robert, and Stephen Pacala. 2006. "A Plan to Keep Carbon in Check." *Scientific American* (September): 50–57.

Solingen, Etel. 2007. *Nuclear Logics: Contrasting Paths in East Asia and the Middle East*. Princeton, NJ: Princeton University Press.

Spruyt, Hendrik. 1994. *The Sovereign State and Its Competitors*. Princeton, NJ: Princeton University Press.

———. 2005. *Ending Empire: Contested Sovereignty and Territorial Partition*. Ithaca, NY: Cornell University Press.

Stern, Jessica. 2002/2003. "Dreaded Risks and the Control of Biological Weapons." *International Security* 27(3): 89–123.

Stiglitz, Joseph, and Linda Bilmes. 2008. *The Three Trillion Dollar War: The True Cost of the Iraq Conflict*. New York: W.W. Norton.

Taylor, A.J.P. 1980. *The First World War: An Illustrated History*. New York: Pedigree.

Thompson, William, ed. 2001. *Evolutionary Interpretations of World Politics*. New York: Routledge.

Tilly, Charles. 1990. *Coercion, Capital, and European States, AD 990–1990*. Cambridge: Basil Blackwell.

Tuchman, Barbara. 1962. *The Guns of August*. New York: MacMillan.

Tversky, Amos, and Daniel Kahneman. 1981. "The Framing of Decisions and the Psychology of Choice." *Science* 211 (January): 453–58.

Ullman, Richard. 1983. "Redefining Security." *International Security* 8(1): 129–53.

Van Evera, Stephen. 1985. "The Cult of the Offensive and the Origins of the First World War." In Steven Miller, ed., *Military Strategy and the Origins of the First World War*. Princeton, NJ: Princeton University Press.

———. 1997. *Guide to Methods for Students of Political Science*. Ithaca, NY: Cornell University Press.

Vernon, Raymond, ed. 1976. *The Oil Crisis*. New York: W.W. Norton.

———, ed. 1983. *Two Hungry Giants*. Cambridge, MA: Harvard University Press.

Victor, David G., and Danny Cullenward. 2007. "Making Carbon Markets Work." *Scientific American* (December): 70–77.

Victor, David, Sara Joy, and Nadejda Victor. 2006. "The Global Energy Regime." Draft paper. Program on Energy and Sustainable Development, Stanford University, 16 January.

Vogel, Steven. 2006. *Japan Remodeled*. Ithaca, NY: Cornell University Press.

Wade, Robert. 2003. "What Strategies are Viable for Developing Countries Today? The World Trade Organization and the Shrinking of 'Development Space.'" *Review of International Political Economy* 10(4): 621–44.

Wallerstein, Immanuel. 1978. *The Modern World System*. Vols. 1–2. Orlando, FL: Academic Press.

Walt, Stephen. 2002. "The Enduring Relevance of the Realist Tradition." In Ira Katznelson and Helen Milner, eds., *Political Science: The State of the Discipline*. New York: W.W. Norton.

Waltz, Kenneth. 1959. *Man, the State, and War*. New York: Columbia University Press.

———. 1979. *Theory of International Politics*. New York: Random House.

———. 1986. "Reflections on Theory of International Politics: A Response to My Critics." In Robert Keohane, ed., *Neorealism and Its Critics*. New York: Columbia University Press.

———. 1990. "Nuclear Myths and Political Realities." *American Political Science Review* 84(3): 731–45.

Wara, Michael, and David Victor. 2008. "A Realistic Policy on International Carbon Offsets." Working Paper 74. Program on Energy and Sustainable Development. Stanford University, April.

Weaver, R. Kent, and Bert Rockman, eds. 1993. *Do Institutions Matter?* Washington, DC: The Brookings Institution.

Wendt, Alexander. 1992. "Anarchy is What States Make of it: The Social Construction of Power Politics." *International Organization* 46(2): 391–426.

Whitley, Richard. 1998. "Internationalization and Varieties of Capitalism: The Limited Effects of Cross-National Coordination of Economic Activities on the Nature of Business Systems." *Review of International Political Economy* 5(3): 445–81.

Williamson, Oliver E. 1975. *Markets and Hierarchies: Analysis and Antitrust Implications.* New York: Free Press.

Woodward, Colin. 2007. "Oceans in Crisis." *CQ Global Researcher* 1(10): 239–63.

Yarborough, Beth, and Robert Yarborough. 1987. "Cooperation in the Liberalization of International Trade: After Hegemony, What?" *International Organization* 41(1): 1–26.

Yergin, Daniel. 1991. *The Prize: The Epic Quest for Oil, Money, and Power.* New York: Simon and Schuster.

York, Herbert. 1970. *Race to Oblivion.* New York: Simon and Schuster.

Young, Michael, and Mark Schafer. 1998. "Is There Method in our Madness? Ways of Assessing Cognition in International Relations." *Mershon International Studies Review* 42(1): 63–96.

Zacher, Mark. 2001. "The Territorial Integrity Norm: International Boundaries and the Use of Force." *International Organization* 55(2): 215–50.

Zacher, Mark, and Richard Matthew. 1995. "Liberal International Theory: Common Threads, Divergent Strands." In Charles Kegley, ed., *Controversies in International Relations Theory.* New York: St. Martin's.

Zimbalist, Andrew, and Howard Sherman. 1984. *Comparing Economic Systems.* Orlando, FL: Academic Press.

Zysman, John. 1983. *Governments, Markets and Growth.* Ithaca, NY: Cornell University Press.

INDEX